WHAT YOUR LAWYER MAY NOT WANT YOU TO KNOW

WHAT YOUR LAWYER MAY NOT WANT YOU TO KNOW

BILLY F. BROWN

abbott press®

A DIVISION OF WRITER'S DIGEST

Abbott Press books may be ordered through booksellers or by contacting:

Abbott Press
1663 Liberty Drive
Bloomington, IN 47403
www.abbottpress.com
Phone: 1-866-697-5310

ISBN: 978-1-4582-1091-3 (sc)
ISBN: 978-1-4582-1090-6 (hc)
ISBN: 978-1-4582-1089-0 (e)

Library of Congress Control Number: 2013914555

Printed in the United States of America.

Abbott Press rev. date: 08/30/2013

TABLE OF CONTENTS

"Most people place themselves into considerable danger attempting to use what they think they know; however, they usually encounter immediate, impending disaster with what they don't know!"—BFB

COMMENTARY

This is a book about lawyers and understanding how they operate and communicate, and what they do for their clients.

You will be delighted to know that this book attempts to assist the client in understanding and communicating with their lawyer. This book also discusses what you can do to balance the power in the relationship with your lawyer. You will learn that there are things you can do when you are unhappy with the manner in which you are being represented by your lawyer.

This book covers a host of things, ideas, and secrets most clients want to know about their lawyer. On the other hand, most lawyers had rather you not know these things since you will be in a position to "level the playing field" and compromise the "balance of power" in the lawyer/client relationship with such information.

If you have never been in a position to hire a lawyer, this book may not be as meaningful as it would have been if you had had the experience. Nevertheless, this book will be meaningful to you in learning the culture of what lawyers do and should do in representing their clients.

This book is also for every lawyer who has ever practiced law, for those who aspire to be lawyers, and for those presently going through the embattled process and progression of law school. Every lawyer should refresh themselves about what they are expected to do in their law practice in relationship to their clients. Those who are in the process of "becoming" should be foretold of what is expected of them.

What Your Lawyer May Not Want You to Know! is not about blasting, defaming, or demeaning lawyers and the practice of law. This book is one of comparing what should happen in the practice of law and what sometimes actually occurs in the daily world of reality.

All clients, potential clients, lawyers, aspiring lawyers, and potential lawyers should enjoy reading *What Your Lawyer May Not Want You to Know!*

Acknowledgments

Any effort such as this book would be shallow and obviously inept if considerable and substantial recognition was not given to every lawyer who has ever practiced law. Therefore, those gallant and bold warriors who dared and endeavored to promote the cause of what lawyers do are hailed as heroes and heroines as they have plowed the field of what law practice is and what it was intended to be. Without lawyers and the aftermath of their efforts this book would not have been possible.

Next, appreciation is tendered to my dear and loving wife, Shari, who steadfastly endured my plodding along on a long journey of attempting to find and collect my thoughts in recognizing that many things look a lot easier than they are. She has been the rock upon which I have attempted to lay my foundation of thought and writing not only in this book but in my life.

Along the way on such a venture (if not adventure) there are people who appear with guidance and innovativeness who lend a bit of encouragement to an otherwise dull, boring, and meaningless undertaking. One such person was Doug Sharp of Abbott Press Publishing. His consistent support is sincerely appreciated. He is a true credit to the credibility of the publishing industry.

Then, this project was directed, spirited, and further ignited by my guide, mentor, and director of logistics, Janelle Lim of Abbott Press Publishing. She was solid gold in knowing the why, how, and what was to be done after the cognitive process of writing was finally exhausted. She is a true gem.

The map of acknowledgments would not be complete without the wisdom, guidance, and direction of my editor, LouAnn Lofton. No doubt LouAnn wondered many times, how and why she got involved in such an undertaking. She was true and steadfast to the end and gallantly finished the race. Thanks for you agreeing to accept the challenge and your great contribution to its completion.

Next, the one who pulled all this together to make sure it all fit on the printed page is Brandi Savant. I never ever wanted to know how she did what she did because I was too afraid to ask. She was truly wonderful in finishing out the formatting of the book's journey on its way to the publisher. Thanks for your tireless efforts in getting the job done.

Great credit goes to those many people behind the scenes at Abbott Press Publications no one really knows, sees, or contacts. They are the unsung, unheralded heroes and heroines who undauntedly complete the process of getting the book published. Thanks to these wonderful people who know who they are.

Lastly, credit and acknowledgment goes to the many who have inquiring minds looking for knowledge that leads to understanding about the many activities and processes of life. Some of these processes are essentially integral to the sustaining of life. Hopefully, those of you who decide to read this book will be among those who believe that the practice of law in a civilized society is that activity that sustains, perpetuates, and guards the gate to ensure the preservation of that which we all believe to be important to each of us.

Hopefully, we all agree that freedom, liberty, equity, civility, and the pursuit of happiness are the goals of any model society. If you believe in those values, you should, likewise, be acknowledged as attempting to contribute to maintaining the ideal life we all seek.

DEDICATION

This book is dedicated to all the good, great, and gifted lawyers who every day steadfastly represent and protect their clients' rights ethically with integrity, honor, fairness, and a dedication to putting forth their best in the best manner possible.

This book is also dedicated to the lawyers who were there from the beginning, almost 250 years ago, when our American system of democratic government, and its rules and laws, began to emerge from the abyss of discontent with the status quo in a time and place now far removed from the contemporary world we live in.

After this lengthy, ongoing evolution of a legal system designed to preserve and protect humanity from its innate quest for unyielding self-indulgence and self-degradation, lawyers—in spite of some who would disagree—continue in their drive to maintain a system of justice, equity, fairness, and order in the greatest nation in the free world.

This dedication goes to all of the above without reservation or doubt.

Without lawyers the world would not survive, irrespectively of those who would deny and rebuke such a notion.

Lawyers deserve the recognition, respect, appreciation, and accolades they don't often get.

That's the foundation and basis for this dedication.

PREFACE

This book is about the "way it is" in terms of the legal profession and its lawyers. This book is not about the law, nor does this book give any hint of advice on what you should do about any particular legal problem you might encounter. This book is not about helping you learn how to practice law. You need your lawyer. So any reference to the law, advice, or what you should do in any situation is not intended as a lawyer's opinion or counsel and should be disregarded in any such perceived manner. This book is about how to work with and understand the relationship with your lawyer through appropriate communication.

Once you have had an opportunity to reflect on what's being said about the nature of the legal profession and the lawyers of which it is composed, you'll understand and agree that this book is about *What Your Lawyer May Not Want You to Know*.

Candidly, this book is about "stuff" you need to know. Your lawyer is not going to tell you what's in this book. You probably have figured it out by now that this is the reason you need to read and understand this book.

Some things in life you just have to learn for yourself through the experience of others. You don't have time nor can you afford to experience them all firsthand. Reading this book can add to your knowledge, appreciation, and understanding of what you need to know in the relationship with your lawyer.

What Your Lawyer May Not Want You To Know! puts you up front in knowing what to do and knowing what to expect. Enjoy the learning experience!

When you finish this book, you will walk away with a better understanding and appreciation about lawyers, yourself, and the legal profession. You will find and discover some empathy, sensitivity, and admiration for what lawyers do.

As life should always be, you may not agree with everything that transpires in the process but you, at least, can try to understand. That's what this book is about!

This book is not just about lawyers but about the circumstances, situations, and environment in which they perform their professional responsibilities. Over time, lawyers have executed their behavior consistent with prevailing opportunities for their survival as well as their own personal gain. Before embarking on any disclosure about the legal profession—the law, lawyers, courts, judges, and the rules and procedures that comprise it—allow me to forcefully make this declaration. The point: Most lawyers are honest, hardworking, diligent, competent, and professional people. There are some, just like doctors, priests, preachers, engineers, dentists, machine operators, restaurant owners, merchandisers, and otherwise, who are dishonest, lazy expediters, and take shortcuts to enhance short-run profit maximization. Lawyers are no different than many other professionals who have no tangible product to sell. These professionals sell their advice hoping to give the client peace of mind and spirit. This solace can take the form of a monetary reward for injury, relief of oppression of the client's well-being, or their quality of life. The lawyer's skills and contribution in service to the client have myriad forms of benefit.

In *Henry VI*, Shakespeare was seriously amiss when he suggested, "The first thing we do, let's kill all the lawyers." If we are to remain a society of law and order, lawyers are a necessary part of those ingredients. Even during times of unfavorable discourse in the evolution of judicial history when the "tail seemed to be wagging the dog," there always seemed to be a force of equalization whacking away as a counter force to swing things back to some position of reasonable equilibrium. Most, if not many, do not want to acknowledge that these forces creating balance in life have been the legal profession.

Good or bad, right or wrong, liked or disliked, lawyers are a dominant force in your life. They have been and always will be. This has all arisen because of the nature of life. We as the human race tend to degrade ourselves to that of the lower animals when we acknowledge that life's processes are made-up of disagreement, conflict, and man's battle for space, equality, property, and freedom, but "that's the way it is." Lawyers did not create the problems or, at least, not all of them.

The contribution in this book concerning the legal profession is not one of "lawyer bashing" but addresses the greatest problem between the lawyer and you, the client. This problem is not an exclusive one for lawyers in our society. It is a problem that engulfs primary interest and attention from the bedroom to the United Nations and all points in between. However, this problem postures and presents itself to some arenas more than others. This problem is well-known, but not-so-well recognized or acknowledged. It is a problem more often denied than admitted, more often shunned than addressed, and camouflaged with crafty mechanisms from rhetoric, humor, and sarcasm. The problem strikes at the heart of life. The problem presents itself from sex to singing. The problem is that of "communication." That's what this book is about.

How well do any of us communicate to get what we want? Somehow, in some way, and at some time, each of us becomes conscious of our ability to communicate. Many, if not most, consider communication to be a given, granted, and unconscious activity. "It just comes out." One of the greatest keys to success is in learning and planning to communicate. Most of us don't think like this nor do we want to. Just saying what's on your mind is usually a bomb ready to explode.

Taking the time to think, evaluate, and plan to communicate are probably the vital forces in anyone's life. However, few of us engage in such activity. Oh, sure we think about sex, creature comforts, security, and our next meal but who really sits and becomes a problem-solver with deliberateness, direction, motive, and purpose?

If you read this book as part of your problem-solving approach to life, you will advance to the front of the pack. This book is one that is loaded with real-world caveats about the reality of the legal profession and life.

Understanding leads to the appreciation of, respect for, and sensitivity of any activity. This book does not promise to be a paragon of wisdom about the legal profession, revealing the whereabouts of the Holy Grail or the direction to King Solomon's mine. This book is intended to be practical, insightful, and informative, hoping that along the way you will have a eureka moment. That point in time will be worth the entire journey because you can take the insight with you as valuable reference to life and its reality.

The problem of communication this book deals with has persisted in the legal profession since the beginning of time. However, as well as nevertheless, it has been almost always inappropriately addressed by almost everyone and anyone who has dared to comment on the profession. Even such a noteworthy man as Clarence Darrow was not highly complimentary when he said, "The law is a bum profession. It is utterly devoid of idealism and almost poverty stricken as to any real ideas."

This book can change some of the perceptions of what the legal profession is about and what it does. This can be accomplished by attempting to address a few problems of communication and understanding between the legal profession and the clients it seeks to guide, direct, and protect. Unfortunately, most often the most authoritative premise for whatever we believe is that "the perception is the reality." Unkindly, Orson Welles exclaimed, "The law and the stage—both are a form of exhibitionism." Is this the reason for those perceptions that cast lawyers often in unfavorable reviews? Maybe lawyers are just "bad" actors!

If perception is the reality, the legal profession will continue to remain on the lower end of the spectrum of respectability. What the legal profession has exhibited is not what was intended and certainly not what should have been construed by those it serves. Thus, what's the problem?

The problem of communication between the legal profession and the world has been the profession's greatest continuing concern for many decades. There seems to have been little done to address this problem except an unwritten, unconfirmed, and unsubstantiated positional proclamation that the "good" has outweighed the "bad" in the course of the human drama being carried out.

Why have lawyers been given a bad rap for so long? In review and retrospect, many (and not most) times and circumstances have deduced that the legal profession has brought such dastardly acclaim on itself. This did not have to be nor should it have been.

This book addresses the issue of relationships between lawyers and their clients. Hopefully, this effort will provide a clear and direct road map for a better and easier path ahead in the relationship between you and your lawyer.

This book is no panacea and is not offered as the last vestige or paragon of truth about lawyers and the legal profession. This book is no "idiot's guide" nor any "Made Simple" treatise to help you destroy, control, or manipulate your lawyer. This book is about communication in relationships as the essence of understanding for a high quality life.

Most lawyers experience law practice from the broadest spectrum possible. The practice of law by a majority of lawyers is experienced via nickel and dime cases that are not worth the effort for the client or the lawyer to cases where poor indigent clients were awarded money beyond their wildest dreams for injuries they actually suffered.

Then, on the other hand, every lawyer handles cases for clients who receive justice or a monetary settlement they don't deserve. The lay person (a person of the street who is not in the profession) attempts to compare their situation with that of someone else's case. This is almost impossible and clients usually acquire a perception that leads to unsound and unreasonable expectations. So, when a client goes to a lawyer they are mostly "pre-set" in their mind about what they want from their lawyer. Lawyers are thrust quickly into a dialogue of communication essential for the mutual understanding between themselves and their client. Many (and, hopefully, not most of the time) get off to a bad start from the beginning. This book and its contribution are geared toward attempting to prevent such a disastrous journey in the months ahead for the client and the lawyer.

Every lawyer has hundreds of stories, from some that are outrageously funny to ones of tragedy and heartbreak. This book is not about those war stories. This book is about how the legal profession works, and it may assist you in surviving its wrath while also helping you understand and appreciate *What Your Lawyer May Not Want You to Know*. This is not a book all about the secrets of the legal profession. There are some, of course. Once you read it, you'll recognize that the revelations are obvious. The reality is that no one from the profession has dared to state the "way it is."

INTRODUCTION

W ords seem to be the most popular means of communicating ideas although they may not always be the most effective. You have probably heard the well-known, well-worn idea that, "What you are speaks so loudly, I can't hear what you are saying." The nature of what the legal profession is, and how it has been perceived, has caused it to suffer in terms of credibility and respectability. Understanding how this has been derived is important from the perspective of the lawyer and the client.

The legal profession, and those lawyers who comprise it, are victims of being placed in a position where the spoken and printed word, both good and bad, are the vehicles on which they travel to get what their clients want or in attempting to avoid what their clients don't want.

This "game" of language with lawyers can be a most tricky endeavor when their position assumed for the benefit of a client is met by another lawyer who has the same purpose in life of getting what his client wants. Thus, what follows is a "game" of "wordsmanship" where each lawyer is seeking a position of advantage over his opponent because that's how he gets what his client wants. Clients don't care how their lawyer wins. Just win! This begs the age-old question, "Would you rather have an honest lawyer who plays precisely by the rules or would you rather have a lawyer who will try to win in any manner necessary?" Lawyers don't want to think about this question. However, most lawyers attempt to play by the rules.

You are probably beginning to see the picture a little clearer. The matter of what the client has demanded from their lawyer has created much of the fervor about what lawyers do to satisfy their clients. We all recognize that "consumers" (and clients are "consumers") are demanding more and more at a cheaper price at their convenience now. This seems to be the way of the world. More, Better, Now and conveniently at a Cheaper price . . .

Clients are more demanding, better educated, and are exposed to what is happening in the legal profession. Clients consistently think their cases are worth considerably more than they realistically are. Clients think in terms of lottery jackpot verdicts and think they know more than the lawyer does about what should be the result of their legal situation. Clients shop lawyers to hear the words they are looking for the lawyer to say. If they do not hear what they are looking for they will move on to another lawyer looking for those "magic" words. Lawyers and clients alike are aware that this "sought-after" communication is taking place more frequently than ever before in the legal profession.

Competitiveness in the world has become ubiquitously obvious from lawyers to medical doctors. The problems that arise from fierce competition to represent a client searching and seeking to weigh his options for a lawyer has caused the client/lawyer relationship to suffer in terms of communication.

Lawyers, in their defense, often seek to avoid such conversations with clients who are fresh from hearing their neighbor tell of how successful their lawyer was in getting a zillion dollars in just a few weeks over only minor injuries. The legal profession, as honorable and laudable as it was intended to be, has been molded, tempered, and cast by unfavorable publicity, competitive advertising, and rampant criticism highlighted in every form of communication.

All of the successes and failures in the legal profession are tied to the involvement, implementation, and execution of some form of communication. Of course, the tidal success of all language ebbs and flows with the use and misuse of language. The use of language is the basis for communication, in terms of being effective or ineffective. Language is the basis for relationships. Sometimes, the language is spoken. Other times, the language is implied. Other times, you just know. Then, sometimes, you don't know what you have heard and the communications remain blurred and neither party has much basis for knowing what the parties have attempted to communicate.

Language has never and will never be an exact science, and we can only find any consistent and irrefutable meaning in its simplest uses. We all would probably argue eloquently and continuously about what is meant by "simplest" or more contemporarily what is meant by "sex." Sometimes, we just know it when we see or hear it.

The most obvious statement to be made about language is that language is a society's common expression of speech all made in an effort to communicate. But so much for all of this discourse about language! What the point? The point is, "Why do we spend so much time studying and reviewing language in our lives?" Of course, the answer is "to more effectively communicate." Then, why do we communicate? The threshold answer in life to this question is "TO GET WHAT WE WANT!" Think about it! We communicate in life "TO GET WHAT WE WANT." Unquestionably, there are some who will read this comment and immediately try to consider that this remark must not always be true. Well, you think about it! It's always true. Your communication with your lawyer should be "TO GET WHAT YOU WANT."

Life consists of relationships. The life you live may contain relationships with a spouse, children, your parents, your relatives, your friends, your neighbors, church members, and on and on. You even have a relationship with inanimate things such as a favorite chair, a favorite food, or a special pair of shoes. Some people have a favorite song. We form these relationships because we are attracted to those objects which form the basis for the relationship because we perceive "utility" in the relationship. Don't be too critical! I'm not suggesting that you run around talking to your favorite objects, such as a pair of shoes or your favorite piece of music. I am suggesting, however, that you do think about these objects as something you want, use, and enjoy. Most of us work diligently at preserving and maintaining the things we enjoy. To do this, we employ the art of communication in some form, either to other people or even to ourselves. Have you considered that every time you have a thought you are communicating?

The point is that all lawyers in life are positioned to help you get some of what you want or to help you avoid what you don't want. You probably haven't perceived lawyers in this sense. Lawyers are "word-merchants." Rights, duties, and obligations are always articulated in the form of words properly aligned to reflect the truest intent of the communication between people who are concerned about getting "what they want." That's the only reason in life that you would ever want to see a lawyer: "to get what you want or avoid getting what you don't want." That's a tough position to take but many believe that lawyers don't make good friends—or good pets for that matter.

The banter of "lawyer-bashing" has been loud and clear for years now. Why? There are so many of them! The cover of the May 23, 1995 issue of *Financial World* depicts five grumpy old men under the caption, "Lawyer Glut!" Turning to an article on page 52 of that same issue, Debra Sparks writes, "By the year 2023, Harvard Law School Dean Robert Clark predicts there will be more lawyers in the U.S. than people. Within five years there will be over a million lawyers in this country. That means roughly 70% of all the lawyers on the planet will be plying their trade in the U.S."

Lawyers are a prominent part of life in the world. As a matter of fact, in the United States the lawyer population has doubled in the last 30 years to approximately 1,245,205 lawyers. This equates to one lawyer for every 300 citizens in this country. In 2005, 70% of lawyers were male but figures currently show now that out of the 146,288 students in law school, 47% are female. In the past 30 years, female lawyers have populated the ranks by a 266% increase. The population of lawyers has grown around 2% per year since demographic data has been retained about the growing inventory.

"Just too many dogs and not enough meat," could be an artless way of suggesting that many lawyers are conducting themselves in creative positions of advocacy. The implication here is that some lawyers are looking for lawsuits against corporate giants which have little, if any, precedent in common law or any statutory law whatsoever. Some lawyers exercise vigorously in "creative advocacy." This attitude often leaves little time to honestly and realistically communicate with the client. As a result, the broad segment of the client population gets to view the innovation of advocacy allowing them to believe that everything is "fair" game in the battle of litigation. Lawyers and clients who are overly zealous in pursuit often fail to communicate. Many have alleged that lawyers have brought their failure to communicate on themselves.

The point here is not to solve the ills, woes, and rigors of the overall legal profession and our society's negative response to what it sees. The thrust of this offering is to help you survive your lawyer. Forget about all the stuff you can say about lawyers that has actually shown some negative creativity from those who have sought to disagree with the legal profession rather than understand it.

This book is about helping you understand your lawyer and helping you help your lawyer in helping you. Lawyers need help, too. They live in a specialized world of communication and conflict. If you are better informed and able to bridge the gap you will know what to expect, what to look for, and how to communicate with your lawyer. Remember, most lawyers are honest, hard-working people who have your interest at heart. Those times when the situation and circumstances seem to dictate the contrary are usually a result of poor communication, not communicating, or some misconception between the two of you.

There is one thing that stands irrefutable in the bridge of the relationship between a lawyer and his client: the lawyer and the client experience a disproportionate amount of power in the relationship. This imbalance of power is the most important thing for you, the client, to understand. That position will not change, but there are ways for you to swing the pendulum a little more in your favor without hurting the lawyer/client relationship. Communication with your lawyer is what this book is about. That's what you need to know. *What Your Lawyer May Not Want*

You To Know! for the first time ever talks about what your lawyer is thinking and how he is communicating. When you know that, you are more balanced in your relationship with him and can help in the communication process.

You are about to embark on a study of that communication process. To do this you must first learn what you can expect from your lawyer and what you have no right to expect. Your success in life at everything is relative to your expectations. **LET'S SEE WHAT YOU CAN EXPECT FROM YOUR LAWYER . . .**

CHAPTER 1

THE LAW, LAWYERS, AND YOU

There is an old adage—and if there isn't,
there should be—that says, "There are some
things so complicated they are not worth
getting involved with."—BFB

T he law has been spoken about with irreverence, sarcasm, contempt, disdain, and rebuke. Conversely, on other side of these positions most would agree that the law should be idealized as a symbol for order, discipline, and control of certain relationships in society. The law represents the maintenance and enforcement of some structure that provides for defined relationships between people and things affecting ownership, freedom, and the rights of the individual in an organized society. Once you recognize that the "law" is a mere structure for promoting conformity and compliance in a civilly organized society, there is much less sting in the pain of one's criticism. The "law" represents what should be the rules of society to lead, guide, and direct behavior between the individuals of a society in their personal lives and the life of a society. These laws are promulgated by those in positions of power, charged with the responsibility for deciding what the law should be.

The "law" standing without the benefit of interpretation would be mute and would carry no meaning. We derive meaning out of life in all its aspects from the interpretation of the language conveyed. Our judicial system has evolved over many years, and has been concerned about the interpretation of language. You are familiar with some of these words: "freedom of speech," "freedom of religion," "due process," "civil rights," and on and on.

1

This process of interpretation is a daily struggle in the life of a judicial system. As a sophisticated society, we have grown very concerned with what is being thought by those in positions of judicial power about what certain things should mean. However, in reality, there is a practical balance of opinion on almost every public issue that accounts for a stalemate in the weight of any one favored direction. So, everything eventually tends to equal out in the position between extremism and the state of being conservative in our society as a part of the social process. Irrespective of this balance in the societal arena, there is still a continuing squabble over those who have the power to influence the swing of the pendulum in the judicial process. Ideally, the judicial process should mirror the profile of the society in which it operates.

The more direct and immediate impact affecting the ascertainment of the values considered essential and important in any society is the vastness of diversity in its morals, dogma, and culture.

In the society of which you are a part, there is one idea, one underlying process, one persistent driver, and one non-eroding quest that remains a steadfast, insidious goal of many of its members. This goal is the discussion of this book.

Noteworthy and obviously noticeable, this one word has been intentionally omitted from the previous paragraphs. This word has caused more problems in the history of mankind than any other word. Even though this word is a part of freedom, it is also a part of bondage and slavery. There has been a continuing fight to maintain this word's influence in our life and in our society. This word represents and means responsibility and what's necessary for stabilizing a reasonable balance between polarized forces that grind toward making new ways and new ideas in our society. On the other hand, a vigilant lamp is always lit to impede the overzealousness of manipulation to assure that there is never an irresolvable barrier in the direction of anyone's destiny. This word that has been the biggest catalyst for changes in the life of mankind and the world is "control."

Control inevitably is one of the major components in life. There are those who seek to control and there are those who resist control. There are those more in control and there are those in less control. There is an underlying belief in any civilized society that lawyers are in control of many things influencing the society's freedom, liberty, peace of mind, well-being, and the security of its property. Lawyers have played a decisive role in the development of a modern way of life in this world.

Control Is Everything When Moderated

The major involvement in the development of a modern civilized society is how "control" is going to be balanced for the mutual benefit of all the interested parties involved. When you study the United States Constitution, you realize the document creates a central government of "enumerated" powers. Regardless of what culture you emerge from, "power" has always been equated with the "capacity to control." Control, as noted above, is the quality that a government must have in order to fulfill its mission to its citizenry.

When you trace the history of the development of power between any government and its citizens, you will eventually discover an evolving struggle between the two. This is an ongoing process and should never be expected to terminate. Aside from the long process of how a national government has evolved to its position of exercising its powers, states likewise were vested with the power to control their own survival and the relationship of peaceful civility between their citizens. The establishment of both national (Federal) laws and state laws is the essential means by which the governmental systems, both state and Federal, survive. States allocate authority to counties within the states to exercise power in the form of establishing laws to promote, protect, and provide for their citizens. Then, municipalities are further given authority to pass their own laws to regulate civil life in the community.

So, we all have to recognize and acknowledge that laws are ubiquitous. Without laws, there would be no organized control of our society. Without the necessary structured efforts being made to promote civility in our society, there would be only a low quality of life without safety, security, peaceful enjoyment, tranquility, or peace of mind. Whether you like it or not, control through execution and enforcement of the law is absolutely essential to continue in the style and quality of life we have so progressively acquired. This has not been attained without conflict, difficulty, struggle, and consternation. Mankind has fundamentally resisted most efforts to control his basic behavior from the earlier time of *homo erectus* up to the current time of the latest celebrity resisting a charge of D.U.I. When you think about it, the entire history of mankind has been a struggle over "control"—from religion to politics to the institution of marriage.

When you stop and realize that, overall, the law represents a form of control, you should instantly recognize that the internal effects of control and its aftermath must cause conflict.

Lawyers Are Bridges Between You and the Law

The lawyer is perceived as one in society who has a unique relationship with the law. Most of us don't think much about the fact that the law is so inherently interwoven into the heart and fabric of our lives. The law is an essential part of all of our lives to a real extent. Some people are luckier than others in that they may go through life without ever having to consult a lawyer. Others become very familiar with lawyers and their role in society as having the means and ability to help you avoid conflict, minimize conflict, and minimize the damaging effects when conflict arises.

Lawyers have learned how to deal with power. If you had the ability to deal with power and conflict, you would not need a lawyer. The point is that lawyers are essential to the preservation of life and society. Some even reflect that the legal profession and its lawyers are a necessary evil. However, lawyers are "conflict" specialists. They deal with power on a daily basis to assist their clients in restoring the status quo in their lives.

There are many treatises on the shelves of bookstores blasting lawyers as thorns and weeds in the garden of life, thieves with a license to steal, betrayers of the justice system, diabolical perpetrators of injustice, out to destroy the family and promote moral decay. The list could even go on. The truth is that some of this is true but most of it is not. These broad sweeping generalizations really aid no one. No system is perfect. Doctors, engineers, preachers, and even salespeople have similar problems because they are in service businesses where people enter into the relationships with different expectations and perceive performance beyond what is often considered reasonable and appropriate.

When You Need a Lawyer, You Need a Lawyer

There are also many books loaded on the shelves of bookstores which attempt to broadly and generally advise you on various legal matters. These books serve a good general purpose but most offer the proviso and admonition that such a book should never be construed as a replacement for a lawyer. When you need a lawyer, you need a lawyer. There is no attempt here to advise you of the general principles of law. Most of us are surprised about how much is known in society about child custody, accidents, contracts, bankruptcy, divorce, employment rights, malpractice, real estate, corporations, insurance, patents, copyrights, wills, workmen's compensation, product liability, and even estates. You likely read newspapers and magazines and watch TV just like everyone else. You probably know a little bit about all these areas.

The point is that if you are not a lawyer when you have a legal problem, you need a lawyer. Then, on the other hand, when you are a lawyer and have a personal legal problem, you still need a lawyer. Someone wisely stated that the lawyer who acts as his own lawyer has a fool for a client.

You can read all the books from the bookshelves and may not be able to advise yourself if you actually do need a lawyer. To be able to render competent legal advice, a lawyer must not only know the basic principles of law involved but must also understand the practicalities of pursuing a remedy or solution in terms of the overall benefit for the client. These are questions which are not answered merely by reading *Everyday Law Made Simple*. Legal advice is more than just knowing the right answer, as you'll discover ahead. Don't let this admonishment be a downer. Go buy all the legal encyclopedias and law guides you want, but never ever think, even in the slightest of moments, that you can decide if you can handle your own legal problem. If you think you have a legal problem before you try to advise yourself, rest assured, you will after you take your own advice. Giving yourself advice is often on the order of a self-induced lethal injection.

The market is plentiful with "do-it-yourself" kits covering everything from setting up your own corporation to crafting your own divorce settlement, estate plan, and will to filing your own personal injury suit. These initially inexpensive shortcuts are green pastures for lawyers. Lawyers love for you to "do it yourself."

Can you do it? Sure, you can, but you don't know what you are doing. All you are doing is filling in the blanks. It's like learning to fly a plane by passing the written test or like learning brain surgery by reading the surgical procedure book. Knowledge should always be accompanied by common sense. Common sense dictates that just because you have a surge of "feeling your oats," you don't go and try to do your own thing. If you do, it just may take two lawyers to get you out of the jam you put yourself in when you were dreading seeing just one lawyer. Now follow this to the next chapter and be glad that you decided not to do yourself in by acting as your own lawyer. You are worth saving from yourself and your lawyer.

Watch for Mr. or Ms. Lawyer "Know-It-All"

One final note here: when you finish reading this book you'll really appreciate the complexities of the legal profession and the difficulties all lawyers have with it. If the lawyer you have chosen after reading Chapter 3 tells you that he or she has never had any problems understanding the law and its application, thank him or her and then get out of that office immediately. You would probably be well advised not to even take the time to retrieve your hat and coat. Competence, training, and education are very important but they are not absolutes and no one seems to have ever cornered the market in knowing all things and doing all things to the full satisfaction of everyone. Arrogance can be rampant in the legal profession. Better luck on your next shopping trip . . .

CHAPTER 2

DO YOU REALLY NEED A LAWYER?

There is an old adage which says,
"People are afraid of what they don't
know." This needs some modification
to a new adage which allows that, "Most
people are afraid of what they don't
know only if they realize that they
don't know."—BFB

D o you really need a lawyer? At times, this question is not easily answered. Sometimes it is obvious. Every time, it should be carefully analyzed, studied, and evaluated from a number of perspectives which we will attempt to examine. There are those who avoid lawyers when only a lawyer could possibly solve their problem. There are others who call their lawyer at every slight incongruity in life that might not meet their exact expectations. This latter group is better labeled as "P.I.T.A.s" which is an acronym for "pain in the anatomy." In some circles the last word in the description is substituted with another. P.I.T.A.s are difficult people to work with since this lawyer is steadfastly attempting, at least initially, to maintain good public relations with all of those who would darken his door seeking representation. Lawyers want clients who will place confidence and trust in his legal abilities to thwart any of life's aggravations which could be soothed by application of good representation in the legal process.

You Will Not Have a Problem Getting to Talk to a Lawyer

A lawyer, most often, will talk to a potential client about almost anything regardless of the subject's level of stupidity, ignorance, or even irrelevance. However, you are not required to use much of your imagination to appreciate that lawyers are looking for a legal problem that not only has some substantive issues which can appropriately be dealt with using their skills, but a problem that also is of some gravity and import worthy of engagement. When the case is of such significance, the lawyer can then be justified in applying their system of receiving fees for his or her services. Otherwise, the case problem is one of a nuisance which will net little satisfaction for the client and only a small fee, if any, for the lawyer. You'll discover that the smaller case is often as difficult to solve as the larger one, and more often than not is more difficult for the client since no lawyer wants it and the client does not know how to go about getting it solved.

Let's Talk About a Potential Legal Problem

An example might be if you own a home in a subdivision where the yards are separated by a common fence. However, there is a tree in your neighbor's yard that is leaning over toward your house. If the tree is blown down because of a strong storm the tree would fall across your house. You have asked but the neighbor refuses to cut the tree down even though you have continued to lose sleep over your anguish. You want to sue to make the neighbor cut the tree and for money damages for the resulting mental suffering you have endured because of your neighbor deliberately refusing to cut the tree. When a lawyer is presented with the psychiatrist's bills along with prescription costs, it is difficult to deny that the client is serious about their legal position. A lawyer's dilemma here is whether this case represents one within his skills, ability, and training, whether he believes the case has any merit for which a reasonable legal solution may be acquired, and whether the case is worthwhile for the lawyer and the client. Don't scoff at these facts! People every day in life are burdened about situations for which they have no apparent solution. This brings us to the point of this chapter.

Will "Common Sense" Do the Trick of Solving My Problem?

The question in every potential client's mind is whether a lawyer should be consulted, or can I, as a reasonably intelligent able-bodied human being, make application to my own reservoir of common sense to solve the problem? The question of "common sense" is a tough one. The most difficult problem for the lay person is to compile an inventory of reasonable approaches based on education, training, and experience to assist him in solving his particular problem. This not only takes considerable experience in life but some rudimentary familiarity with legal principles and procedures. Even a little knowledge can be a most desirable and useful asset in a life problem/solution. However, there is a "catch-22" here because the old adage about a little knowledge being a dangerous thing looms heavily, just waiting for its chance of application. Most of those who know more than a scintilla about their legal rights and the practicality of pursuing them have had some experience in the legal arena and base their reasoning— right or wrong—on what they have observed. Where do we go from here in evaluating whether or not you need a lawyer?

Lawyers, Lawyers EVERYWHERE!

The legal profession in the last several decades has gone through some drastic changes. Some have been more catastrophic than others. Of course, what's unimportant to one lawyer may be a monumental boon for another. Lawyers are not all created equal nor do they want to be.

A godsend for some, and a plague for others, was that lawyers were allowed to advertise beginning in 1978. Your own imagination and your ability to watch TV lets you know what happened next. Lawyers seemed to start coming out of the woodwork and some even came out of the woodshed. Some, at least so it seems, were heard of for the first time ever. Advertising ran across the whole spectrum since some were new, some old, some experienced, some inexperienced, some good, and some not so good. It was really difficult to know the difference and still is. Their creativity and salesmanship would lead you to believe that only the best lawyers advertise. This is not necessarily the case or the truth. More and more, lawyers are beginning to find their way into your living rooms. Be easy; don't just blast the lawyers for getting involved in the social processes of selling their alleged skills and abilities via the airways. Doctors representing everything from the delivery of babies to brain surgery are also doing the same thing. Competition—and sometimes greed—in both the legal and medical professions has caused this to come about.

Now, more than ever—and please pay attention to this—lawyers are advertising that you, the potential client, can have their first-time consultation FREE. Old Abe Lincoln would roll over in his grave if he heard this, since when he was around he advised, "A lawyer's time is his stock in trade." I am sure that you are beginning to see where I am going with this. SHOP LAWYERS! Learn whether or not you have a problem that needs the attention and assistance of an attorney. Listen to more than one lawyer. Get their advice and counsel. Use your common sense about the affairs of life and judge whether your legal concern is worth the legal fees and whether the end product of your pursuit is worth your time and aggravation in dealing with the legal system. LISTEN and LEARN! In advising you to do this, I am assuming that because you are interested in reading this that you are at least a couple of notches (and maybe more) above the level of a buffoon. If what you hear doesn't make any sense to you, whether or not it makes any sense to anyone else doesn't matter. It's your money, your time, and your potential aggravation that's at stake.

Clear Signals for When You Need a Lawyer

To those who couldn't care less about the legal system and those who are not interested in "what your lawyer may not want you to know," there are some clear and irrefutable signals about when you should see a lawyer.

First, when you are served as a defendant with legal papers, called "legal process" or "summons" in a civil lawsuit. Second, when you are arrested on a warrant containing a criminal charge. Third, a witness in a court case who receives a subpoena often will seek out a lawyer to fully understand the circumstances of being a witness. Fourth, when you know that you have a legal problem, or are looking for a legal solution, in some situation of serious significance where your common sense and savvy street gamesmanship will not suffice.

It has become a "do-it-yourself" world and everyone seems to be getting along with this idea. However, the legal arena is no place for amateurs. When the novice self-helper jolts into the world of legalisms, they usually end up "doing it to themselves" (i.e., hoisting themselves on their own petard). This just may be apropos and befitting, since the point here is that all you have to do is ask and learn to understand about your legal problem in that first interview and consultation and then you can make an informed decision whether or not you need a lawyer.

Good things often come from circumstances which on first impression don't appear as being in the best interest of society. In the case of advertising and increased competition in the legal profession, the potential client now has an opportunity to become an informed and intelligent decision-maker as to what they want to do in response to their perceived legal problem and whether "they really need a lawyer" before they ever hire a lawyer. This represents an opportunity for the client you may not have had before the arrival of increased competition and advertising. Lawyers want your business so they'll talk to you about your legal problem. They want to make the best impression on you so they can get your business.

Don't Stop Reading—The Best Ideas About Lawyers Are Yet to Come

This all sounds too simple! Something must be wrong. Usually when it sounds too good to be true it usually is. Since you are beginning to understand a little of how the world of business is involved in the legal profession, you may think that the task is simple. Keep in mind that the practice of law is a business. If you hold this idea in your mind, you will understand how lawyers work and why they do what they do.

Now, since you are looking for a lawyer, venture out into the world of "FREE" consultations until you get want you want. Unfortunately, it's just not that simple or easy. Just wait before you start deciding that this is the answer until you hear the rest of "what lawyers may not want you to know." You are not ready yet, but you'll be there soon!

Good luck to you as you find out whether or not you really need a lawyer. Sometimes, luck is better than a little skill . . .

CHAPTER 3

WHAT KIND OF LAWYER DO I NEED, AND HOW DO I FIND THIS PROBLEM-SOLVER?

"One of the most distrustful people
you'll ever know is that person who
is clever, inventive, eloquent,
intelligent, and knowledgeable, fulfilling their ambition of being
financially successful by selling
their time and services to ignorant
and stupid people"—BFB

"The only time most people will take
or seek advice is when they recognize
that they are in trouble; otherwise, their
own advice is the only advice they think
they need".—BFB

O nce you have decided that you have a legal problem, your lawyer momentarily becomes the most important person in your life, notwithstanding your spouse, your kids, your dog or cat, or the I.R.S. In the last chapter, you were advised to learn about your perceived legal problem by searching out those who would render assistance in an initial interview which would give you guidance and direction without charge. This should have helped you set the stage for making the decision of whether you need a lawyer for your problem. This suggestion about going to those who would not charge for the initial interview is not intended to encourage you to seek free legal advice. If and when you choose a lawyer, the lawyer's fees must be paid if you are going to keep that lawyer on your case and if you want that lawyer to give your case the interest and attention it deserves.

On the other hand, every lawyer in the world has given free legal advice but most of them do not know that they are giving free legal advice at the time they are giving it. I am sure you get the drift of this. Lawyers who are unpaid for their legal services are not happy lawyers. They are not unique. Everyone who is not paid when they should be paid feels the same way. So, don't be unnecessarily hard on lawyers for this.

Lawyers Are Looking for the Right Case

Don't be misled or don't misconstrue the lawyer's intentions in providing a free first consultation. The lawyer is not playing the role of "Mr. or Ms. Charity, Compassion, or Generosity." The lawyer is looking for those special legal circumstances, a level of involvement, a certain problem, a particular kind of conflict, or a unique situation the legal profession calls a "case" which presents to the lawyer a matter where he or she can competently, reasonably, and effectively represent the client for a fee. No lawyer wants to take a case considered to be a "dog." A "dog" case is one that doesn't have great value for a lawyer in terms of earning a decent fee or one that doesn't have the potential of being reconciled to the reasonable satisfaction of the client. "Reasonable satisfaction" for the client can be justly described as attaining the approximate desired outcome that the client expects at a fee the client would consider reasonably justified. Ideally, all lawyers want their clients to receive value in the attorney-client relationship. There is often a great gap between what clients expect and what the legal system (via lawyers) delivers to meet clients' perceived expectations. Later, considerable discussion will be offered on this very important aspect of the attorney-client relationship.

Most lawyers don't like to acknowledge the fact that all lawyers "pan for gold" in the form of looking for the "Big Case." Without hearing the suspicious descriptions of how, where, when, and who contributes to these acquisitions, your own imagination will suggest that some lawyers look harder, longer, and more than other lawyers. These "rainmakers," as they are often called, are likely to show up unannounced at major outings where major calamities and national cataclysms are in progress. These are probably not the lawyers you are looking for to solve your legal problem because if your legal problem was one of sufficient magnitude, they would usually find their way to you.

Legal Specialization Means Focus

Lawyers over the last few decades have begun to emphasize specialization of professional services. Lawyers have finally and gradually realized that the more you try to do in terms of a variety of services, the less you are able to know about each of them. There are only so many hours in a day and you can only read so much to keep abreast of the expeditious evolution of changes taking place almost on a daily basis. Simply stated, lawyers are beginning to recognize that the idea of "more" in many areas of the legal practice means less competence which leads to diminished satisfaction for the client. When lawyers specialize, they maintain a confined, centralized focus on that area of defined legal activity. Lawyers are recognizing that they can't be all things to all people and it's better to be good at one thing than only acceptable at many things. Think about it—would you want to go to a psychiatrist for brain surgery?

This is not to say that you need a specialist for every legal problem. Every lawyer can make out a will and prepare a power-of-attorney. Those who say that they don't do those things just don't want to do those things. Usually, lawyers, like any other citizens, do their best at what they like to do. When you discover that a lawyer does a great amount of work in domestic relations cases, for instance, this means, in most situations, that the lawyer has acquired a reputation for those kinds of cases.

This can mean at least one of two things. First, this is what that lawyer likes to do and is seeking this kind of case, or secondly, this lawyer has established a good reputation based on his or her experience in handling these kinds of cases. Often, a lawyer will learn to like whatever business he can attract as a distinct area in the overall practice of law. The more he handles a particular kind of case, the more he gets a reputation for that area of the legal practice—unless he's incompetent and/or consistently fails to meet a client's expected level of satisfaction, or both. This may come as a surprise to you: yes, there are actually incompetent lawyers who are successful in keeping their clients happy and satisfied. This seems paradoxical and is something you need to understand. This will be fully discussed in the next chapter.

Don't Just Sit There; Take Some Initiative Yourself!

You have gleaned by what's been said above that you are looking for a lawyer who has a reputation for handling the type of legal problem you perceive yours to be. Ask your neighbors, ask your relatives, ask your grocer, ask your hair stylist, ask your minister, ask your postman, and/or ask your boss who are the best lawyers they know for drawing up a will, getting a divorce, or whatever. Get some opinions! If you don't want to reveal the nature of your problem, just tell them it's personal and then ask them for the name of a good lawyer.

Then call that lawyer and tell him or her that you have been referred by your friend or neighbor, etc.—state the person's name and the lawyer will usually acknowledge the name whether the lawyer remembers or not. Next, ask the lawyer if his office closes real estate loans, or deals with whatever legal problem you have. If you are told that he does not close real estate loans or does not deal with your particular legal problem, ask who he would recommend. Every lawyer knows someone who handles the type of legal problem you think you have.

Now, this next part is important. When you call this lawyer you have been referred to, advise the secretary that you called the first attorney (be sure to give his name) and were referred to this law firm and told to ask for (the name of attorney recommended) who would do a good job for you at a reasonable fee. This is important! All lawyers want, beg, seek, solicit, and covet referrals. There isn't a greater compliment among lawyers than to have one lawyer refer legal business to another attorney unless it's junk business, which we'll discuss later.

The manner in which you have handled the telephone call and related that you are coming to the referred lawyer's office by way of advice of another attorney makes you special and more than likely to get the V.I.P. treatment. If you didn't get the "red carpet" treatment or were not treated in a way that met your expectations, wouldn't it be embarrassing to the referred attorney if you went back to the referring attorney and told him how "snobby, uncaring, inconsiderate, rude, and degenerate" the referred lawyer was? How embarrassing! Not only will the referred lawyer not want to confront the referring lawyer but the referred lawyer will realize that a great source of future business has been lost.

Believe it or not, most lawyers have fragile egos and must, at least in their own minds, be held in high esteem by any and all subjects. Believe me, if the referring lawyer and the referred lawyer are not golfing buddies or blood brothers or sisters, the referring lawyer will usually never take a chance on any lawyer referral blowing up in their face in the future and especially with this alleged airhead who didn't take the time, patience, and consideration not to come across as a snob and degenerate lawyer among other things. The same is true with medical doctors. How would you feel if you referred a friend to your plastic surgeon who failed to show the proper regard for your friend? You would be embarrassed and feel insulted that your recommendation had been treated with such considerable disrespect. Remember, your opinion of someone is based on that person's most recent behavior you know about. Once a nice person doesn't mean always a nice person.

To summarize the point, lawyers are a great source of referral to other lawyers. Lawyers who do not perform a particular service enjoy referring clients to other lawyers who do that specific thing. If you make the right connection and use the right approach, the referred lawyer may be your choice of attorney. Once you get in the referred lawyer's office and discover that for some reason they cannot handle your case, ask them to refer you to someone who can. Then, when you approach the other lawyer's office, start the approach again as we discussed before but without telling them about the first lawyer you called. You don't want to raise the flag that you have a problem case that no one wants to take. We'll talk more about problem cases later.

Don't Be Afraid to Talk to a Lawyer! Ask! Ask! Ask!

When a lawyer talks to you about your case and later in the interview advises that he cannot take your case, don't just say "thank you" and sojourn out the door. Ask the attorney whether or not he believes you have a case worthy of hiring a lawyer. Don't sit in the chair like a dummy and accept some generalized lame assessment. Find out why the lawyer won't take your case. Is it because he doesn't know what to do? Is he afraid? Does he think you can't pay? Does the lawyer consider that this type of case is a loser for the client and the lawyer? Do the cost for the client and fees for the lawyer outweigh the benefit for the client? Is it a no-win situation for the client? Does the lawyer think that it is a loser case? Ask him! If you leave the office without getting some idea you are the dunderhead, not the lawyer.

Another Source for Finding a Lawyer

Now, there is another source for finding your lawyer but you must know that it may not be any better than the first one suggested above, even though it appears to have the legitimacy of the some structure with which we are familiar.

When we were coming up as kids, we became familiar with the word "clinic" as a part of our developing lives. That's because our parents had an opportunity to frequently take us—obviously against our will and wishes—to a medical clinic. This was perceived as a place of various services of medical care short of having to go to the hospital. Today, we see auto clinics, credit clinics, computer clinics, and, of course, legal clinics.

Legal clinics advertise as being one-stop shopping places for the searching client with a legal problem. These clinics usually advertise on TV as to their variety of services and often emphasize the discounted fee as an enticement for the weary potential client. These legal clinics perform a valuable legal service to the client population and one should not lose sight of this. However, you, as a potential future client, should also recognize that this level of legal service is almost equivalent to the same situation you would confront if you required a major overall of your automobile engine. Would you take your car to a car care clinic to do this? Some would but most would not. The same is true with the legal clinics. Their modus operandi is to attract legal business around the perception of the discounted fee. In life, most of us have learned that you always pay for what you get but you don't always get what you pay for. This is to say that these legal clinics are geared to processing smaller and lesser complicated areas of legal service which lend themselves to being accomplished through the aid of paralegals and word processing equipment.

The bottom line for potential clients about legal clinics is: 1.) Know what kind of legal problem you have, 2.) Know its relative complexity, and 3.) Know broadly what is involved in its solution. Remember, whatever a lawyer is doing is what he is good at doing or eventually will be good at doing. This is not to say that there are not exceptions to what is being said here. Please do not construe that the legal clinic is to be avoided. This is not the case. They are performing a valuable service to the client community. However, remember—would you reasonably expect to get heart bypass surgery at an out-patient clinic?

Who Knows a Lawyer Best?

Finally, those who know lawyers best are the judges and court clerks. Often, you may have an opportunity to call a court clerk and ask them which lawyer handles a particular legal problem. The first lawyer that comes to his or her mind is the recommendation. Judges are reluctant to recommend a lawyer since they may have the opportunity to have you point your finger at them later. A judge can't take a chance on recommending a lawyer. (At least, most of them wouldn't.) I'm sure you understand the reasons why when asked, often many lawyers don't want to recommend another lawyer.

"No One Is Looking After Your Interest Until They Have an Interest in You"—BFB

In the end, what kind of lawyer do you need? You need a lawyer who is interested in your case and will see it through to the end, a lawyer who is compassionate with the issues of your case and is not solely representing you because you can pay his fees, a lawyer who has the legal capability to handle your legal problem, a lawyer who is mature in judgment and can act towards reaching the best solution to your legal problem, and a lawyer who understands you, the client, as a frightened, apprehensive, and frustrated person who is seeking a legal solution in a scary, time-consuming, inexact, aggravating, and often dispassionate legal system and who is sensitive to those feelings.

Shopping for a lawyer is simple but not easy. Most people don't have a clue about where to start. Learn one of the most important lessons in life—learn to ask! Remember: one of the greatest statements ever made was, "Ask and ye shall receive." Remember lawyers are in this world to serve clients. When you know how to make that happen, you can engage in the legal process with some equality. Until you learn about the legal profession and how it works, you are at its mercy! Amen!

The "Junk" Case

Every lawyer greets clients with open arms before he knows what the case or concern is about. A lawyer soon learns whether the situation is worthy of the lawyer's time in terms of money, efforts, success, or overall involvement. Some lawyers have a difficult time directly and appropriately communicating the potential about how the lawyer really views the client's predicament. Lawyers are reluctant to tell a client that his or her case is one that can be unattractively described as a "junk" case.

To every client, his problem is real, confronting, worrisome, and agonizing regardless of its magnitude or what anyone else thinks. No client thinks his or her case is a "junk" case. Lawyers cannot be brutally blunt with a client in casting off the problem as one of no or little consequence. Clients still feel the pain, pressure, and perplexity regardless of whether their lawyer feels they should or should not.

A lawyer will never, or at least should never, tell a client that his case is not worthy of representation and is a "junk" case because regardless of what a lawyer thinks, the situation giving rise to the case is real, painful, and agonizing to the client. A lawyer must tread lightly if he or she is going to reject representation of the client.

In every lawyer's mind is the looming concern of how to tactically and tactfully communicate to the client the lawyer's honest assessment of the situation, if it's not favorable for the lawyer's involvement, without completely destroying any future potential of evaluating another opportunity to represent this client.

Clients don't know or don't care that their case is really a "junk" case to the lawyer. They want a solution irrespective of the lawyer's potential benefit at a reasonable fee or no fee.

The Lawyer's Dilemma

First, the lawyer must hear out the client with all the nuances of detail to allow the potential client to believe that the lawyer has heard "everything." (This is exhausting for the lawyer, since the lawyer knew in the first two minutes whether the client was presenting a "junk" scenario.)

The second part is how the lawyer must steer the client towards encouraging the client to solve the problem himself without the lawyer being obvious in not wanting to handle this situation for the client. This effort to steer the client toward self-solution is usually couched around saving the potential client lawyer fees as well as the lawyer not being able to place the case into his present inventory of an excessive work load. There are a myriad of reasons the lawyer can give but most of them are not honest or real. The lawyer may even develop a conflict of interest with some of the parties involved in the adversity.

Third, the lawyer must be careful not to tell the client he will try to get this "taken care of," fully realizing that he does not plan to do anything. Some lawyers believe if some problems are left alone they will go away, abate, vanish, or disappear into thin air. (Believe it or not, some do!) But most won't.

The lawyer who is the "Mr. or Mrs. Nice Person" who volunteers to take on the "junk" cause invites trouble with the client for two reasons. Foremost, the small problems are often the most difficult to solve and require a considerable about of time, which do not justify a legal solution. Then, a lawyer cannot appropriately and correctly charge a client for the amount of time required to obtain a solution or satisfaction without incurring the client's disfavor. Thus, the rendition of a "catch-22" for the lawyer. More lawyers gain bad reputations for taking on "junk" case clients than gain good reputations for doing so.

The bottom line is that lawyers should take notice about their own thought processes in how they deal with clients. Consciousness is the beginning of awareness and response in human activity. Potential clients must be aware of how lawyers think of case situations so they can, at least, understand more about lawyers. You, as a client, may not agree but you can lessen the anguish with your understanding.

Potential clients must be aware that every lawyer greets clients with open arms before knowing what the case or concern is about. A lawyer soon learns whether the situation is worthy of his time in terms of money, efforts, success, or overall involvement. Every lawyer has a difficult time in directly and appropriately communicating the potential about how he really views the client's predicament. Lawyers are reluctant to, or totally refuse to, take on a client's case if the situation can not be mutually beneficial to both the client and the lawyer.

Even to a lawyer no case is ever a "slam dunk" or as easy as it may appear on the front end.

Lawyers must keep an ever present vigil and steadfast determination in attempting to sort out whether the lawyer will represent the client. Lawyers think about three things: (1) Good cases mean fees for the lawyer, (2) Bad cases represent fees for the lawyer + P.I.T.A. (pain in the anatomy), and (3) Can I help a client with a minimum of involvement irrespective of the fee?

Lawyers are usually good people who have been trained to assist in solving problems on behalf of mankind. However, a lawyer and his practice is a business. If a lawyer is working only for the good of humanity, the lawyer may be dragging his staff and other workers who depend on a livelihood into the same *pro bono* relationship. This is more often than not unfortunate but a realistic fact of life. Revenue−expenses = profit (survival). (This is the way of the world and a lawyer is no different.)

"The Law of Waning Interest"

You as a client should understand the "law of waning interest." If you pay a lawyer $500 to engage in representation, the lawyer estimates how much time it will take to reach the solution required to bring the situation to a conclusion. If, however, unforeseen glitches appear, the "revenue−expenses = profit" formula goes awry and the efficacy of it is disrupted. Consequently, the fee is no longer adequate enough to meet the reasonableness of what is expected of the lawyer to justify the fee quoted to the client. This is a crucial point in the lawyer/client relationship. Many lawyers do not want to confront the client and reveal that the fee is inadequate for the time being spent, but will temper their efforts in resolution according to what they have been paid. They don't intend for this to happen but as a natural law of compensating balances this often happens. The lawyer drags around feeling scorned because of not being adequately paid, and the client become disenchanted because of the lack of closure on the part of the lawyer. Whose fault is this? Obviously, it is the lawyer's fault. The client doesn't know and is not supposed to know. Is it the lawyer's position to know?

Not always, but an experienced or semi-experienced lawyer should realize that there are glitches everywhere and in every situation. You can not always anticipate where they will appear or come from but at least, as a lawyer, give yourself some space and some discretion to return to the client and ask for a greater fee to cover your representation.

So, a wise and experienced lawyer will tell a client upfront that the fee being asked for will cover the representation as anticipated. However, if certain conditions, circumstances, and interventions present themselves, you may be advised that greater attorney fees are being incurred. An attorney owes this to a client because being foretold is being forewarned. Nothing is worse to an attorney/client relationship than the element of surprise. A lawyer has a duty to the client to advise him or her when circumstances change the terms and conditions of representation.

To allow the "law of waning interest" to creep into representation of a client's interest is a disaster for the lawyer and the client.

Reason, logic, rationality, and common sense are all premised on U.F.A.C. (underlying facts and circumstances). Even the best lawyer can not always make silk out of a sow's ear. What makes complete sense to you can be considered idiotic to someone else.

Life Is Almost Always Wonderful in the Beginning

In the beginning of almost everything, everyone seems to be happy, optimistic, and filled with high expectations of outstanding success. If you think about such an idea, this kind of feeling exists in situations as varied as getting married to walking through the doorway of a casino seeking a great fortune. Regrettably, the gleam of favor on the side of that which would meet your ideal wishes is often fraught with disappointment.

When the client first realizes and discovers a need for an attorney, the search is often very frustrating and cloaked in stress and anxiety over what lawyer to hire.

This experience is not much different than a person seeking out a medical doctor or a dentist. Usually, a person in need of professional services asks a friend or a relative for a reference of a professional they know. Any recommendation is mostly based on the experience they have had or the reputation they know regarding the practitioner. This process is certainly unscientific and a guess, at best, on the part of the person asked. But, no one is going to recommend someone they don't know or trust.

A reputation is what other people think you are. Character is who what you really are. So, it behooves any professional practitioner to engage in an all-out effort to be as blemish free as possible. Reputation should be in the consciousness and present a need for a driving awareness on the part of any professional. Little things often carry the entire perception of one's reputation, and command that one engaged in presentation of a public image maintain a continuous vigil of impeccability as much as humanly possible.

Nevertheless, clients choose lawyers for their own personal reasons. If a client is smart, he will tell the lawyer that he was recommended to the lawyer by a former client of the lawyer or some such person who knows the attorney. Regardless, a client can better bridge the attorney/client relationship by giving the lawyer a familiar reference. This can often cause a lawyer to feel somewhat special toward you as the client since the lawyer wants to please his/her previous client knowing that you will certainly relate what you think of the lawyer you have hired based on their recommendation. This comes out of the old adage, "As a friend, if you have a friend then that friend is a friend of mine."

Maintaining personal relationships is extremely high on the list of things sought in life in every aspect of living. Lawyers and their clients are no different.

As has already been expressed, there is no science that completely explains how law practice, lawyers, the law, the court system, its processes, and the manner in which all of this works together.

Some lawyers consider law practice to be a game in dealing with all the forces of influence that act as barriers or obstacles standing in the way of getting what they are hired to get for their clients. However, many realize that the totality of law practice provides that everyone participating be able to maintain a position to get their piece of the pie. This is really the situation from judges, defense attorneys, personal injury (P.I.) lawyers, and office lawyers.

Law practice represents one gigantic eco-system where everyone in a sense depends on everyone else. If it were not for personal injury (P.I.) lawyers, defense lawyers would not need to exist. If it were not for lawsuits, trial judges would not need to exist. If it were not for human conflict, chancery judges would not need to exist. They all need to exist for the system of justice to exist. Clients make the world of law practice survive and if it were not for clients, all lawyers would have to find another job.

So, as lawyers, we all have to be ever so mindful of what goes through the minds of client in terms of what they want, what they need, and what they expect. Continuous vigilance, self-evaluation, and consciousness are key determinants in whether a lawyer remains aware of what the client perceives when dealing and working with a lawyer. Such conditioning of a lawyer's percepts regarding his clients is a major contributor to what the image and reputation of the legal profession is and has been. For a lawyer to get inside the mindset of his client will never be an easy task but an effort should be made to, at least, understand what processes occur in the scheme of a client attempting to find a lawyer.

An Unfortunate Scenario

The scenario below has appeared comically in some legal publications depicting what a client endures in getting involved in trying to hire a lawyer.

Day 1—I need a good lawyer.

Day 2—I think I have found one.

Day 3—I think I have found a good one.

Day 4—I got in quickly to see the lawyer.

Day 5—My lawyer is great!

Day 6—He/she is absolutely the best choice I could have made.

Day 7—My lawyer is attentive and on the ball.

Day 8—I will get quick and great results.

Day 9—No other lawyer would have been as good (I appreciate my lawyer!).

Day 10—I guess I will hear back from my lawyer soon.

Day 11—I know my lawyer is busy.

Day 12—I haven't heard anything. I will give him a little more time.

Day 13—Wonder when I will hear back.

Day 14—I wonder why I have not heard back from my lawyer.

Day 15—I will call my lawyer. (Can't get through so I'll leave a message.)

Day 16—I know my lawyer's busy and can't return every telephone call.

Day 17—I will call again. (Did not get a call back but, at least, he/she could have asked the secretary to call me back.)

Day 18—I wonder if I should make an appointment to see what's happening.

Day 19—I got another legal fee statement from my lawyer and he/she hasn't done anything. What the heck is going on?

Day 20—I am not sure about this lawyer but I know I am getting the "run around." I am wondering if he/she is concerned about how I feel.

Day 21—Looks like I made a mistake in hiring this lawyer. (My lawyer has no idea how important this is to me and probably doesn't care.)

Day 22—I am worried now if I am going to be left "holding the bag" and paying for the legal service I don't get.

Day 23—I should have been more careful in hiring a lawyer who cares and is more responsible.

Day 24—How can I hire a lawyer who will do something? (I am really sick about the whole thing!)

Day 25—A friend of mine has recommended another lawyer and he says this lawyer is really good.

Day 26—I guess I should make an appointment to see my current lawyer and fire him/her and try to get my money back.

Day 27—My old lawyer does not want me to have an appointment with him/her but the secretary says that he/she is working on my case.

Day 28—I have had enough. I will see a new lawyer and ask him/her to advise my present lawyer that he/she is my new lawyer.

Day 29—My new lawyer seems nice and concerned. I wonder if I will have to face the same circumstances of the last 29 days.

Day 30—I will give my new lawyer my case and hope that these last 30 days are few and far between and that no one else has to endure such anguish, uncertainty, and frustration.

Day 31—Today is the beginning of a new experience (hopefully!). I had heard about lawyers before but I guess I had to learn for myself. Hopefully, my new lawyer will be different.

This is a horrible scenario. Does it happen? Yes, it does. Should it happen? The answer is absolutely, "No!"

Clients, regardless of the quality of their case, believe they are important as clients. Most of the lawyers you will ever know feel, believe, and think that a client deserves the respect, courtesy, attention, and professionalism as established by the Model Rules of Professional Conduct for lawyers, medical doctors, dentists, and other professionals. Lawyers are charged with the obligation to act professionally, responsibly, and ethically. As you know, life is replete with idealisms. Reality is what counts with the client.

Sometimes in life everyone gets busy and fails to realize that everyone else is basically the same, having similar goals, pain, values, pleasure, and sensitivities. Life is about treating people fairly, empathetically, and with accord and respect. A lawyer's relationship with his or her client should consist of expressing the highest human qualities possible. Empathy, understanding, respect, and care are the highest qualities one human being can express to another. Every professional should be reminded of their influence, responsibility, and dedication every moment of every day.

Lawyers should never abandon their consciousness and sensitivity toward their clients regardless of how important or unimportant they think a client's case is. A lawyer's duty to the client is to be diligent, honest, and open in communication, and to realize that communication takes place in the mind of the client even when nothing is said.

CHAPTER 4

WHAT DO LAWYERS DO—ANYWAY?

"If what you were asking your lawyer to do was
easy, a lesser person could perform the task and
a lawyer would not be required."—BFB

"Lawyer: A person who believes they are as
important as they think they are."—BFB

R emember when you were a kid, you played with silly
little puns like: "What's up in the road—ahead?," "Look
what's back—behind," and "What do you have on—your
mind?" "What do lawyers do—anyway?" could also be read,
"What do lawyers do—however?"

The bad raps against lawyers contain some very humorous
stories and often the stories are more packed with some spackling
of truth than fiction. (At least, from the standpoint of the law
profession's overall societal perception.)

One of the humorous stories that I enjoy telling on an occasion
of a public presentation is the one about Lagoster Medical Research
College no longer using rats in their experiments. The rats have
been replaced with lawyers for three reasons:

1. There are more lawyers than there are rats and therefore,
   lawyers are more easily available.
2. There are fewer conflicts with the use of lawyers since rats
   are now being protected under the watchful eye of the
   A.S.P.C.A. (American Society for the Prevention of Cruelty
   to Animals) and lawyers don't have this protection. (Thus,
   fewer legal conflicts.)

3. However, the most important reason at the research college is that there are certain things they could not get the rats to do and lawyers are more than willing to do almost anything.

What You Hear May Sound Logical, but Is It True?

Often times, we accept fables, legends, folklore, fantasy, fiction, rumor, and humor as fact. Fortunately, reality always abides close around to bring thinking back into the mainstream of life where we hopefully deal with the truth and practicalities. What is real is what's important.

Lawyers, in our society, have been the butt of most of the good and bad. Unfortunately, they have not been given the deserved credit for all the good things they do, from forming the government and establishing the United States Constitution to helping sustain our free enterprise system of commerce where every individual in life is given the opportunity to be rich or go broke trying. Most people had rather remember the "not so good"—stuff like "Watergate," the "O.J. Simpson trial," and later "Whitewater." All of these somehow involved lawyers who seemed to be a guiding influence in shaping public perception.

Unfortunately, in many situations, everyone doesn't have the same ability, training, background, and education to delineate, dissect, distinguish, and appreciate the sordid details for what they really are and not what someone else says about them. This someone else takes the form of national media as presented on your TV set, your radio, the magazines and newspapers you read, and of course, your boss, your spouse, your relatives, or your neighbor next door.

You are not alone. Everyone seems to be trying to get our attention. Most of us have great difficulty in penetrating the world and its events to see them for what they really are because of the influences around us which attempt to guide our opinions of things before we even have one.

Lawyers, in many instances, have been treated no differently. Much of the dissent, disenchantment, unfavorable discourse, and profession bashing has been deserved, but much of it has not. The resulting perceptional problems stem from the same problem one experiences when a bad apple is found in a barrel of apples, or one rotten fish in a bucket of fish. The whole barrel or bucket becomes tainted. Some presumed logic follows that if one is bad, they all are bad. Then, perception becomes the reality and this perception becomes irrevocable in the perceiver's mind until there's sufficient experience that would lead to a position to the contrary.

Most Lawyers Work Within the Boundaries

A lawyer is duty bound in the legal profession by rules, regulations, procedures, codes of professional responsibility, ethics, a sense of personal morality, and the law. Obviously, all lawyers don't perceive each of these with the same meaning, the same sense of responsibility, or the same spirit of dedication. Each one's perception of these standards becomes his or her reality. Not only are lawyers different in skills, training, education and ability, but they have separate and distinct philosophical differences about the practice of law.

This philosophical dissimilarity is what makes your lawyer unique to you. That's the reason you chose a particular lawyer and this becomes more apparent to you depending on the level of case you expect him to handle for you. When the magnitude of your case becomes larger, you look closer at the qualifications of your lawyer. Going back to the car clinic, you know it's no big deal to change the oil, but changing out the motor is not in the same category.

What you can expect from your lawyer is not a lot different than what you can expect from your physician. The first thing a physician wants to know is if you are in serious trouble. That's one reason the nurses take your temperature, check your blood pressure, and count your pulse rate when you arrive in the clinic or the doctor's office. Almost everything in life takes on a relationship of relative urgency. This applies to nearly everything from getting the roof repaired to going to the dentist. If your tooth hurts, you'll be seeing your dentist sooner than you had probably planned. If you have been served with legal papers, you'll be seeing a lawyer sooner than you would have had you waited until you finally got around to making out a will.

Lawyers weigh this relative urgency immediately when you arrive in their office. There are some things that require immediate attention. From the moment you receive legal papers either in person or through the mail, time begins to tick away on the period of time you have to make a response to those claims that are being made in the papers you received. Some people put seeing a lawyer off until the time has almost expired before they go in search. Some people don't appreciate that the papers mean what they say when you are advised that you must make an answer or response to the "Complaint," "Declaration," "Summons," or "Legal Paper" within (so many days) or you will have a judgment (a decision) rendered (made) against you by the court (really meaning the judge).

The wording on the papers you receive is not complicated, ambiguous, or misleading. If you speak the language in your jurisdiction you'll know what it means. If you don't speak the language and receive papers personally or certified through the mail, call the court from which they were issued and ask what they should mean to you as a party who just received them. They will probably tell you to go see a lawyer. The "notice" of a lawsuit reads simply and directly. The lawsuit itself may read like a map of the galaxy. This is what you need a lawyer to define for you.

Time is of the essence, and can either be an ally or an enemy! Because of this factor, some lawyers won't take your case even though in most circumstances the lawyer can always get additional time to make a defense or response for you. The lawyer can readily perceive that if you are careless, disregarding, lackadaisical, and nonchalant about the legal papers you have received, you will be even more that way when they start representing you. You can get labeled as a "trouble" client with a capital "T." Lawyers don't like "trouble" clients since most lawsuits or cases require the client's unyielding cooperation throughout a long, arduous, and laborious process of getting the case ready for a trial, court hearing, or whatever.

We'll talk extensively later about those things you as a client need to know about the legal process before you think you want to go to court, and those activities which potentially will tax you, the client, into possible premature relinquishment, submission, regret, or withdrawal short of the actual proceedings in court. This will be of great interest to you.

The point is that you as a client must also be diligent concerning your legal problem. So many clients believe that once they have seen a lawyer, the client can drop out of the picture. Wrong! Even after hiring a lawyer, you are still responsible. Often you may have to keep advised of what your lawyer is doing. Even if you don't have to, it's good business on your part to do so. So many times, clients don't have a clue as to what's happening with their legal representation. If your lawyer doesn't help you keep informed about your representation, you should be highly and keenly interested and plan to visit with your attorney at the scheduled commitment times you have established during the initial interview (this will be discussed later).

What can your lawyer really do anyway? You can imagine that not all lawyers do the same things. Some lawyers go to court. Some don't. Some lawyers take divorces. Some don't. Some medical doctors perform surgery. Some don't. Some automobile garage mechanics work on transmissions. Some don't. You get the picture! The kind of lawyer you are looking for is the one who can help you with your legal problem.

The Beginning: The Review Stage

The first thing you can expect from a lawyer is for the lawyer to listen to the nature of your legal problem. Once the problem has been heard, at least to some extent, the attorney will diagnose, categorize, and preliminarily prescribe in his or her own mind where the legal problem fits in the overall scheme of his or her law practice. This is the review stage of the initial interview when the lawyer begins to size up whether he wants to take the case based on the nature of the legal problem.

Here, the lawyer may explain to the client the legal principles involved in the various courses of action which may be open to the client in seeking satisfaction of his legal problem under the law. There may be several courses of action for the client that can be usually be explained by the attorney. The client may also have facts and circumstances which may contraindicate any further pursuit of any legal recourse. In other words, facts may present themselves which may practically render inoperative the client's opportunity to pursue any realistic path of legal solution.

For example, a woman could potentially have some difficulty seeking a divorce from her husband if she was pregnant with another man's child. Unfortunately, the attorney seldom ever knows all the facts and background before agreeing to take a client's case. This is partially the reason for lawyers receiving errant criticism by clients and the public for results and circumstances which are beyond the lawyer's knowledge and control.

Sometimes, in the review stage, legal recourse for the client is often a best guess until the attorney has had time after taking the case to study all the facts, events, and circumstances, and how these assessments are affected by the existing decisions which have been decided in similar situations and the law of the jurisdiction. Sometimes, the review stage only leads the client and the lawyer to the advising stage. "Sometimes a question will exceed the scope of its answer."

A lawyer doesn't take every case that an opportunity presents to him. Lawyers refuse cases for various reasons. Sometimes, they don't know the reasons. Sometimes, a lawyer's intuition leads him into deciding not to involve himself in a case because of the personality of the client. Chapter 5 discusses the various types of lawyers in terms of their personalities. Here, we are talking about what lawyers do regardless of who they are. Often, you'll discover that lawyers are what they are because of who they are. When a lawyer decides not to take on a client in an attorney-client relationship, the attorney may simply attempt to advise the client about the nature of the legal problem in an attempt to either assist the client in handling his or her own legal problem with a non-legal solution or the lawyer may refer the client to another lawyer.

This is an interesting point. When the lawyer believes that advising the client in a manner that will potentially result in resolution of the client's concern in a non-legal manner, a client will, more than likely, be charged for the legal services of the lawyer unless there was a prior agreement that the client would not be charged for the initial consultation. If the lawyer refers the client to another attorney, seldom, if ever, does the lawyer charge the client.

Retainer Relationships

Some lawyers enter into long-term relationships with clients and continuously review, advise, and guide the clients in a representative relationship. The guiding stage of a lawyer/client relationship is more comprehensive and demanding. A lawyer's worst nightmare is to be responsible for all the legal advice that a client could get, need, anticipate, or encounter. Sometimes, a lawyer engages in a relationship with a client around an understanding characterized as a "retainer." A retainer represents a partial payment for work that may be required for the client. More importantly, the lawyer is bound not to take a fee from anyone having a conflicting interest with the party employing him. This guiding stage is built around a long-term relationship and involves the lawyer assisting in helping make decisions in the client's overall course of actions.

The Representation Stage

The last stage is when a lawyer enters into a representative relationship with the client. This is called the representation stage. In this stage, the full responsibility and duty for making things happen falls squarely on the shoulders of the lawyer. The lawyer is in the driver's seat and has the client's fate in his or her hands. As with the surgeon with scalpel in hand, the lawyer may act for and on behalf of the client and ultimately determine the client's fate—good or bad. Literally and figuratively, the lawyer has a life in his hands. Once the lawyer/client relationship is born, all the forces of the mandates required of the legal profession are put into action.

You now have a lawyer. Be attentive, be aware, be responsive, be loyal, be honest, be understanding, be supportive, be inquiring. Learn! Know what's going on with your case. This is a time of relief for you, but not a time to relax. Don't let ignorance be blissful. You are responsible for what you don't know since you have the God-given control, power, and ability to ask if you don't know what your lawyer is doing to represent your interest.

Congratulations on your decision to hire a lawyer. Be good to your lawyer and your lawyer will, more than likely, be good to you! Remember: goodness begets goodness.

CHAPTER 5

WHAT KIND OF
LAWYERS ARE THERE?

A s there are many varieties of fish in the sea, there are many types of lawyers. Contemporarily, the most often thought of phrases when a lawyer is described are honest, dishonest, sleazy, questionable, money grubber, and sometimes an "ambulance chaser." Hopefully, this is not what "lawyering" is about but as was stated earlier, your "perception is your reality." Life deals some funny and strange cards. How you and everyone else read those cards is based primarily on how you expect to read them, among other things. After all, isn't your happiness based on whether or not the bulk of your expectations are being met as you sojourn through life?

Anticipation Can Be the Root of All Evil!

Every person who has ever or will ever use the services of a lawyer has some preconceptions of what they are going to encounter. Sometimes, anticipation of circumstances and events cause more apprehension than the problem with which you are attempting to deal. Seriously, what do you expect?

Lawyers are pictured with gigantic egos and are also credited with more power than they deserve or actually have. One of the reasons they have been enamored with this assessment is because, in the legal arena, only those who are licensed to practice law are generally allowed to participate in representing other people. This, by no means, is to say that on any day of the week you may not represent yourself in the gladiator's arena. By the way, I must remind you, consistent with previous admonishments, when you buy the self-help books *Practicing Everyday Law Made Simple* and

How You Can Be Your Own Lawyer, go on and make a day of it and purchase *Brain Surgery Right in Your Own Home Made Simple.* These books are usually found in the same area of the book store, in the section labeled "monkey business" (and this is not to necessarily put "monkeys" down).

Where are we going with this discovery about your lawyer? This is leading to the discourse of "how to communicate with your lawyer" and what you need to talk about to have a good understanding to effectuate a good satisfactory attorney/client relationship. But before we engage in those suggestions of how to do that, you need to know a little more about lawyers.

Lawyers fall into a number of categories of personalities, as all people do. A lawyer's personality is not unlike the variety of people around you everyday at work, around you in social organizations, or around you in everything you do. Look around! Some people favor chameleons, lions, foxes, dogs, and even some would suggest that some of the people they know act like buzzards, monkeys, piranhas, and jackals. All of these types represent a behavioral style which is displayed through an individual's personality.

How Would You Define Personality?

Often, people have some difficulty trying to define personality. Webster says that it is "the visible aspect of one's character, as it impresses others." In other words, it is the manner in which a person presents their behavior in relationship to another person. Argumentatively, a person on a deserted island would have no personality. However, that discussion and debate will be left to those philosophers who are interested in such endeavors. The point here is that you are reading this in attempting to understand your lawyer and in that quest you should know something about behavior as exhibited through personality. The reason for this is that in many situations, what is being communicated is not what is being said. For you to understand your lawyer, you should know the differences between how certain personality types communicate and what they mean.

There are some common acknowledgements that can be made about the concept of personality:

1. Everyone has a personality whether they know it or not.
2. There are individual differences in personalities.
3. The displays of individual differences are consistent.
4. Personality types communicate consistent with behavior.
5. There are a vast number of personality styles.
6. Communication style is consistent with personality.
7. Personality is based on communication style.
8. People judge other people based on personality.
9. A personality tends to like others of the same personality.
10. All lawyers have personalities.

The knowledge that people tend to communicate consistent with their behavioral characteristics which are observed through personality is a good starting point for discussion.

The First Influence: "Personableness"

Those who have researched and studied communication styles tend to agree that there are two primary variables that influence communication. First, there is the aspect of a person being "personable" which is observed in someone's willingness and responsiveness to developing relationships with a display of feelings and concern. What do you think about when you consider a person to be personable? Let me suggest the traits of warmth, kindness, considerateness, and gregariousness, with an outgoing, charming, friendly, cordial, sensitive, and approachable nature for starters. This lawyer is accessible, hospitable, amenable, and receptive. Sounds like that this is the ideal, doesn't it?

These qualities of personality and behavior are often the lawyer's greatest character weaknesses. Often it is difficult to be kind, understanding, compassionate, and caring and at the same time, present the image of no-nonsense toughness to the client. This requires a delicate balance of behavior on the part of the lawyer. You'll see later how this is achieved by one of the lawyer types.

The Other Influence: "Authoritarianism"

The other primary variable of behavior exhibited through personality is that of being "authoritarian," which is often characterized by behavior which appears as assertiveness in controlling other people through the exercise of force, will, power, aggressiveness, and authority traits in conflict situations.

Understanding Your Lawyer's Behavior Is Worthwhile

You are beginning to get the picture. No one can escape what and who they are. Every personality displays behavior which has a varying degree of each of these forces. You have probably heard the term, "more or less." Well, this is an ideal place to make it have some application.

Why are we taking time out to concern ourselves with how lawyers communicate? Don't we just have to accept what we get? I certainly hope not! Would you continue to go to a physician if he continuously failed to communicate with you about your medical condition? Probably not! But you may decide that's just the way your physician is and accept him as your physician without thinking about his communication style. It's all a matter of what you expect in a person's communication style.

Here's the point and the cardinal rule (and please don't fight me on this since there's plenty of evidence to back it up): "like attracts like." I know what you're thinking—all your life you have heard that "opposites attract." They possibly do, but not for the right reasons. Don't you enjoy being around a friend who is very much like you? Don't you enjoy being around someone with whom you have something in common? The differences in life cause conflict.

When you look for an attorney, you are looking for someone you feel comfortable with and can be honest with, and someone you can share your legal problem with without fear of the attorney being critical or judgmental. Think about it! You married your spouse because you thought you had something in common. If you are not married and are looking for a mate, you are looking for someone who has something in common with you. If you like opera and your spouse likes country and western music, you are not on the same page and probably don't attend too many concerts together. You get the idea. People who have rapport have some commonness of thinking and behavior. They appreciate similar things and have some common ideas. Lawyers are like that, too, so let's look at how they communicate based on who they are.

The First Lawyer Type: "Mr. or Ms. Personality"

The first type of lawyer is best described as "Mr. or Ms. Personality." This lawyer is outgoing, charismatic, sociable, emotional, personable, persuasive, people-loving, dynamic, and is a risk-taker. This lawyer is a "lawyer for all people and all reasons" (at least he thinks he is). This type of lawyer falls midway between being the highest in "personableness" and the highest in "authoritarianism," and has wide latitude of behaviors they can display from their behavior inventory.

Lawyers who display behavior through this communication style have several problems because of an unyielding propensity for expression. First, they have a tendency to stop listening to the client after a few minutes. They had rather do the talking and have the client listen to their point of view. This lawyer may form an early opinion about a client's case on insufficient information and will then often become outspoken to the point of being offensive, using exaggerated gestures and facial expressions to make his point. Often, you'll notice that this lawyer will try very furiously to promote his point of view using considerable emotion. Never lose sight that this lawyer is a charmer and usually has a "house full" of clients because clients will buy this lawyer's enthusiasm and energy. This lawyer can also be very forceful in legal matters exercising the same personality powers with other people that attracted you into letting him or her represent you.

One downside of working with this lawyer is that this type has been known to lose interest in difficult cases and has some tendency to become attracted to easier cases because of restlessness and liking change, variety, and anything new or different. This person also has problems with time management, wanting to do too many things at the same time, attempting to please all people. Obviously, there's a high degree of ego here consistently displayed in this style of behavior. Paperwork is not one of the favorite things this lawyer likes to do.

The "Personality" lawyer can become easily bored with your legal problem if it can't be solved in short order. But remember, this lawyer type is vulnerable to the need of being consistently liked and respected because of his own ego demands. So, remind this lawyer of the trust you have placed in him should such circumstances arise that would dictate such a confrontation. Look for signals of this type of lawyer such as a disorganized and cluttered desk (makes them look busy), awards, certificates on walls, motivational plaques, pictures of the attorney shaking hands with political figures, and an office arranged and decorated spaciously with a comfortable seating configuration. Don't forget that this lawyer is a sales person and can charm the boots off of a goat. They are also capable of handling your legal problem. In legal circles, this lawyer is often known as a "rainmaker," meaning a source of drawing clients to the firm.

The Second Lawyer Type: "Mr. or Ms. Dictator"

The second type of lawyer operates on a lesser level of being personable than that of the "Mr. or Ms. Personality" type and could not care less since this second kind is the least personable of any type. This lawyer is the "Dictator" type who displays himself in most relationships with the air of being the first and last "word" of authority. This makes this type the strongest displayer of authoritarianism. This lawyer is most often not liked by other lawyers.

The personality is characterized by such behaviors as being always correct and in control, irrespective of whether they are right or wrong or in doubt. These lawyer types are impatient and have a tendency to require perfection from everyone including themselves. They have very little sense of humor in their fast-paced competitive style of working. Few people, if any, enjoy working for these types since they are overly demanding and exhibit a lack of acknowledgement of work well done, even when the work meets their approval. In all respects, these lawyers are "P.I.T.A.S."(see chapter 2) to other lawyers, their clients, and sometimes to their spouses. These people are self-ordained and appear to need only themselves. They have a "god" image of themselves which serves to mask their own personal insecurities. They have anti-social tendencies in relationship to other lawyers, bar associations, and the world-at-large.

If enough has not been said already, this lawyer is task-oriented rather than people-oriented, likes power and prestige, frequently wants to change things, and has a tendency to be quick and direct. Where you, the client, may have problems is in this lawyer's restlessness and aptness to be impatient, impulsive, abrupt, and arrogant. All of these things can get in the way of your attempts to communicate with your lawyer. If your personality is of a different style, you'll have difficulty accepting the "Dictator's" lack of empathy and rudeness. These lawyers are not good listeners except when they are listening to themselves.

They are extremely competitive and will never admit to being wrong about anything. This pattern of repetitive behavior is easily perceived as the basis for their coldness and lack of feelings when dealing with their clients. Know and understand this type of lawyer so when you hire one you are prepared for this behavior. The "Dictator's" attitude and behavior can be a shock to you!

However, there are upsides to working with this type. This lawyer likes the challenge of accomplishment, is decisive, can argue one moment and laugh the next, and has the ability to juggle many tasks at once. Don't get the wrong idea—these lawyers are usually very successful. They are fighters. They are determined, tenacious, and unyielding in their bold efforts on behalf of their clients. Sometimes, one of their philosophical problems is that they are not very compromising and do not see, or are reluctant to see, gray areas. Remember, right or wrong, they are seldom in doubt. They can be the most effective attorney you can hire, but they also can be the most frustrating since they will return your phone calls only when they choose to do so and on their own schedule. They are not "hand-holders" but can get the job done for you if you can understand how they behave through their personality in working with their clients.

The Third Lawyer Type: "Mr. or Ms. Intellectual"

Our next type of lawyer is a far cry from the ones we have already discussed. This lawyer is the "Intellectual" type whose behavior is characterized by a reflective and analytical disposition. This lawyer will be one of the most non-emotional lawyers you have ever met, displaying a stiff and formal posture during social relationships, and even calling you Mr. or Mrs. in their office. They are well respected in the legal community for their astuteness and excellence in solving legal problems. These lawyers want to avoid confrontation because they dislike any form of carelessness or disorder. They run from overly aggressive people and seek to proceed at a cautious pace, being well planned and prepared to effectuate a legal solution in a most precise and professional manner. These lawyers like problem-solving activities and usually ask specific questions to get specific details in order to get down to the "nitty gritty" while the two previous types of lawyers discussed are often mislead by their efforts to hastily get the "big picture" first and the details later.

The "Intellectual" type believes that the devil is in the details and is unrelenting in pursuit of facts and data. They are very time disciplined, structured, and organized because of this drive for details. These people are generally very neat, well-groomed, and precisely organized in dress, desk, home, and with their automobile. These lawyers are not extemporaneous and do not fly very well "by the seat of their pants" or "off the cuff." Their whole life is knowledge, preparation, organization, and thinking par excellence. Another lawyer seldom out-prepares this lawyer nor is this style of lawyer rarely bluffed since the "Intellectual" type is perceived as having a "mind like a steel trap." This type of lawyer is usually an outstanding lawyer, lacking the quest for being either "personable" or "authoritarian." In fact, they are about as low as you could get on either scale. Be aware that this lawyer can "out-lawyer" other lawyers but recognize that there are some situations which are better represented by one of the other types.

This lawyer is often unwilling to make a decision, displays a strong dislike for change, and often gets so absorbed in details that he or she cannot see the proverbial "forest for the trees." This lawyer has a tendency to worry about things for which he has not prepared and, therefore, likes back-up solutions for the situations he encounters. These lawyers always desire to have a plan "B" in their inventory of plans to bring about a legal solution for the client. However, consistent with their "worry" states of mind is the condition that they are sensitive to criticism and abhor making any errors. These lawyers are often not good fighters and will avoid conflictive confrontation and combat when possible. This attitude is attributable to their desire for harmony and organization. These lawyers are generally critical, picky, and hard to please. They don't generally like cases that turn on factual situations, but had rather deal with cases turning on the interpretation and analysis of the law. Lawyers of this variety like stable situations and display a strong dislike for change. They lack balance and versatility which causes them worry, resulting in quiet, unreleased and unexpressed inner anxiety.

There are benefits to working with this type, though. These lawyers are controlled, deliberate, cautious, structured, organized, precise, disciplined, serious, industrious, scientific, and planned. They have a "show me" attitude which accompanies their questioning attitude as a thinker and an analyzer who pursues facts and logic. This lawyer represents the epitome of quality control and accuracy who will analyze a case situation leaving no stone unturned.

These lawyers are competent, predictable, and very successful in the legal arena. Don't ever underestimate this lawyer! You may have a wizard who never appears that way who can handle your legal situation without some of the behaviors that you would have to contend with if you chose other types. Remember! Life is a continuous flow of trade-offs. Think about which type may be a good lawyer in your situation and pick the lawyer most appropriate for the circumstances. Most often, you will be the best judge of this, and if you are unable to do this, just pick the lawyer you like best. This is not necessarily scientific but it beats no suggestion at all.

The Fourth Lawyer Type: "Mr. or Ms. Hand-Holder"

The last category of lawyers to be discussed is that of the "Hand-Holder," who displays their behavior in the form of being amiable and supportive to the client. This lawyer is exactly opposite of the "Dictator" type who exemplifies the purest form of the "authority" force and influence in behavior. The lawyer who falls into the category of the "Hand-Holder" is the strongest proponent of the "personable" force and influence. This lawyer has a good sense of humor and is lighthearted, passive, warm, supportive, sensitive, patient, friendly, kind, open, attentive, and loyal. They never seem to get in a hurry and they operate at a slow pace sharing personal feelings and emotions. These lawyers are very relationship-oriented, and they emphasize listening to the client, asking many questions, and expressing a caring concern for the client's legal problem and the client's well-being. This lawyer is a high and steady performer as an individual or as a team player with the qualities of being modest, unassuming, and patient while being dependable and responsible. Lawyers of this variety are genuine people who have little care or time for show-offs or pretentious people but are generally very supportive of others or a cause. A "Hand-Holder" is a true friend. What you see is what you get. Many people like the rapport that a lawyer of this type renders during their time of perceived legal crisis or problems. Clients of this lawyer know that they are being represented by a person of great integrity and sincerity.

Of the four types of lawyers presented here, the "Hand-Holder" appears to be the most mature and the best listener as a lawyer. Is this the best lawyer?

It might seem so, but there are some downsides to consider here. This behavioral type is not a risk-taker and, in fact, will avoid recognized risks as much as possible. This lawyer appears easy-going, mild-mannered, and is often seen as a push-over. Don't be misled by this appearance! This lawyer can be extremely responsive when pressured by assuming a stubborn posture of being uncooperative. If anyone ever crosses the "Hand-Holder" type, the event may be forgiven but will never be forgotten in the mind of this behavior type. They are always concerned about security and good performance and resist sudden changes in their job, location, and friends. Their biggest weakness is their tendency to agree with almost everyone. They are not highly assertive or individualized.

Characteristically, these lawyers have difficulty in taking a strong stand because they do not want to offend anyone, which supports their over-anxiousness to win the approval of other people. These people need an uplifting of confidence on a regular basis and you can generally observe that they constantly ask for reassurance. They obviously have some difficulty with making decisions and consequently are not very decisive. Anyone can easily understand why these behavioral types seldom make strong leaders, but they may make strong lawyers because what a particular type of case situation may need to properly and appropriately support the client's needs might be consistent with what the "Hand-Holder" has to offer.

This lawyer type is a model for how the legal profession should extend a caring and concerned attitude toward its profile of a lawyer who can communicate with a client on the highest level. With this type of lawyer, you should never have miscommunication or a misunderstanding regarding communication about your case. But you will have miscommunication and misunderstanding because that is the nature of the communicational conflict between a lawyer and a client. They arrive at the point of communication from two different cultural backgrounds. The problems that inevitably exist between a lawyer and their client are not necessarily the consequence of inattention or indifference on the part of either but as a result of the two of them not having common meanings and each carrying different expectations about what the solution should be and how it should be brought about. However, the "Hand-Holder" lawyer type fits very easily into many legal situations that require continuing contact with your attorney where the legal solution requires an ongoing involvement and discussion between the client and the lawyer to reach reconciliation. This is the type of lawyer that will see it through to the end with the same steadfastness you first recognized when you hired them.

So when you hire this lawyer, don't expect the dynamic bravo of "Mr. or Ms. Personality" with more "personable affect" and "authoritarianism" than the rest. Don't expect the strong-willed determination of the "Dictator" who exudes a persistency of more "authoritarianism" than other lawyers and is characterized by

Billy F. Brown

decisiveness and dominance and being the least "personable" of all lawyers. And don't expect the organized preciseness and cautiousness of the "Intellectual" who most often will display less "personable intimacy" and less "authoritarianism" than any other lawyer type. Know that the "Hand-Holder" is more consistent than other lawyers in being "personable" and you can benefit from this in certain types of cases and situations. So, therefore, it will behoove you to know your case and then to know your lawyer!

To Worry or Not to Worry

Most of life involves the decision of whether to worry or not to worry. The basis for all worry in life is the assessment of risk involved with what you are worried about. When there is no risk there is no worry. The aspect of a legal problem is no different. If there are no consequences of a legal problem, a client does not worry about the problem. If there are consequences, a client worries. When there are consequences, a client goes to see a lawyer.

A lawyer deals with a client's concern with a number of different philosophies depending on the mindset of the lawyer hired by the client. Take a look at the various approaches different lawyers take:

1. Deeply Concerned

This lawyer is a serious lawyer and considers the client's problem one of great consequence and often has a "sense of urgency." This lawyer has the ability to make and take the client's legal problem much more seriously than it really is. Often this lawyer is "hotter than the fire." This lawyer has the tendency to be dramatic, intense, and may actually scare the client more than the client was before he or she came to see the lawyer. With this

52

lawyer, you need be leery of over-dramatization (dramaturgy!) and exaggeration.

This lawyer is capable of extracting a larger fee from a client because of inducing more fear into the mind of the client than would ordinarily be justified or expected. Often this lawyer is a doubter about what can and cannot be done. This lawyer is often skeptical, negative, and unsure about the outcome of representing a client.

Further, this lawyer can be unsure about himself. When a client encounters this type of lawyer, the client is seldom at ease about the outcome of his or her situation and will continue to worry long after having put the case in the hands of the lawyer. The client will often maintain close contact with the lawyer over the case, which over a long period of time, can become troublesome for the lawyer and the client. This lawyer has the intention of being effective and efficient often at the cost of outcome in the legal representation, as you will understand in the next "mindset" of the "No Problem" lawyer.

2. No Problem

This lawyer is a "smoothie" and communicates a "feel good" ease of tensions with a client. This is a confident lawyer regardless of whether he or she should be or not. This lawyer always has a feeling that the case, situation, or conflict can be resolved for the client in the client's favor. This is a confident lawyer who will share that "good feeling" with the client. This lawyer will often convince a client that there's nothing to worry about. This lawyer is worth his weight in gold because of the ability to relieve the client of the drudgery of worry over what the client cannot control. When the client leaves the presence of this lawyer, he or she is relieved, relaxed, and has a feeling of being "worry-free." Clients want to willingly pay this lawyer because of the benefit bestowed on them by the lawyer's self-assurance. Regardless of whether this lawyer is right or wrong about how the case will turn out, this lawyer seldom exhibits doubt as to the outcome because this lawyer understands his or her M.O. (*modus operandi*) in making problems go away.

This lawyer knows that time is an ally in the legal profession. The further a client and lawyer get beyond the initial impact of a situation, case, or conflict, the less intense the confrontation will be. Over time, all problems tend to become fragmented, modified, solvable, diffused, diluted, redefined, and spread out to change from their initial presentation. In other words, time changes almost everything. Nothing, good or bad, is as important later as it is now or today.

Consequently, the "No Problem" lawyer uses time as a very crucial and important ally. When there is an opportunity to delay, stall, postpone or continue a confrontation of issues, a "No Problem" lawyer will delay the proceedings until another day. The longer a case, situation, or conflict is delayed the more likely the results of such confrontation will be more easily managed, manipulated, and compromised. The key to negotiation is compromise. The longer any of us indulge in anything, the more likely we are to seek reconciliation, compromise, and alternative resolution.

The resulting effect of elongated and prolonged involvement tends to cause considerable wear and tear on the nature of resilience, stamina, endurance, patience, and motivation. In other words, the "No Problem" lawyer intends to forebear, delay, procrastinate, and seek as long possible before confronting any issue of conflict. By the time most people get to the point of having to deal with an issue they are tired, exhausted, and disgusted beyond wanting to deal with the original issue. The philosophy of the "No Problem" lawyer is that a postponement is often a partial victory for their client.

A man on "death row" seeks the same sort of compromise in trying to avoid the death penalty. If he or she gets enough delays, postponements, and stays of execution, he or she just might eventually die of natural causes.

Be careful not to fault a lawyer for not wanting to "throw down the gauntlet" and charge into battle. There might be a chance that the problem, if allowed enough time, might just resolve itself. This is probably not realistic but at least the problem will have had time to become diminished. At least the fervor of the initial charge will have had time to dissipate.

3. Let Us Reason

This lawyer is fairly logical, reasonable, and rational person. He or she believes that a client should understand fully about the case, the law, and the methodology of solution he or she proposes to solve the problem. These lawyer types are excellent lawyers, but are often overzealous in attempting to convince a client that the lawyer has a vast knowledge of the law, tactics, methodologies, and a strong grasp of the psychological understanding of human nature. This lawyer wants to convince a client that the client is going to get a full bang for the buck. This lawyer is very knowledgeable, capable, understanding, and patient. However, probably too much so.

Most people don't care about how a watch works. They just want to know if it tells "time." Most people don't care how a computer works. They just want to know that when they turn it on, it will work. A client doesn't need to understand everything about his or her case. A medical doctor does not need to explain to a patient the mechanics of taking out his or her appendix. A doctor does not have to explain everything to a patient for the patient to have confidence in the doctor. The same is with a lawyer.

Many clients think that a "Let Us Reason" lawyer charges by the word. Clients on the front end sincerely appreciate a lawyer who is concerned about a client understanding everything about the case, but eventually get tired of hearing about how and what the lawyer is doing. Much would be the same for a medical doctor continuing to talk about how the appendix would be extracted from the patient. Enough eventually gets to be enough.

However, there are those clients, as well as patients, who want to know every "bit by bit" of the wherefores, when, and how. So be it! If that's what the client or patient wants, there are those who are willing to oblige.

All Are Different

Can lawyers be categorized? The answer, of course, is "yes" and "no." There are broad categories that clump lawyers together but lawyers are individually unique—much like snowflakes in that all snowflakes are the same because they are made of ice and have six sides. After that, they are all different. Fingerprints have the same analogy. Don't try to say that all lawyers are the same any more than saying that all people are the same. When you begin to understand differences in lawyers and in life, you begin to appreciate what each distinctive difference brings to the front, an advantage as you go about selecting the lawyer that best suits your particular needs.

Just Maybe, Nothing Seems to Fit With These Lawyer Types and Your Lawyer

Now, some pages later, do you think you know your lawyer? I can hear you now lamenting about how your lawyer doesn't fit any of these descriptions. Of course not! No lawyer fits squarely into the model and mold of any one of these types. The point is that lawyers, because of their training, experience, and frequency of dealing with people of every kind, shape, and description, become very adept at being almost anything necessary in conducting business in the process of human conflict. Most lawyers have a little of each behavioral style in their inventory but each has a primary base of behavior from which they operate. They each practically have the ability to be, at times, wizards, lovers, dreamers, clowns, artists, engineers, scientists, preachers, teachers, dramatists, poets, healers, educators, friends, humorists, and most of all of those things in between. But lawyers have an ability to "flex" their styles of behavior. However, each has a behavioral philosophy of who they are and how they conduct their practice. They may not know what it is but it exists as a matter of fact and human nature.

Why do I think that lawyers can be all of these things? Because that's the way they are because of who they are, what they are, and what they do. The way a lawyer relates tells you who that lawyer is. Is there one best style of lawyer? Absolutely not! You may have heard that a lawyer is a lawyer is a lawyer! That's not true. Lawyers are different; they are just like any other profession whose membership is made up of all kinds. Get to know your lawyer! No, there is no one best behavioral style of lawyer. The best style depends on the type of "lawyering" you need. You can decide who you need as a lawyer by understanding the personality style of the prospective lawyer.

Which Lawyer Will You Get Along With Best?

What style of personality behavior gets along best in the working relationship with the client? That depends on you! What personality behavior could best describe you? You will probably respect the type that more closely matches yours. Think about it for a minute. If you are the "Dictator" type (and will admit to it), just how long do you think you will get along with "Mr. or Ms. Personality," "Intellectual," or "Hand-Holder?" Not long, I'll assure you—already you are thinking that you could eat each of these lawyers for breakfast any morning. Remember, we all identify with people who are much like us. Sometimes, this is a most difficult idea to accept and admit.

There is no magic wand to wave in understanding human behavior and how it manifests itself through personality. You need to understand yourself first to appreciate how you behave. We all generally respect, admire, trust, follow, and want different people for different reasons. The key to understanding people is in understanding "differences." The differences you contrast between your behavior and someone else's is your basis for identifying that behavioral style of personality. Most of life's decisions are made only in comparison to similar situations in our inventory of experience and organized learning. When you choose a lawyer, all of this experience and learning will come to the front of your decision-making process and will be used by you, often unconsciously and subliminally, in making the selective decision.

The same mechanism of comparison based on our experiences is alive and well when we evaluate the lawyer types and how they are perceived by you when compared against your own behavioral patterns. The whole idea makes sense, but you have to observe and be aware to evaluate what you now understand. Sometimes, it's important to like your lawyer and other times it's not, but most of the time it is.

Communication Is the Essence of Life

Those who don't learn to communicate in life don't get along well in life. Can better communication be learned? I think the answer is "yes" and "no" and could be a "maybe yes" and a "maybe no." At some point in life, we stop worrying about repairing those deficit areas of reading, writing, spelling, and arithmetic, and just focus our direction and interest toward doing whatever it takes to survive and maintain. Little attention is made or paid to the efforts of improvement and the enhancement of ambition or anything else for that matter. Such may be true with communication. Each of us just may continue to communicate in the manner we do now for the remainder of our journey in life. That doesn't spell disaster for even the worst of communicators if you will recognize your own style of communication and those of others with which you will be attempting to communicate. This is especially true with lawyers since you are being invited to communicate in what is essentially the equivalent of an unknown foreign language. What's even worse is the reality that you are usually involuntarily subjecting yourself to this new experience in communication. The key to life is understanding and not agreement. If you understand about lawyer communication styles, you are about halfway there in surviving the relationship with your lawyer. As you know, there are no guarantees, but hopefully your trip will be as painless as possible.

The next chapter discusses the most prized possession of the lawyer. But don't lose a single thought about this present chapter. The two chapters mesh together to bring you the complete picture of what kind of lawyer you will be looking for, or to help you understand the lawyer you have already hired. Lawyers are different. So are politicians, school teachers, preachers, policemen, firemen, physicians, and spouses. I hope you have a clue as to why. Knowing your lawyer is important!

You'll now see why!

CHAPTER 6

THE LAWYER—
A WIZARD OF LANGUAGE

"Often a lawyer has no way to communicate
to the client what the client does not
want to hear."—BFB

A Lawyer's Warning to His Client:
"Any assumptions you make based on what
you think I said are totally your
responsibility and consequently any
resulting damages arising from such
assumptions are and shall be immediately
and directly deemed attributable to your
own stupidity."—BFB

F
ew would argue with the contention that communication
is the most essential activity in life. Everything in life
begins, continues, and ends around communication. Your
personal happiness in life depends primarily on your ability to
communicate with yourself and your fellow human beings. Many
life forms communicate, but the human is the only fortunate
species to be allowed the gift of language in verbal and written
forms. Therefore, the position is not profound proclaiming
that communication is a basic life skill which determines your
relative success and happiness in everything you do. Some
believe that nothing happens in life until there is some form
of communication. Even ancient religious writings reflect that,
"A word is the source of every deed, every thought, and every
act." This seems to indicate that we, as humans, are exclusive
in thinking only with words. This would lead logically to the

position that words which are stored in our minds are the source for all of our personal behavior.

Language is the conduit of communication. The dominance of language in life is reflected by the number of dialects in the world varying from approximately 20,000 to more than 50,000. All of these languages were developed for no other purpose than to enable people to communicate ideas to one another either in audible speech or in the written word.

The greatest conflicts in life arise over communication as expressed by language. Language, in fact, is very inexact and lends itself to wide interpretation using language itself to deal with language. In the dictionary on my desk are 1,664 pages containing approximately 120,000 words. This is a nice dictionary for home use but pales by comparison to the 16,500 pages of the Oxford English Dictionary which is reputedly the undisputed supreme authority on the English language and is the size of a set of encyclopedias.

Why so many words, when they add more confusion to the solution? It's obvious that someone could not have been satisfied with just a few, so more must be better. With life's rules, procedures, and processes all wrapped around the use of language with its abundance of so many words all meaning something different, the same, almost the same, and even some which none of us can agree on, guess what? Here come the lawyers!

Are Lawyers the Elixir of Life?

The quotes are legion about the legal profession since the beginning of recorded history. Some are noteworthy for their efforts in attempting to hail the profession as having contributed to the great evolution of our government, freedoms, and the quality of life in the United States. Unfortunately, that was some time ago and has since been almost forgotten.

Law has been heralded as the "essence of life." Lawyers haven't! Maybe, as Clarence Darrow, one of the greatest lawyers ever, said, "The trouble with law is lawyers." This seems to be consistent historically and goes downhill from there. Even such an old acclaimed figure as Thomas Jefferson observed, "It is the trade of lawyers to question everything, yield nothing, and to talk by the hour." More directly to our chapter discussion, John Gay noted, "I know you lawyers can, with ease, twist words as you please." Will Rogers had a keen insight about lawyers. He on many occasions in his public appearances talked about lawyers and what he thought of them. Once he said, "The minute you read something that you can't understand, you can almost be sure it was drawn up by a lawyer. In fact, lawyers make a living out of trying to figure out what other lawyers have written."

Why has society continued to blast these "wordsmiths" of life? Someone has offered the suggestion that it is in the nature of the beast because of what lawyers do and how it is perceived by those for whom their behavior is presumed to help and by those whom their behavior is not intended to help. Any theory is almost as good as any other. And the beat goes on, on, and on . . .

Know When You Need to Make a Trip to See a Lawyer

You can do what you want to do, you can say what you want to say, you can feel what you want to feel, and think what you want to think, but when you have a legal problem you are not going to your baker, hair stylist, or your butcher for advice and counseling. You are going to see a lawyer—good, bad, or indifferent. So, here in this chapter, let's get you prepared to make the trip.

A World of Words

Lawyers are forced by the nature of the legal profession to dabble in the most dangerous of all worlds—a world of words, a world of abstractions, a world of intangibles, a world of perceptions, a world of interpretation, and most importantly, a world which is guided, directed, influenced, and led by the mind of the beholder. At least several thousand quotes could be offered to establish the importance of language, made up of many words, as the most essential, vital, and critical ability of mankind. I hope that proof won't be necessary and we will be allowed to travel on the presumption that language's importance is acknowledged by everyone. This is not just idle talk. Some people believe that lawyers are responsible for every screw-up in life because of their advocacy in manipulating the language we all live with to get what they want.

Lawyers use language probably more than any other profession as their primary tool in trade. Professional writers are, of course, a serious consideration but recognize that their trade does not contain adversarial discussions about what language means and what it intends to convey in terms of a message representing an understanding, information, or an agreement between people attempting to communicate. Professional writers are attempting to communicate unilaterally. Although it could be argued that reader feedback is a form of communication in the writer's world.

In the lawyer's world of communication, there are many things that have prepared each of us, including the lawyer, for the way we see, the way we hear, and the way we communicate. All of us are a compilation of many influences which has produced an ongoing set of values we all use in assessing what we see, hear, and experience in the everyday life of living. These influences consist of all of our perceptions, motivations, attitudes, needs, and experiences we have learned since we came into the world as a human being. A lawyer is no different than what's been said. The prime distinction between a lawyer and the client arises from a lawyer's training for the legal profession, his experiences in dealing with and working in the arena of human conflict, and those temptations he confronts which are not offered to the mass of population outside the workplace of the lawyer.

Most of our behavior in life is learned; some of it is conscious and much of it is unconscious. Many lawyers are not aware of what they have become and how they fail to interrelate with clients because of poor, faulty, and inappropriate communication. Lawyers forget that the person responsible for the content, reception, meaning, and clarity of communication is the lawyer. Why have lawyers lost insight into how to communicate with clients? The answers are not obvious. They are not necessarily simple. Lawyers are often, likewise, victimized by the communication process when the client decides to hear what he or she wants to hear.

Often, regardless of how clearly, concisely, and directly a lawyer communicates, clients want to hear what they want to hear, irrespective of what a lawyer says. Clients want lawyers to say those things which meet their own preconceptions as to how a legal problem can be successfully solved and they want such a solution to be immediately forthcoming without hassle and at a cost that meets their expectations. One of the lawyer's continuing problems in communication is the failure to help the client in establishing reasonable expectations about the case at hand and its many possible outcomes.

Clients are people, who, like most of the people you know, think like they think, feel like they feel, believe like they believe, and want what they want regardless of who deems that they should or should not! That's life and that's the way it is. The sooner we all recognize that we all have to deal with differences, the process of attempting to promote understanding will get easier. Clients may not agree, and lawyers may not agree, but they both can bridge the gap of disagreement with understanding. Of course, you and I know this is much easier said than done. At least, we can understand what the goal is.

Lawyers are usually in a position of a no-win situation with the client in communications. If lawyer is straightforward and realistic about the difficulty with a client's legal problem, the client often gets a negative impression about the lawyer's expectations of success, based on how the client believes the legal problem should turn out. The client may thereafter decide that this is not the lawyer he is looking for, and go down the block looking for a lawyer who will, instead, agree with his (the client's) own assessment of the case.

In some ways, many clients ask to be taken advantage of by some lawyers in the legal profession. Often, clients are overzealous and unrealistic about the satisfaction they seek. In many ways, the legal profession has failed to practically, realistically, and directly communicate with the mass of clientele who seek out lawyers everyday about reasonable expectations as they may be found in the legal arena. Clients need to be aware that they may have a case but the satisfaction they seek cannot be had reasonably, practically, sanely, and exactly without the efforts on the part of the lawyer costing them excessively beyond the satisfaction they seek.

The Lawyer's Paradox!

Often, it is difficult for a lawyer to be honest with a client in discussing his or her case with them.

First, the client does not want to hear what a lawyer would say if it does not agree with what he, the client, has already determined the answer to be.

Secondly, the client is going to hastily exit out of the lawyer's office if the client determines that the lawyer does not believe that he has a "good" case.

Thirdly, the lawyer business is founded on being able to represent clients and a lawyer knows that all clients are not "good" clients and that all cases are not "good" cases.

Fourthly, competent lawyers know that they often don't know what the real expectations and potential outcomes are of some cases. Cases evolve around the facts that are developed and the law of the situation. Therefore some lawyers have a tendency to "hedge" with the client. This is often dangerous for the lawyer and the client.

If the potential client hears the lawyer suggest that his case is not good because of the facts and/or the prevailing law, there is a tendency to want to shop for a lawyer that hears or sees something different. When you think about this situation, it is reasonable that a lawyer does not want to blow himself out of the case because of what he first hears from the potential client. Wisely, a lawyer will want to first understand and check out the facts and then see how the prevailing law will influence the direction of the case if certain facts are developed.

Whether you believe this or not, lawyering is not easy, simple, or as "sliced pie" as you see on TV's lawyer shows. Many hours, days, and months go into the preparation of a case to get the posture of such to a reasonable and satisfactory conclusion. Often the client does not understand or appreciate the time it takes to reach a successful conclusion. Many times this is the lawyer's fault because he fails to communicate the on-going process of bringing a case to the end. Also, the lawyer with a "slam-dunk" attitude on the front end of a case often creates a client expectation that is unrealistic in terms of the time allocation needed for the case to be concluded, and likewise, in the ideal results the client wants. Clients have to be conditioned on the front end of a case so they remain steady and calm during the time of processing the case. This "conditioning" is accomplished by the lawyer taking the time to fully and adequately explain all the "ins and outs," wherefores, and intricacies of what the lawyer has to do to represent the client.

When a lawyer hedges because of the uncertainty of what is going to happen, the client hears what he wants to hear and hires the lawyer who has some reservations about the case. Then, the client leaves the lawyer's office with high expectations that the lawyer knows to be unreasonable if not impossible. This is usually a bad beginning of a lawyer/client relationship. Eventually, in the sequence and process of reaching some resolve of the client's problem, a moment of reality will present itself and expectations will come face to face with the outcome of what is posed as a solution to the client's concern.

"Lawyering" Is a Business!

You must remember that lawyers are in the business of representing people for money. They are in a business. They are the business. When you face a lawyer, you are going to have to listen to what he or she is saying to you about your case to establish and understand what your reasonable expectations should be.

This is a most important point! You are happy, depressed, or sad about life only in relationship to your expectations. An old proverb says, "If you don't expect anything, you'll never be disappointed. If you expect everything, you'll always be disappointed." When you think about the idea of expectations, it makes sense to be practical, realistic, and reasonable. Your lawyer will definitely agree with this idea.

There are seldom any ideal cases. In other words, there are few, if any, true gifts, absolutes, ultimate rewards, unmistakable positions, and exact patterns in life. Any case can have an "Achilles heel." If any lawyer tells you that your case is "lead-pipe cinch" or a "slam-dunk," you should be put on notice that your lawyer is either inexperienced, naïve, stupid, or all of the above. (It would not be unreasonable for you to "run"!) Those cases are extremely rare indeed.

Listen to what the lawyer is saying. Good lawyers "C.T.A." (cover their assets). Recognize this when your case is being discussed. A good lawyer is a master at language and will qualify the communication with you about your case. Listen! Listen! Listen to what they are saying. You'll have a tendency not to listen to the exact words being communicated because you are trying to grasp the bigger picture of your overall case and its chances for success at a fee you can afford.

Some clients just want to dump their case on a lawyer's desk and run out the door as fast as possible. Most people who employ a lawyer are at their wit's end. They want relief by passing their "mess" on to someone else. Consequently, clients don't listen and lawyers don't communicate.

The Lawyer's Wonderful Words of "Supposition" and "Qualification"

There are no magic words! But all words can appear magical if you are not carefully listening to how they are being used and injected in the right places. Many words used by lawyers are called words of "qualification" and represent a partial disclaimer by the attorney regarding your case. Logically, the lawyer doesn't want you to hold the idea, feeling, or perception that everything about your case is perfect. A lawyer might build doubt about your case by speaking in terms of "conditioning" the quality of your case by using such qualifying words as "maybe," "when," and "if." Other words of limitation, qualification and conditioning are "probability," "potentially," and "possibility." Listen for these words and know what is being said. The lawyer invites many words into the discussion that relate to conditions known as "contingencies," meaning they may or may not happen. These words help the lawyer be truthful in talking to the client but most clients do not realize the importance of such words in the understanding of representation between the lawyer and the client.

The greatest word of qualification in the English language is "if." If elephants could fly, we would all have to carry umbrellas. If we are successful with your case, you will have lots of money. Would you like to have lots of money? You see, you are so enamored with the question that you have forgotten about the suppositional statement made before the question. The client is capable of "preemptive self-deprecation" as well as "self-deception." Remember, we all hear what we want to hear.

Clients are often their own worst enemy. They will swear that their lawyer told them that they had an outstanding case and could not lose. Many times (this is a qualifier), lawyers and clients will fall into that agreed understanding with the lawyer saying, "I know you believe you understand what you think I said, but I am not sure you realize that what you thought you heard is not what I meant." Is this comical? No, it's tragic!

Remember, even good lawyers don't always know the answer to your legal problem, but every lawyer can postulate, guesstimate, surmise, approximate, conjecture, estimate, speculate, hypothesize, imagine, theorize, and suppose, if you push them hard enough for an opinion even when they are not sure. However, you can be assured when good lawyers don't know, they are going to qualify their communication. Listen for doubt in communicating with your lawyer. When you don't hear the magic words of doubt, you should be concerned about whether your lawyer has had enough experience to under-stand the nature of doubt and uncertainty in the outcome of conflict in the world of litigation. Now, if you are dealing with the proactive aspects of the legal arena such as preparing an estate plan, will, or a testamentary trust, you can substantially discount this discussion. Hopefully, at this point in your visit to a lawyer, you are enjoying peace, solitude, and the avoidance of conflict.

Listen for these words: often, sometimes, maybe, slightly, a few, could be, likely, generally, largely, perhaps, somewhat, soon, sooner or later, sort of, so-so, so to speak, seemingly, thereabouts, approximately, give or take, virtually, what have you, roughly, possibly, primarily, probably, proportionately, occasionally, often, mainly, just about, essentially, here and there, fairly, reasonably, before long, and broadly. These are only a few. There are many others. These words are inexact words. They are not absolute words but words with variable meanings. They are words of perceptions. What does "just about" mean? To you, it means one thing based on your own perception. To someone else, it means something different. Who's right? Both parties are. Who is wrong? Neither party is wrong but conflict is produced when expectations, understandings, and meanings do not have a common identity. If you go back through the five chapters preceding this one, you will notice that I have used words of qualification considerably. Words of qualification leave room for error on the part of the communicator.

Here's a good example of vagueness: "When will you leave?" Answer: "Soon!" When is "soon"? You have an idea and I have an idea about what's being communicated. If they are not the same, you and I are potentially going to have conflict because our expectations are not the same. This can be avoided by the client! The lawyer is probably not going to change how the legal profession has learned to communicate since its beginning. A wiser, more aware, and diligent client can protect himself or herself from illusory expectations. Unmet, unfulfilled, and unrealized expectations are the lawyer's and client's biggest nightmare in their relationship.

The motto "be prepared" has some high relevance in the relationship with your lawyer. To promote good lawyer/client relationships, lawyers must learn to mean what they say, say what they mean, and do what they say. Clients must also do their part in this relationship by listening, asking questions, and keeping a steady hand on their own expectations to ensure that they do not become illusions. Illusions most often precede reality. After the event and the confrontation with reality, your illusions may become disillusions. This disillusion arrives when you know the truth of your unrealistic expectations. Arriving at reasonable expectations is one of the most important concerns between a lawyer and a client. Both suffer in the communicational relationship when there isn't a clear understanding of what the expectations are. Don't be guilty of not listening to your lawyer and don't be guilty of allowing your lawyer to fail in discussing the many possible options of outcome with you concerning your case.

Appreciating, understanding, and being sensitive to all the discussions in this chapter are not simple and easy tasks, but you must prepare yourself for your own preservation in an unfamiliar world. Remember, the thrust of our charge here is not to bridge the gap of agreement in what you are hearing but to link and span the bridge of understanding.

When you learn to understand, you can then learn to communicate!

Chapter 7

What Can You Expect From Your Lawyer?

"Desperate people will accept a reassuring
word from almost anyone regardless of
qualification."—BFB

"There is no one who cares as much about
what you care about as you do."—BFB

Most people expect their lawyer to be all things dealing with all things. I hope you have begun to diminish this illusion by now. Lawyers, like everyone else in other occupations, are better qualified at some things than others. Thus far, you have been encouraged to be aware that lawyers have tended to become specialized. The tendency toward focusing one's ability in the direction of a reasonably defined area of the legal practice has been brought about because of the expanding complexity of the legal intricacies which have invaded each category of the law. So you have to know what your lawyer's area of emphasis and interest is before you engage his representation. However, and irrespective of the lawyer you are looking for within an area of specialty, you are looking for a lawyer who will "shoot straight" with you in your preliminary discussions prior to you hiring him or her. This is really the crux of the matter, isn't it?

Is the lawyer you are talking to in your search for a lawyer telling you like it is or like he perceives it to be, or is he simply leading you to the frightful edge of being totally desperate to the extent that you'll buy any hope of reprieve or reconciliation?

This is the most important answer that a lawyer can give you in helping you decide whether you are going to allow the one with whom you are talking to represent you.

Why Do Lawyers Practice Law?

There are all kinds of motives for why lawyers practice law. The most logical thought is that just happens to be the reason they went to law school. Well, that's not true! When "would-be" lawyers enter law school they don't have even the slightest clue as to what law practice is about. Most of them don't even have a clue when they get out of law school.

Then, some of them never get a clue the entire time they are practicing. Law school is a place on the order of a dungeon providing a dubious but serious environment where probably only about 40 to 50 percent ever make it out. Perhaps the others are chosen by divine destiny to be delivered from the trail of purgatory; those remaining are directed, destined, and determined to endure and dedicate their lives to the practice of law. For some, it will just be a short time as they find out that they don't like the practice of law because it's not what they thought it would be. The idea of what you hear and see in the media is not at all what it's like. Some, before they get in the arena of law practice, think of the business as one of high prestige, charm, power, and great fortune. Most lawyers know this is not necessarily the case. Of course, some of them live high-profile lives, with great prosperity and substantial power. The rest do not. The remaining force, outside just a few, are sincere, hard-working, caring, and diligent people trying to make a living practicing law.

Remember, lawyers are not in the business of practicing law for the humanitarian rewards of life. Sure, there is some of that in the satisfaction and gratification part of the business but it's not the focus of their involvement. Just like medical doctors, they have a sense of purpose, but they are focused on never getting to the point of not thinking about the business of making a decent living. That's the reason the lawyer you go to see is going to listen carefully to your problem. The worst scenario for a lawyer is to chase an empty covered wagon and not realize it was empty until he catches it. The lawyer has wasted considerable time and money while he or she could have been in a revenue-generating endeavor and now has a highly upset client because of the empty run. Of course, you know in the client's mind, the lawyer hired was not the right lawyer for the case. The lawyer is scorned and the client is unhappy. It's just not a good time for either of them.

Lawyers often get a bad rap for not bringing home the bacon but lawyers can't talk about clients even if the client has given the lawyer a bad steer initially about the facts of the case. That's the reason a lawyer has to look long and hard before he or she takes on a client's case. If you understand this reality, you can have more respect, empathy, and understanding of what your lawyer has to do before he or she takes your case. Buying a "pig in a poke" is not the way for a lawyer to make a living.

Law graduates are a unique product of our educational system. They are expected to practice law, and perform with some of the training they have received, as well as continue to practice, practice, and practice. There are a host of expectations that the legal profession and its lawyers place on themselves and the business. They are perceived by society, so they think, as making lots of money and enjoying a position of prestige in society.

Things have changed, though, in the legal profession. Distinctly, there are gigantic amounts of prestige that have now fallen and waned from the legal profession's ranks in just the last few decades. There are many lawyers who make lots of money. There are many lawyers who make good money. There are some lawyers who make some money and then there are some lawyers who just get by. Sometimes, it is difficult to know the difference since most of them try to live a life of pretending to be prosperous and successful beyond their level of accomplishment. The reasoning behind this pretense is two-fold: first, they want their clients and "would-be" clients to think that they are successful because they are good lawyers, and secondly, they want other lawyers to think that they are successful. There is a pride and ego among lawyers about who is a good lawyer and who is not so good.

Lawyers Come in All Varieties and Styles

Lawyers do what lawyers do. There are many who believe that the purpose of "lawyering" is to get and keep a client. Many lawyers and law firms have accumulated a vast inventory of clientele and intend on keeping those clients. Lawyers and law firms have become wise to the various needs of different styles of communication as was discussed in the last two chapters. To bridge the gaps of communication, lawyers and law firms have become very diverse in the types of lawyers in their associations. You'll now find minority and ethnic representation in the law firm which, until a few decades ago, was primarily dominated by the white Anglo-American. Remember what was said earlier. People like to communicate with people they have something in common with. People like to communicate with someone much like themselves.

Regardless of how much diversity there is in a lawyer's office, the question remains—how can you know when a lawyer is going to be forthright, honest, direct, candid, and responsive to your interest in knowing about the severity of, and potential for legal resolution of, your problem? What makes this even tougher is the fact that you now realize that lawyers are most often propelled by some mandate or manifesto to make as much money as they can since they are trying to live up to the multiple expectations of society, friends, spouses, clients, other lawyers, and themselves.

You now realize that an ego can be a sword or a shield. There are many lawyers who use the ego as a sword only. These are the ones who will most likely give you the realistic assessment you are looking for on the front end of your lawyer's representation of your interest.

But how do you really know before he begins representing you whether or not he is the lawyer you should have chosen? You'll never know until after the representation is finished and only then will you be halfway sure that your lawyer did not expend more effort than was necessary in protecting your interest in the legal matter. There are some types of lawyers that you can be surer about than others but even then there is no guarantee that your representation was done as inexpensively, practically, and as expediently as possible.

Remember, the legal profession is not designed around quantified and structured dictates on how everything should be done. This makes the legal practice, and those activities that go on within its boundaries, subjective and judged in the eyes of the beholders. Seldom is any approach to solving a client's problem absolutely wrong or absolutely right. If the client is reasonably satisfied, that's all that counts to most lawyers. On the other hand, there are some who never seek satisfaction of the client and are the subject of many bar complaints about their behavior. Being tough skinned, having no moral conscience and no consideration or sensitivity for humanity, they return to doing what they do.

Who can you most likely expect to level with you among the lawyer types discussed in Chapter 5? Let's examine and determine what they look like using the Diogenes approach of taking a lantern and going out into the city streets looking for an honest person.

Are You a Thinker or a Feeler?

Before our journey takes us into these communication types and how they communicate openly, thoroughly, and honestly to the client, you, the client, should recognize that people have a tendency to either be weighted more as a thinking person or as a feelings person. No one is a pure thinker without some feelings and no one uses feelings as a basis for their behavior to the total exclusion of thinking.

In considering this idea, draw two circles and have them slightly overlap each other. You now see that there is an area in the middle between the circles that has the influence of both thinking and feeling. When you go back to Chapter 5 and analyze the lawyer types, you can easily see how this has application to the "thinking" and "feeling" characteristic of personality. A look will be given to the effect and influences these states will have on your attorney in giving you a straight answer to your inquiries.

A note of caution is expressed in the idea that the law is the foundation for our society, its freedoms, and its governance. Regardless of what the law is, if your factual situation does not fit within the meaning of a particular law then all the law in the world will be inapplicable. If you don't know by now, facts—not necessarily the law—make lawsuits, determine equities, and govern what advice a lawyer gives a client. Please don't misconstrue what's being said. You must have the application of the law but that only has relevance and reference to your particular factual situation. Discussion will be made later about how facts are those quantities and qualities which are the subject of a constant and continuous search in a lawsuit.

Do Appearances Speak the Truth?

"Mr. or Ms. Personality" appears in your initial conference of representation as "too good to be true." He or she exercises such confidence, concern, and charisma with the client that the client already feels much better about the entire situation.

These lawyer types are often ideal repositories for a client's problems. Lawyers of this type speak in generalization and platitudes. Watch for war stories. These lawyers are extremely elusive and command a mastery of communication far superior to any other type. This fact does not, by any means, make them a better lawyer but they will help you think that. In your representation interview with "Mr. or Ms. Personality," you will encounter countless words of "qualification" as was discussed in the last chapter. This lawyer is hard to nail down but be careful not to judge too quickly since this lawyer can be totally outstanding. Pay attention in the next chapter when we discuss the questions to ask them to tie them down enough to give you sufficient information upon which you can base your representation decision. Remember again, this type of lawyer specializes in the art of communication often to the extent of engaging in "B.S." This is not a consistent characteristic, but this type operates from a base of behavior which displays the capability of being the broadest in capacity utilizing the full range of both sociability and dominance. This lawyer can really appear to be all things to all people and can very easily display any one of the other behavioral styles of lawyers because of the ability to adapt and control behavior to match the communication needed to establish rapport with a particular client.

Can you believe what this lawyer is telling you? Just like the nature of this lawyer, the answer is "yes" and "no." This lawyer often has some set opinions on almost everything. If this lawyer is too "quick-triggered" before you even have an opportunity to tell your story, you should consider that this lawyer wants your case and your money—and not necessarily in that order. In other words, his or her eagerness to get your case should show you that there are motivations of attraction other than wanting to help you solve your legal problem. Think about it for a moment! Eagerness is often a compulsive reaction we all use in not letting something slip away. Ask yourself whether the lawyer you spoke with was cautious and seemed genuinely concerned about the facts of the situation. This is extremely important!

These lawyers fall into the category of being equal as a thinker and a feeler. They are adept at being whatever they need to be. However, this is not where their downfall lies. If anything, they get over-involved in expressing their point of view, being outspoken, using gestures, and being dramatic and enthusiastic. Be careful not to buy their energy. They are generally very capable lawyers so be sold on the idea that you are buying their ability and not hearing what you want to hear. Remember, they are very capable of helping you hear what you want to hear.

Is This the Real Thing?

The next behavioral style of lawyer you'll consider as to whether you can get straight "stuff" from is the "Dictator." This lawyer could also be called "Mr. or Ms. Straight Stuff." Unlike "Mr. or Ms. Personality," who when wrong blame the client who didn't reveal all the facts, the judge who didn't know the law, or the jury who didn't listen to the case, the "Dictator" is never wrong or, at least, refuses to acknowledge being wrong. These lawyers plan and design their behavior so that they will always be observed and reputed as a powerful thinker.

When you look back at what's been previously said about this type of lawyer, you'll not be surprised that this lawyer is as straightforward as can be. This type is known for decisiveness, dominance, and competitiveness. This lawyer will probably not attempt to sell you on anything about your case and will tell you if he thinks you have a case or not. However, the prime motivation behind this often rude, blunt, short, and direct assessment is not your interest but their own. Remember, also, that these lawyers' behavior is that they are never in doubt, whether or not they are right or wrong. These lawyers draw quick conclusions about the quality of your case. This stems from their being dictatorial, bossy, in control, and probably selfish. Often, this behavioral type will be deliberately premature about the assessment of a case because that's the way this type operates. These lawyers are fast paced, aggressive, impatient, and quickly decisive. As you can see, these lawyers are almost always compulsive, and maybe even impulsive, when it comes to making up their minds about things. If you continue to express the facts representing your case after they have made up their minds, they'll be quick to tell you either not to worry about your case, they'll handle it, or they will often stand-up and tell you that you don't have a case.

Seldom will you leave this lawyer's office not knowing where you stand in regard to his or her impressions of your case. These lawyers are not particularly interested in selling you on their abilities. They're not storytellers and do not pretend to be other than what they are. They are not high in versatility when it comes to making clients feel comfortable, relaxed, or knowledgeable about their case. This lawyer does things his or her own way without regard to your expectations, your personal needs, and any regard to those things which might militate against the success of your case. This lawyer is going to give you a great feeling of confidence or going to scare the hell out of you. First, you have not gotten accustomed to their brisk, blunt, and cold manner so discount your first feelings of being "not so sure" about this lawyer. You'll know a little more about how to talk to this lawyer after the next chapter. Remember, these lawyers are not "bull-shooters" because that's not the way they are or the way they believe they need to operate.

The "Dictator" has a strong personality and will often appear to be indomitable, ruthless, obstinate, and unyielding. Recognize these as personality traits and not necessarily features of character. Make sure that you are choosing this lawyer for his ability and interest and not buying the glowing aura of his powerful strength of character.

Remember, there is no one perfect or best behavioral style of lawyer. The value reality of your representation is found in your personal evaluation of "tradeoffs." Each lawyer described here has a unique set of qualities, abilities, skills, and ideas which help them be successful. Do you want your lawyer to be kind, nice, sympathetic, sensitive, empathetic, or mean, tough, rugged, uncompromising, pushy, daring, and bold? It's difficult to find a lawyer that can consistently be all of these. It's like asking someone to love and hate at the same time the same person or idea. Here again, there are no pat answers about the kind of lawyer you are looking for.

Most people would agree that you are looking for a lawyer you feel good about. I suggest that your "feeling" good is more important than what you have reasoned, what your logic would dictate, or what you think. The head is the only part of the human body that is capable of lying, being deceived, and making decisions on what only appears to be in the human's best interest.

Feelings about people, ideas, and things are those qualities that control most of our lives. Most people have gotten themselves into most of their troubles by making decisions through the thinking process. Most of our ill-produced feelings have appeared because of the way we think about things. Look heavily toward how you feel about the lawyer you are about to hire. If it feels right, more than likely, it is.

Can a Lawyer Be Just Too Honest?

The third behavioral type we are evaluating for the ability to "shoot straight" is the "Intellectual" type. When you look back over Chapter 5, you'll remember that this type of lawyer has difficulty making decisions. This gives a big clue as to what you can expect at the representation interview. If this lawyer requires preciseness, is very cautious, and only acts deliberately after he has acquired all the details, you already can imagine what to expect in the initial interview. "Let's wait and see what develops before I give you my opinion," is not very satisfactory to the client who is sitting on the edge of his or her seat with heightened and intensified anticipation and anxiety. The "Intellectual" type is not very reassuring, to say the least. Their world is filled with doubt, skepticism, and wonderment. They are not risk-takers nor are they speculators about anything or everything. Is the "Intellectual" type of lawyer a "straight-shooter?" An absolutely and unequivocally "yes" would be the answer to the question, but so what. It is almost like saying that the person who never says anything always tells the truth. So what? Well, based on what's being said, should this lawyer simply be written off from consideration in handling your case? Absolutely not! This may be the lawyer you are looking for.

Why do I say that? Remember, this lawyer is extremely deliberate, organized, precise, slow-paced, cautious, and wants to be right. This lawyer prides himself on his problem-solving skills. There will be no "rush to judgment" here. There will be a distinct reservation of opinion until this lawyer has had time to study, contemplate, evaluate, and analyze the factual data and the law in your case, in order to rend an informed and rational basis for an opinion. As was suggested earlier, don't count this lawyer out.

Many receive and support this lawyer as a breath of fresh air after having listened to "Mr. or Ms. Personality" and the "Dictator" with their assertively overt communication styles. Now, you are listening to an introvert who is interested in listening to you tell about your perceived legal problem. The "Intellectual's" easygoing style is often misleading to the client who gets restless and wants some immediate communication that will get him or her premature and preliminary "peace of mind." This lawyer is probably not going to be much help here and you are going to have to have confidence that this will come in time because of this lawyer's brilliance and problem-solving ability. Why might this be the best lawyer for you?

You Have to Know Something About What You Are Trying to Do

The point is that this lawyer may not be the best one to handle your legal problem. This is not a flip-flop, dodge-around-the-issue situation. At some point, in dealing with a lawyer, you have to assume some responsibility for where you are going and what you are doing. At some point, you have to begin making decisions. You will no longer be able to hide, stand behind, and excuse yourself relying on your perceived "Forrest Gump" syndrome which allows you to get away with looking, acting, and being stupid and ignorant about what you are doing.

Do you know the size of your problem? The legal world being participated in by the legal profession is made up of the same level of problems that life is made up of. There are some little problems, there are some medium-sized ones, and then, there are some big ones. The legal practice and its machinery are no different than life in the difficulty of trying to decide which are the little ones, the big ones, and those in between. Often, you are probably like most people—you never know whether a problem is big or little until you start trying to solve it. Law practice and its relationship to clients are often no different that what you have experienced in life.

Your finding time and making an effort to go to the grocery store might be a small problem but no one would conceive it to be a large one unless you were physically disabled and did not have transportation or anyone else to go for you. Every problem in life carries with it a unique set of circumstances often distinct to that problem only.

Whether or not you know it, you are held responsible for many things you don't even know about. You have heard that "ignorance of the law is no excuse." This is true but there is one important distinction and provision that no one ever states when this is said. Ignorance is an excuse unless you have a duty to know. This opens Pandora's Box! Most of the laws which you are charged with having the duty to know are those which lead to the establishment, maintenance, and preservation of the order and discipline of an organized society. In other words, don't do anything which could hurt, harm, injure or damage property or people. Arguably, every law in our country could be construed to fit this admonition.

Where does this leave you in your search for a lawyer on whom you can rely for an evaluation of your legal problem? Confused? Perplexed? Frustrated? In doubt? Often, this is unavoidable! But, it's no different than when you have a problem with your car. If your tires need balancing, how much time do you spend trying to decide what to do and where to take your car? Admittedly, this is not a task that requires the skills of a rocket scientist or a stone-cutter. If your car is leaking oil, you move to a higher concern and are more cautious about your decision in taking your car to a mechanic. You may shop for references and opinions about what to do and where to go.

Looking for a lawyer may not be any different. Remember, almost any lawyer can make out a will or a power of attorney, prepare a deed, and handle an uncontested divorce. Some of them may not do this because they don't want to. But, you must begin to know what is more complex than other things in dealing with the legal profession. There is a wealth of knowledge in the form of books, special programming, and public lectures on the nature and general practice of what lawyers do. You can get a little informed almost by osmosis. You are not allowed to stand around in life and proclaim your ignorance and stupidity about some things. The law, the legal profession, and the nature of legal problems are moving up the ladder of public knowledge at a rapid pace. Ignorance was once said to be bliss. Now, being ignorant about what's happening in the legal arena is stupid.

The Simplest Problems Often Do Not Have Easy Solutions

The behavioral type of a lawyer represented by the "Intellectual" is one with which you can identify if you have some understanding about your legal problem. Be cautious here; I am not suggesting that you must or should know how to solve your own problem. However, you should know if you perceive your own problem to be one of a little, medium, or big magnitude in terms of difficulty. Please understand that there is a profound paradox waiting for your enlightenment which can be simply expressed that some of the smallest legal problems may be the most difficult to solve. Often, magnitude may not have anything to do with and any relationship to the ease and simplicity of a solution to a legal problem.

Where does all of this lead us? By now, you are probably beginning to think like a lawyer and recognize that the "Intellectual" type is the lawyer you should perhaps employ to represent you when your legal problem is not typically solved or described in a *Lawyering Made Simple* book you bought on sale down at your local book store. What's being said here is that this type of lawyer is usually interested in very involved, atypical lawyer work and situations where there are no clear answers. You get the point that this lawyer likes study and research. This is how this lawyer "out-lawyers" other lawyers.

Of course, the "Intellectual" type can, like all lawyers, perform a plethora of services, but is not generally interested in the mild satisfaction of routine activities in their law office. They like the excitement, challenge, and perplexity of difficult involvement. They may appear to be dull people by some standards but under this facade is the quest to solve some difficult challenge of a higher legal problem. If your legal problem is routine, don't waste this lawyer's time and patience. If your problem is one which requires taking risk, a swift decision, confrontation, and aggressiveness, don't hire this lawyer. Some responsibility is here placed on you to know what your problem is and what should you reasonably expect in terms of who should help you achieve some satisfaction from its solution. These lawyers should be hired for their "thinking" ability and their propensity to be attracted to the "letter of the law." I believe you get the picture! Don't underestimate these lawyers but, at the same time, hire them for what they are and what they can contribute to your unique type of case and not for what you want them to be. You'll get exactly what you see, no more, no less!

The "Hand-Holder"—Straight Shooter or Coward?

You'll probably remember the last category of lawyer types as the "Hand-Holder." They are closely kin to the "Intellectual" in the capacity of decision-making when you are involved in the initial conference, attempting to decide on hiring your lawyer. They are slow at taking action and making decisions. Whereas you saw the "Intellectual" as a thinker, the "Hand-Holder" falls on the high spectrum of being responsive as a "feelings" person. This lawyer will listen, empathize, agree, console, and share a commonness with you to make you feel good about someone listening to you, maybe for the first time in a long time. Rapport is one of the strongest traits of this style and the lawyer will most likely assure you that the problem will be worked out without giving you any specific details in many instances. Watch your vulnerability! This lawyer means well and does not intend to convey any false impressions to you about your case. You will perceive these things on your own because of the "Hand-Holder's" style. People who have legal problems are often desperate because they feel alone and, except for their lawyer, helpless.

The "Hand-Holder" communicates compassion and understanding to the client. This is often perceived by the client as being a mark of competence, intensity, and concern. In many instances, this is a true feeling being expressed by this lawyer. However, there are some characteristics you should not lose sight of in selecting this lawyer. Sometimes, these lawyers are not very creative and are not self-starters in handling the super involved complex litigation that takes place today in big court cases. Sometimes less is more and more is less!

Often these lawyers are somewhat disorganized, weak in establishing a theory of a case, dilatory about responding to those necessary matters that take place in some cases, and are often insecure about handling the "big" case. These lawyers are excellent counselors and in giving advice. Realize that sometimes, this is all you need. These lawyers are usually excellent "office" lawyers. This means that they had rather stay in the office and talk to clients than go to court and deal with all of the ambiguous, iffy, problematical skullduggery that goes on in cases of substantial litigation. This lawyer goes to court on many cases but picks and chooses which ones. For this lawyer, there is nothing worse than the folderol of a bunch of lawyers dumping on each other and using the court as the place for drawing blood.

The "Hand-Holder" is usually an excellent negotiator, since he or she supports and actively listens to other people, which gains him or her excellent support in return. Negotiation, mediation, and compromise are big parts of law practice, and any lawyer who doesn't understand this will waste a substantial amount of your money and your time. The lawyer here has the skills to help you compromise the conflict which has caused your legal problem.

On the other hand, settlement may not be the result of where your case is going. The "Hand-Holder" is going to make a serious evaluation of your case when you first interview with him to determine if your case can be handled on some basis less than mortal combat. This type's philosophy is that cases that end up in the litigated court room produce causalities and losers on both sides. These lawyers also know that cases that are settled will seldom, if ever, end up in the appeals court unless there has been some gross and substantial misunderstanding or fraud on the part of one of the parties in the conflict.

This is a most approachable lawyer. These lawyers are a pleasure to talk to. They have few "airs" about them. They are kind, affable, amiable, friendly, and genuinely interested in other people. Their ego satisfaction is achieved by being helpful without hurting other people. They display an ideal image of what a lawyer should be like in terms of being a humanitarian. Is this the lawyer you should hire?

All of these accolades for this type of lawyer are not to say that this is the lawyer you should hire. You should be getting the picture by now! Each different case may require a different type of lawyer.

Ideally, the recommendation is that you know what kind of case you have. But, you can't know that. You are not supposed to. If you did, you probably wouldn't need a lawyer. Be honest! You have some idea about your case. If you don't, get one. Try to figure a little for yourself. Ask about the situation. The "Hand-Holder" will tell you. You'll appreciate this more in the next chapter.

Remember, this type of lawyer is a "feeling" lawyer. His main concern is his own sensitivity about the client and doing the right thing to bring the client satisfaction, except getting in the arena of interpersonal conflicts. If you know this, you'll be wise to keep this in mind in evaluating your case in relationship with what you can reasonably expect this lawyer to do in helping you solve your legal problem. When you know what's being said here about this lawyer, you can reasonably expect them to do certain things and understand that they are not geared to do other things.

Don't be disappointed in your lawyer. They are what they are and you have to live by the old adage that being, "Foretold is being forewarned," if you expect to get your expectations met by your lawyer. However, you must appreciate that the "foretelling" is in how the behavior of these lawyers is seen in how they act, what they say, and how they respond to you, the client. If you are looking for the direct communication from a lawyer saying, "I am not the lawyer for you," you are dreaming. You have to assume some responsibility for the lawyer you are about to hire.

There Is No "The Answer!"

How much do you know now that you didn't know before you read the discussion about how lawyers communicate with you as represented by the different styles of communication? I hope, by now, you recognize that there is no "the answer." If you think there is, please go back and start again from the beginning. Life is about judgments and opinions!

Lawyers are different just as all people are different. People tend to become categorized somewhat in terms of common traits, but even then on closer inspection we all appear very different, much like what is said of snowflakes. No two are supposed to be exactly alike because that's their nature.

Some lawyers present themselves with high ambition, some with medium ambition, and some with low ambition. Isn't that the way all people in life are? Ambition is common to all. It just happens to be in varying degrees. With your lawyer, you'll never really know the intensity of their ambition since looks can be deceiving. Unfortunately or fortunately, you'll know soon enough after you hire him or her.

Some lawyers get right to the task while others attempt to refortify the all too prevalent reputation of lawyers as being procrastinators, slow-starters, and being dilatory. What's been discussed here has been with the purpose to help you know what you can expect from your lawyer. Let's see if you do.

Off to the Races!

What lawyer would you expect to be immediately on the "ball" and get your case off to a roaring start? If you guessed the "Intellectual," you are correct. This lawyer has their quiet ego at risk in satisfying the client and will see the case through unless the case leads to those pesky and tedious areas of the practice where this lawyer does not like to go. Then, you might expect this lawyer to call on the skills of another lawyer for the purpose of helping them bring the case to a conclusion.

Off to the Races #2!

If you guessed the "Dictator" as the answer, you are also on target. However, there are some things to look for. If the case drags out and this lawyer is not able to either see big bucks or is not able to bring it to a conclusion quickly, there is some likelihood that this lawyer may give you a call and ask you to come pick up your file. Don't be shocked; lawyers may fire clients unless the lawyer gets into certain situations where they would be required to get the permission of a court to withdraw from your case. You should not be surprised that the "matter of fact" "Dictator" lawyer gets fed-up with clients sometimes and shows little, if any, toleration and perseverance for the case or the client. Remember, "Dictators" are not particularly good "people persons" and nothing here should surprise you.

Even Odds!

What about "Mr. or Ms. Personality?" You are never sure whether they'll blast out of the starting blocks or not. The answer is "sometimes yes" and "sometimes no." They are moody people and often work in spurts. They rapport nicely with the client and wax eloquently about their abilities in getting things done but reality is often another dimension. If these lawyer types like your case and you as a client, they often begin with an enthusiastic dispatch and initially impress the client. Some of these lawyers wane quickly and lose their zeal especially when the case is not smooth sailing and runs into the hieroglyphics or minutia bordering on the quagmire of mediocrity. Then, this lawyer will pass the case over to an associate junior member of the firm or will attempt to get the case settled on almost whatever basis they can arrange. Often, this may be to the client's chagrin, disfavor, and dismay. The obvious point is that all lawyers in this type category should not be stereotyped in this manner with this behavior. However, this type of lawyer has a greater tendency to exhibit this pattern of behavior more than any other type when such circumstances arise as discussed.

Organized and Ready-to-Roll!

Now, the "Hand-Holder" should not left behind in this evaluation. Already you know that these lawyers aren't usually a "ball of fire" and do not usually "blaze a trail of fire." But these lawyers know who they are even if they won't admit it and surround themselves with support personnel in their offices to "prime the pumps" and do those things necessary in making sure you get representation in what needs to be done and in getting the satisfaction you expect. The lawyer, of course, gets credit for the preparation and the final satisfaction of the client.

Remember, these lawyers don't generally involve themselves in "deep-tunnel, sledge-hammer" type cases, which are long drawn-out affairs taking tons of pleadings and years of time. They, as you will remember, are good office lawyers and want to keep it that way.

"The More You Think Lawyers Change, the More They Remain the Same"—BFB

Remember, all lawyers are basically unpredictable as to what they will do in any given situation. In fact, lawyers even surprise themselves. They, like everyone else, are inconsistent but usually display certain core characteristics and eventually over time, more likely than not, will be repetitive with similar or the same behavioral patterns. All of us, including lawyers, have core characteristics of behavior which show a tendency to be consistent even though we have the ability to digress from that pattern depending on time, place, and circumstances. However, the bottom line says that we all return to rather persistent, consistent, and often predictable patterns of acting and thinking when we display our behavior in ordinary circumstances. Behavior is how we all judge people. We make up our minds about who or what a person is by what we observe as their behavior. After all, behavior is about what a person does based on our observation. We only see a small portion of a person's behavior. What we see is on the order of what we observe about an iceberg. Supposedly, you only see approximately 10% of an iceberg but you can reasonably and logically determine its size and character from that small portion. The idea of determining a lawyer's social or management style from what you observe is based on the same reasoning as one would use in studying an iceberg.

As a factor of experience and learning we assess the behavior of a person from what we observe of that person. Right or wrong, we then "judge" that person's motives and personality based on how we "feel" or "think" about what we saw. In psychological circles, there is some basis for believing that a person behaves consistently with their values and attitude. In separating the various behaviors of lawyers, we see that they tend to be grouped into the four styles based on how they exhibit behavior in relationship to their involvement with other people. After all, people only exhibit behavior in relationship to, and in the presence of, other people.

As you would suspect, some lawyers unequivocally deny they fit anywhere on the communicational grid for lawyers. Most people, including lawyers, believe they can be "all things to all people." No doubt, many can accomplish this incredible feat. Many feel they can zigzag through life being whatever they need to be to accomplish whatever they need to do. Accolades and bouquets should be tossed in their direction.

However, communicational styles over time tend to more concentrated in one group than any other. Truly, a lawyer whose core behavior can be categorized as a "Dictator" will and can exhibit "Hand-Holder" and "Mr. and Ms. Personality" characteristics on occasion. Sometimes, you may even misdiagnosis a style on your initial contact. But eventually, the real and true character comes out and you see it in its purest form. No one sincerely wants to be stereotyped as being a certain type but the reality of being just that speaks so loudly their denial crescendos in support of what they really are. Remember, denial may be your first clue of being on the right track.

"A Lawyer By Any Other Name Is Still a Lawyer."—BFB

Lawyers are trained to be lawyers. If the training did not take place, a person acting like a lawyer would eventually learn to think and behave like a lawyer. Lawyers see things differently than other people. Medical doctors see things differently than other people. Construction workers see things differently than other people. Whatever avocation, position or occupation you are in, you have become trained in a manner and means of seeing things with a view always in reference to what you have learned.

All of us see the world from the platform on which we are standing. A doctor sees the world from the view of understanding, recognizing, and dealing with sickness, illness, diseases, and health. Most of what doctors see in life is in some way influenced by this perception and reflection of what they do. Construction workers are the same way.

Lawyers are the same way. They look at things legally in terms of duties, responsibilities, causation, damages, and liability. This is a way of life with them not necessarily as a matter of choice, but because that's the way they are because of what they do.

Perhaps, you are now getting some insight into the nature of a lawyer's "being" to see and appreciate that lawyers are no different than other people you know. They just do things differently because that's the nature of their business. The thing that's different with lawyers is that they serve in a critical arena of life and have a flair for being more visible than most other professions and are therefore subjected to the whims and opinions of many who in the scope of public scrutiny don't have a clue as to what is involved in the lawyer exercising their duty, obligations, and responsibilities to the client. Remember, the lawyer operates in an inexact, unqualified, non-quantified, and often very subjective world. In other words, the lawyer is subjected to the perception of anyone who chooses to make one. This, of course, consists, fortunately and unfortunately, of those who are knowledgeable, informed, and possessed with understanding and those, on the other hand, who don't have a clue. Hopefully, by plodding through this book you are beginning to get that clue.

Abraham Maslow is credited with having posited some explanation without reference to lawyers but to mankind which might easily be applicable to the legal profession: "If you are a hammer, you have a tendency to see everything as a nail." Do you see how this might have reference and application to the legal profession? If you get the connection, maybe, just maybe, you are beginning to understand "some things your lawyer might not want you to know."

"My Lawyer Sold Me Out"

Your lawyer may not have worked as hard as he or she should have on your case. Your lawyer may have had other cases that took priority over yours. Your lawyer may have felt pressured by you to arrive at a quick solution short of what you thought you deserved. But your lawyer did not "sell you out."

Approximately 95% of all cases, both civil and criminal, are settled by lawyers on behalf of their clients. Another polite word for "settled" is the word "compromise." Compromise is not the equivalent for selling you out, but is the process by which lawyers obtain a satisfactory and amicable resolve between the parties for the benefit of a client. If lawyers were not blessed with the ability to compromise and reach agreements between the parties in litigation, all clients would be considerably less pleased about the results of their case.

Going to trial seldom begets the best results for a client. First, going to the courthouse and initiating litigation requires considerably more time, waiting, involvement, and uncertainty for both the lawyer and the client. Clients want their case to be resolved much quicker than what can be acquired through litigation. So, as a client, expect your lawyer to look after your best interest in attempting to resolve your case, short of placing jurors in a box and trying the case in front of them and a judge. Frankly, that's probably the last thing a client really wants. Of course, they don't always know and understand that.

Even if you go to trial and your lawyer wins your case, you may have the drudgery of waiting out an appeal to a higher court. Now, you are being confronted by having someone else look at the case to decide if the trial court's jury or judge was correct in their decision of allowing you to win a verdict. Higher courts can let your verdict stand, reverse, and even remand your case for the new trial. A higher court could even decide that you got too much money and shave off some of it from your verdict, or the court could say that your case is going back for further review by the lower court. Then, on the other hand, the court might say that your case is affirmed just as easily as they could say it was reversed. Just get the idea that there is considerable discretion on the part of the higher court.

The point you should know as a client is that a lawyer is doing you a tremendous favor by attempting to settle your case at the first opportunity and of course within an appropriate range of what you and your lawyer have decided as being a reasonable resolution to your case. You, as a client, should have some idea of what you and your lawyer are looking for in terms of a solution to your case. If you don't and your lawyer doesn't know either, both of you are just fishing for whatever will bite your hook. Know your expectations. Your lawyer should help you keep your expectations in line with what is reasonable and real within the capacity for what your case is worth. You are not dialing for dollars. Your case must have a firm and factual basis to justify what the defendant is willing to pay to resolve your lawsuit. Make sure that the stars in your eyes is not the sun shining through the back of head. Keep your feet on the ground and know what is realistic and what is not.

Through negotiations to reach a compromise, your lawyer will make a skillful display of facts, circumstances, and context that makes your case worth some money. Your lawyer is an artist who can place your case in the best possible scenario using all the U.F.A.C. (underlying facts and circumstances) at his or her command. That's the reason you engaged a lawyer. To know the law and direct your case in the most favorable light possible is what a lawyer does. A lawyer will work as hard as possible to get the best solution possible for your benefit. Often there is a difference of opinion between the lawyer and the client of what that is.

If you don't like the proposed solution as the basis of reconciliation presented by your lawyer, just say "no." Don't agree! Don't say "yes" when you don't have to or want to. There are many clients who feel that they have to agree in the heat of compromise and then once removed from the settings of settlement, get back to lawyer's office and whine over the settlement blaming the lawyer for making them settle. Lawyers don't or shouldn't make clients settle. That's not to say that lawyers don't have some responsibility to talk "some sense" into their client.

Lawyers know the legal arena. They have "been there and done that" many times. Clients need to understand and recognize that their opinion is mostly unqualified when it comes to what they should or should not get as a reasonable settlement.

But remember, you are the client and have the ultimate decision on settlement of your claim or case. On the other hand, when you are foretold you are forewarned that you may later get less for your case or claim, or in a criminal case, go to jail for three or four times the amount of years being offered in the compromise.

To make an intelligent and informed decision, you need to know what your lawyer knows but you can't and you won't because you are not a lawyer. You can only guess (and hope) that there could be a better solution to your case or situation. Your lawyer should know your situation better than anyone else including what you think you know. Again, if you are not happy with what you are being offered you can "roll the dice." However, you need to know that often when you pick up the dice, there is no turning back. Everything that has happened up until that point is erased. It never happened. Your position is now like leading off of first base looking at the pitcher to see if he is going to try and throw you out. If he tries to get you out, you can always try to get back to first base. In the legal arena of settlement, compromise, and negotiation, once you decide to litigate you are sailing a new course from where you have been.

A lawyer often has a difficult task in attempting to educate a client about the nuisances, nomenclature, procedure, and culture of how the legal system works. (Some lawyers are not sure about it either.) Most times, a lawyer can get on the same page as a client but it takes a lot of patience, time, and understanding on the part of the lawyer. More times than not, a lawyer is successful in doing this. Other times, they are not so successful. Clients will, on occasion, listen to their friends about what should and should not be and what they should do, overriding the advice of their lawyer. Lawyers do not give up in relating to their clients. This only challenges the lawyers to work harder, more persistently, and patiently in relating reality to their client. Lawyers do not want to lose a client over any misunderstanding or non-understanding. Lawyers have toiled, labored, and endured that client's case to this point, so they are not going to easily throw in the towel.

The lawyer/client relationship is much like a marriage in the fact that both are in the relationship for "better or worse." You both are in the situation together in a civil case. If the client loses, the lawyer loses. In a criminal case, if the client loses, the client goes to jail (not the lawyer) but the lawyer thereafter usually works feverishly and tirelessly to get the client free. Lawyers hate to lose, regardless of what you might think. They are not just after the money, reputation, and self-acclaim. They have job to do and usually take it to the end.

In the long run or even in the short run, your lawyer is on your side and never in a million years would "sell you out." Hopefully not to demean you as a client, the client must realize a lawyer's ethics, license to practice law, professional oath, integrity, and sense of seeking justice are far more important than the possible reward of "selling out a client."

Trust your lawyer until you are given a solid reason for not doing so.

Everyone has probably heard this most ridiculous phase. Many clients who don't get what they want at the end of their case sometimes lament that their lawyer "sold them out." They obviously don't have a clue what they are talking about.

CHAPTER 8

LET'S GO SEE A LAWYER!

"People want what they want because
that's what they want and will
continue to want what they want
regardless of who thinks they
should or should not."—BFB

"Attention and concern are usually
in direct proportion to the intensity
of your interest. However, patience
is in direct proportion to how respon-
sively and effectively someone else is
meeting your expectations."—BFB

"People think like they think, feel like
they feel, and act like they act regardless
of who deems that they should or should
not."—BFB

After reading the quotes above, you have probably concluded that you are being prepared to understand and appreciate human behavioral inevitability. This raises, perhaps, more questions than it answers. Have humans, especially those from modern and reasonably sophisticated cultures as in the United States and most of Europe, grown to expect too much from society because of elevated affluent living, lifestyles, and living the "good" life? Everyone will admit that competition abounds dynamically and intensely in every sector of a fast-paced society where everyone is perceived as having an opportunity to get a "piece" of the "action." This fierceness of interaction has caused us all to change and learn new and different expectations from people in business who are making every attempt to survive in the barbarous arena of commerce.

Lawyers are a part of this commerce and things are changing for them as most clients are becoming more worldly wise, multifaceted, and cosmopolitan. This new advanced client profile means a new beginning of equity between the lawyer and the client, which is historically unprecedented in the heretofore workings of the lawyer and their commonly perceived public image profile. This new time in the legal profession is one which inures to the benefit of the client in their relationship with a lawyer. Let's take a look at this new page in the life of a lawyer and discover where the client fits into the general scheme of the relationship.

Hiring the Right Lawyer

Throughout your involvement with the legal system, you will be continuously confronted with two parts of the process: first, hiring the right lawyer, and second, making sure you are able to determine, afford, and pay your lawyer fees. Wouldn't it be wonderful if there was something magic about how to hire the right lawyer and you could discover that magical secret? There's not and you won't! However, there are some systematic approaches that will assist you in that endeavor. There are books out there about "how to hire a lawyer" or maybe even "how to shop for a lawyer." This concern will not be ignored and will be dealt with later but first let's discuss the most important thing you need to know in looking for and establishing a client relationship with your lawyer.

The very eminent American psychologist, William James, is extremely renown for having penned the easily recognizable quotation, "The greatest revolution of our generation is the discover that human beings, by changing their inner attitudes of their mind, can change the outer aspects of their lives." This seems to, at least, imply that an individual's attitude is extremely important as a component of a person's life and accounts in part as a substantial influence and basis for their behavior. Modern theorists perceive that the "attitude" is learned and guides an individual to behave in a particular manner when confronted by particular facts or circumstances. Further, many believe that all of a person's values (which have been derived from their environment, beliefs, needs, perceptions, motivations, and influences during all of their lives) are those things that initiate and reflect a person's attitude which, in turn, produces their behavior.

The most important thing you know about anyone is their attitude. You like or dislike a person because of his or her attitude. You want to be around a person or not based on his or her attitude. You form an opinion about people because of their attitude. It is human nature to find fault with other people. When this happens, it is, most likely, taking place because of someone's attitude. Remember, earlier discussion was make about personality and that the personality was the display of behavior when we are interacting with other people. Attitude is the basis for that display. The point is: YOUR ATTITUDE IS THE MOST IMPORTANT THING ABOUT YOU IN LIFE. Therefore, the most important thing in life is ATTITUDE. Attitudes separate the crooks from honest citizens, those you like and those you don't like, and from those you find fault with and those you don't. Some lawyers have good attitudes and some don't!

A lawyer's attitude about his work, about you, and about the working relationship with a client is a reflection of himself. In life, you have to like yourself, respect yourself, and care about yourself before you can show, display, and share those qualities with other people. Sometimes, who a lawyer is speaks so loudly you can't really hear what they are saying. Some of the greatest truths in life do not require words for their meaning and understanding. Such is the way in the world of lawyers! Most people don't care how much their lawyer knows until they first know how much their lawyer cares about them.

From the simplest apology to the highest call to war, confidence, sincerity, and trust are gauged on the attitude observed in those who are delivering the message.

What your lawyer sows is also what you can expect to reap. If your lawyer cares and is interested in your case, then that's what you can expect during the time of your representation. If your lawyer appears insincere, disinterested, and uncaring, then that's what you can expect to continue during the time of your relationship. Foretold is forewarned! You have to observe, be alert, and be attentive to pick up the clues. They are there and you're your own detective.

Let's Go See Your Lawyer!

First, of all, call the lawyer you want to see and make an appointment with him. Whether the lawyer you are going to see is new to you or an old family friend, call him and show appropriate respect for his schedule. Lawyers are busy people and are multi-taskers, involved in many things. To take time out to see or speak to you imposes on their schedule and continuity of what they are doing. Be courteous as you would want someone to be courteous to you. A lawyer is not running a donut shop and should not be treated in that manner. Courteous pays! Lawyers generally return respect when they get respect the same way you do. Life is much like a mirror. You get back what you give out.

The appointment time you have with the lawyer is your time. No one else will be allowed to have the same time with the lawyer, so be on time. Remember, a lawyer's time is his or her stock in trade. Lawyers aren't selling pickles, jams or jellies. Do your part by being on time.

If you are running late, call the lawyer's office and advise his or her staff of your situation. If you can't make a scheduled appointment, call the lawyer's office as soon as you know your situation. The lawyer appreciates your courteous respect and more than likely you will not be charged for the time that was allotted for you with the lawyer.

If you don't call and are simply a "no-show," you may be charged for the appointment time anyway, when if you had shown up, kept the appointment, and met with the lawyer, you may not have been billed. If you are a "no-show" and don't call when you first know that you cannot make the appointment, you should be charged! It's no different than you preparing dinner for guests and then having them not show up and also not call to let you know.

This discussion is not intended to be tough on clients but you, too, have responsibilities in the attorney-client relationship, and then, on the other hand, if you want to argue that you have not retained the attorney, I would simply call on your duties as a respectable, decent, and courteous human being. Good or bad, you usually get back what you send out.

Many who are specialists in the field of communication say the first 30 seconds in meeting another person is the most important part of the relationship in setting the stage for the matters of understanding and working together in the hereafter. Whether or not you believe that depends on your own personal understanding of how communication works.

Supposedly, most of us have great difficulty giving much more than 30 seconds of our time at a time to almost anything. If you have difficulty believing that this is the way it is when we give our attention, just try writing down a day's worth of activities which take up your time. You will be overwhelmingly surprised. So, if our lives are so briefly interrupted with every kind of minutia possible, what does this tell us? It may tell us that we only pay attention in bits and spurts in an obviously sporadic scattered manner leading to the fragmented justification. But, the real and unfortunate product of all of this is that we have become very distinctly and directly selective in what we want to listen to and what we will decide what's being said means. In some circles of theorization this is called "selective attention" and is closely followed by "selective perception" and "selective retention." Where does all of this lead us in our quest to decide which lawyer should be hired to assist you with your legal problem?

Billy F. Brown

Come Prepared to Your Lawyer Meeting: Listen, Be Attentive, and Take Notes

Most of us are in the habit of not paying attention to the things we hear and the things we observe. The reasons for this condition are probably not of your own choosing.

Remember! Behavior is learned!! You don't pay attention because you learned not to pay attention probably as a defense mechanism against all that you are bombarded with in your daily life. As a result of not paying attention, you have become very unfocused, non-tuned, and disinterested in carefully and skillfully listening. You are not alone! The world has gone in this direction. No longer are we shocked at anything since we have been forced to hear it all. Just think what we have been progressively, incrementally, and perpetually exposed to in the last 40 years. Nothing has been kept secret from your exposure (except, maybe, the truth about U.F.O.s). Advertising, promotion, and even news reporting has been conducted with a flair of sensationalism just to get our "competed-for" attention.

Facts are facts regardless of who thinks, feels, or believes that they should or should not be. Don't scoff at this assessment! The point is that you should be prepared to engage in the process of discussing your case with a lawyer knowing that you are about to engage in a conversation about something you maybe generally know about but not specifically. Much conversation will take place between the lawyer and the client and only a small portion will be heard, a smaller portion retained in memory, and even a smaller portion will be reasonably and correctly assessed and decoded as to what was actually said by the lawyer to the client or potential client. Sounds discouraging, doesn't it?

It can be, but it doesn't have to be. When most lawyers see a potential client, or a client, with a legal pad, their attitude changes. Why? Lawyers really hate conflict especially with their clients. There are rather humorous comments floating around the profession about how great law practice would be if it wasn't for having to "put-up" with clients. Obviously, of course, there would be no law practice if there were no clients. So, lawyers are cautious when they are dealing with a client who is attentive, self-disciplined, controlled, and reasonably informed. Under those circumstances, the lawyer must be as appropriately postured in appearance, respect, communication, and in doing the business of representing the client in a manner that will withstand the careful scrutiny of another lawyer's examination and evaluation.

A lawyer's nightmare is being examined under the watchful eye of another lawyer who is looking to determine the appropriateness of a lawyer's conduct and display of an acceptable standard of legal skill in representing the client. Those lawyers who are not so "up and up" pray that they are not placed under the microscope of a headhunting lawyer.

The days of the client sitting on a stump and watching the world go by while his or her lawyer does whatever the hell he wants to is gradually fading. At one time, the arena was rampant with lawyers who get could away with whatever they wanted to. Still, even now, if the client doesn't know, the lawyer can do no wrong unless the client talks with another lawyer about the case and the conduct of the lawyer he or she has hired. This will be discussed later.

Knowing What to Ask Your Lawyer

Many clients come to the threshold of legal representation with only one question: How much will it cost? To hell with how much it's going to cost. Trust me! The fees will be explained to you by the lawyer. The big question that should be foremost in your mind is whether this is the right lawyer. Remember! Many lawyers perceive that they are only in the legal profession to make money. Why is this such a surprise? It shouldn't be! Everyone goes to work with the expectation of being paid by their employer. If your employer advised that your company would no longer pay you for working, no one would blame you for quitting. Lawyers should not be held to any different standard. However, the problem comes into play over the amount of the fee and how the fee will be incurred and under what circumstances.

Please notice! When I said above that, "the fees will be explained to you by the lawyer," the word "fully" before the word "explained" was not used. Don't get ahead of yourself. There are more important concerns before you get to fees. Keep reading and going straight ahead to understanding about the lawyer you are probably going to hire. Fees will be discussed in the next chapter but first determine if this is the lawyer you want handing your case or representing you in court.

The Most Powerful Word in the WORLD!

The word is not "HATE," "KILL," "DESTROY," "POWER," "FORCE," or "DOMINATION." None of those words are even close. (Nor is the word "sex!") You probably remember what's ahead from grade school. As a youngster, you were exposed to Rudyard Kipling, who is responsible for the contribution: "I had six honest serving men who taught me all they knew; their names were Where and What and When, and Why and How and Who." These are words which give you a key to making reasonable and informed inquiry about anything. They are subjective words which give the person to whom they are asked an opportunity to be expressively narrative about their response. Objective questions do little in providing information to the questioner. They usually begin with "will," "are," "do," "can," "may," "would," "could," or "should." There are others but you get the idea. The responder can answer the objective questions "yes" or "no." By now, you have already suspected that very few of the questions in life can be answered by "yes" or "no." Why? Any answer to any question has multiple influences which affect its outcome. Any "yes" or "no" answer is cloaked in assumptions which are seldom disclosed as the premise upon which the answer is based.

Clients like to get to the "nitty-gritty" with the lawyer they are talking to by listening to the magic words uttered by the lawyer in response to the question, "Do I have a good case?" Frankly, whether your lawyer will tell you or not, this is really not a good question because of its many multi-pronged considerations, and any answer given by the lawyer would only have credibility based on knowing the considerations and assumptions made by the attorney in offering the answer. Any meaningful answer would be so complex, the client could not possibly appreciate all of the assumptions which may later prove to be false, the proposed but pending eventualities of proof which may not occur, and the expected resolution of the variances in revelations of testimony as to what the proposed facts of the case are by different witnesses who each think they are correct in what they believe they saw and heard.

Asking Relevant Questions When You Are With Your lawyer

The questions to ask a lawyer could be called the "right" questions. However, the only questions that are "right" are those which are "relevant" to your reason for seeking the advice and legal counsel of a lawyer. As was suggested earlier, your understanding of what information you are about to receive from a lawyer is no better than your preparation for understanding and getting the necessary information in making an informed decision about your representation. So what are some relevant questions?

Without a doubt, the most important relevant question which has multiple parts, is whether the lawyer with whom you are speaking is competent in the field of your legal problem and whether this lawyer is interested in handling your legal representation on the basis of a reasonable legal fee payable within the terms and conditions of your ability to pay. Obviously, this says it all! How do you make a start in breaking down each of these areas which are important in your deciding to hire a lawyer?

First, discover if the lawyer you are talking to has had some, or even considerable, experience in the area of your legal problem and whether the lawyer would be interested in your case. This is not complicated to discover. A dialogue may sound something like this:

"Before I take up unnecessary time in conferencing

with you, let me tell you that I have a lease problem

in getting a tenant who has not paid rent in five

months removed from my property. Is this the kind

of business you handle?"

Both you and the lawyer know the answer already as to whether this lawyer evicts people who have not abided by the terms of their lease. How do you know that since you have not spoken with this lawyer before? Most secretaries have already screened the problem when you first called to make the appointment. If you have a patent, trademark, or a copyright problem, and call a real estate lawyer, your time and the lawyer's time will be severely and needlessly wasted if that lawyer does not deal with patents, trademarks, and copyrights. The secretary already knows why you are there. There may be exceptions you'll encounter but generally the lawyer does not want to waste their time or your time.

Some clients have a tendency to circle the wagons in getting to revealing what their legal problem is. You know what I am talking about. They start historically from the conception of the relationship, describing the weather, what people were wearing, and the type of car everyone drove. Lawyers don't want to hear this drivel. Lawyers will ask what they want to know so guard yourself on how extreme you are motor-mouthing in talking to your lawyer.

However, you need to recognize that some lawyers want you to come to their office regardless of whether they handle your problem or not so they can meet you and establish a rapport for any future legal problem you may have.

Some, also, make a big payday out of referring you to a lawyer who will handle your type of problem. These lawyers often get a referral fee back from the referred lawyer which usually is a third of the fee charged the client less any "out-of-pocket" expenses.

The referring lawyer will not charge you a referral fee in getting you to a lawyer who will handle your legal problem. However, some lawyers to whom cases are referred add a little "extra" to their normal fee to cover the situation of having to pay a referral fee to the referring lawyer. This lawyer to which your case has been referred will gladly pay the referral fee to the referring lawyer since this may be a continuing source of new business they would not have otherwise acquired.

The lawyer referral business is big in the personal injury area of law practice. Big firms who handle mostly personal injury cases depend on their case load from referring lawyers from a large geographical area. This is not all bad for the small-town lawyer who may not have the resources and the contacts to properly pursue a major matter of personal injury litigation. The client benefits from the reputation, skills, and resources of the major law firm specializing in that type of case litigation. There is no extra fee for the client allowing the case to be referred. Actually, it's a good deal for the client since the referral lawyer remains as the local source of contact for the client while the major law firm prepares the case and spends their resources on behalf of the client attempting to successfully pursue the case.

You, as a client, do not have to accept any referral or advice from anyone unless you have previously agreed to allow your case to be referred in the contract you signed with your lawyer. The contract of hiring your lawyer will be discussed later. You are in control of those whom you employ. Don't lose sight of this fact. That fact alone is probably the most important fact in your relationship with your lawyer. Your lawyer may in charge of your case, but you can be in control of your lawyer!

Help your lawyer help you. When you call for an appointment, don't play coy with the secretary by refusing to tell him or her what your legal problem is. Such a position on your part is not well-received and could possibly keep you from getting an appointment. The secretary is only trying to save time and wasted effort. The secretary is a part of the legal system and has the same obligations of confidentiality as the lawyer has. Some clients get bone-headed and refuse to relate the nature of their legal problem to the secretary. Their refusal often causes everyone involved a great deal of consternation and aggravation.

When You Have Found a Lawyer Who Solves Problems Like the One You Have

There is no more direct route to getting information than the straight question, "How often have you been involved with a lease problem dealing with the eviction of a tenant?" The lawyer will tell you the rest of the story. After he finishes his response, your next question could simply be, "What's involved?" It sounds like to me that you are "off and running," but that's not the end of the story. Often, the key to any situation is in knowing what questions to ask!

There are innumerable questions you could ask your prospective lawyer from what his hobbies are to whether he goes to church or not. Your potential arena of inquiry could border a level of being ridiculous to being briefly relevant. Here's an example of being a bit on the overbearing side: You could arrive at a lawyer's office with a tape recorder, video recorder, a non-introduced witness wearing sunglasses and a trench coat, with you holding a typed list of interrogating questions to ask the lawyer. What would you do if this situation was presented to you? You would run like hell, wouldn't you? The lawyer you are talking will too, unless you have such a severe case resulting from a personal injury where the potential client is in a quadriplegic condition caused by someone who has obviously breached absolute liability and possesses unlimited resources from which to recover a large sum of money.

Each of the four lawyers we have identified earlier will render a different response to your profile. First, "Mr. and Ms. Personality" are curious and would play along with you for a while in getting to understand your scheme and motive.

The "Dictator" would probably throw you out of his office, or alternatively, give you a break and never let you into his office. You would more than likely last only a few seconds in attempting to speak with him. You would probably not get any audience with the "Intellectual," either. You have already exceeded the characteristics in your behavior he or she is willing to deal with. Lastly, then, you can expect the "Hand-Holder" to be somewhat intimidated and show kindness at first, but gradually withdraw from being interested.

All in all, you must remember you are in the lawyer's domain and he sets the rules of engagement, the agenda, and the protocol. Pomposity and arrogance should be left outside the door (at least for now).

Money Makes the World Go 'Round

Whether we all want to admit the position or not, much of life translates into some component dealing with money. You either have some money and want to keep it, or you don't have any money and you want some, or you have some money but want some more. Admittedly, this picture plays out in the daily world of life. You can be sure, the nature and pursuit of money will not be substantially altered in this life.

Money usually gets a lawyer's attention. Most lawyers must tolerate and comfort a great amount of restlessness on the part of clients in big cases. The bigger the case, the longer it often takes to bring the legal process to a conclusion. Remember, everyone must have an opportunity to make their "daily bread" on such a case. This includes the defense firm representing the party accused of causing the injury to the plaintiff. However, in fairness to any defense lawyers, they must check out all the total circumstances of the case, the plaintiff, and the law before they often know their posture in bringing the case to a reasonable and amiable resolution in the form of settlement. The discussion about lawyers, lawsuits, and settlement will be made later, but meanwhile you are still in front of the lawyer you are thinking about hiring. Don't scare them to death with your zealous determination to interrogate them like you are Mike Wallace on "Sixty Minutes." Be easy, relevant, relaxed, and even causal. Don't present yourself as being a "P.I.T.A." Leave your *Everyday Law Made Simple* book at home.

The difficult part of the interview is in attempting to find out as much as you can about the lawyer you are talking to and being relevant about your case. You can find out if the lawyer is experienced in your area of concern, and if he is willing to handle your case, by simply engaging in discussion about your case. Lawyers are seldom asked where they went to law school and what legal fraternity they joined. All a client wants is good legal representation at a reasonable fee. A client will soon discover that "good representation" means that a lawyer is competent, interested in the client's case, and is willing to "take on" the cause. That's what legal representation means in the legal profession.

Chapter 9

Understanding Legal Representation

All Trails Have a Beginning

Once you have begun a conversation with anyone you begin to immediately know whether that conversation is going to be easy, difficult, strained, meaningful, or boring. You have had enough experience in life to know what I am talking about. Obviously, some lawyers are easier to talk to than others, as you'll remember from previous discussions. After a few minutes of conversation, you will probably be asked how you sought that particular lawyer for representation. This reference and recommendation is important for the lawyer in two main areas.

First, if the recommendation has been made from a previous client, the lawyer can acknowledge a common bond with you since you are apparently on good terms with that person enough to take his or her recommendation of a lawyer.

Secondly, if another lawyer has referred you to this lawyer, the lawyer wants to know that so they can either pay a referral fee to the lawyer or, at least, thank them for the referral. A lawyer has an "eye" for future business and always must be attentive to referral cases.

As you can easily see, all of this conversation will lead to many opportunities to direct your inquiries where you want them to go. All lawyers do not accept referral fees if you are referred by them to another lawyer. Some feel they are simply being of assistance in attempting to help you solve your particular problem.

What Will the Lawyer Do for You?

After all, this is what you are there for! What services will the lawyer perform for you and how much will their representation cost you?

Lawyers, sometimes, take a generic approach to answering questions about what they will do and how much they will charge. For example, a lawyer may tell you, "I have been handling this type of thing for 15 years and I'll assure you I can make it go away for you. I'll need a retainer fee of $300 which could possibly cover the entire fee." (Most lawyers ask a client to put up a small deposit for the legal fee which shows and displays "good faith" on the part of the client.) The lawyer may then continue, "The normal fee in the type of case you are asking me to represent you on usually averages around $600. I will try to do the work for less, but a lawyer never knows how much time will be involved in attempting to acquire satisfaction for the client. Let me tell you, Mr./Ms. Client, how I plan to proceed in your representation . . . Do you have any questions about what I have said to you?"

Nothing you see or anything you hear from now on gets any easier for the client. The client finds himself or herself in a closed world of mumbo jumbo, not hearing what was said, and not understanding what he or she did hear. Clients usually know, or sure discover, that what they need they cannot get for themselves. In many ways, they are alone, hanging on only to the hopes and faith they have placed in the hands of their lawyer. Clients don't know what the legal process entails in spite of the fact that some think they do. One of the greatest illusions in life is thinking you know something when you don't have any basis whatsoever for knowing what you think you know.

There are still some good, honest, bright, and sensitive lawyers in this world who will take the time and the diligence to advise you of your legal options and what options they would recommend on your initial interview with them.

Lawyers are more cautious than ever before. Why? The situation is very much like safe sex. Why has society gotten so concerned with safe sex? Obviously, the answer is because there must be some kind of problem which would necessitate more concern. Lawyers are under public scrutiny more than any other time before. A lawyer will be careful in telling you the likely result of filing a lawsuit and how much and what you can expect from a lawsuit. Lawyers are careful in telling you what they think a jury would return in a client's case in terms of a successful verdict because they know that such representation could come back to haunt them later.

In life, if you just listen long and often enough, you can probably hear just about anything you want to hear. That's just about the way it is with lawyers and "lawyering." There's always a lawyer just up the street, down the road, or across town who would have gotten you more money in a lawsuit or charged you less in another matter. Clients will shop lawyers to see who will say the best "words."

"Lawyering" is no different than going to buy a car. Of course, you and I recognize that the subject matter is different. After you have completed the purchase of a car most all of your friends and neighbors will tell you that you they could have gotten you a better deal. That's why people lie about the deals they get or the amounts they pay their lawyer.

Once You Have Determined What Your Lawyer's Going to Do . . .

Most of life takes on the old good news or bad news scenario. The good news is that your lawyer says that he or she can be very effective in representing your interest and that the case looks like a "sure-shot." The bad news is that the fee in this kind of case is equivalent to the expenses of undergoing cancer therapy. Great Holy Smokes! How can you win? You can, but you need to know what to expect from getting involved in the legal process from the position of what you are going to be expected to contribute to your case and from the standpoint of how much this whole thing is going to cost.

Sometimes, in some situations in life, you'll discover that life would have been a little more pleasant and your "grief factor" would have been less if you had decided to not get involved and abandon your quest to seek justice and retribution. If there is such an animal as "justice" and you do experience its influence, the acquisition can be expensive.

The Most Important Question in a Relationship With a Lawyer

Foremost, can I get along with my lawyer? You are going to be working with your lawyer and he or she will be working with you. Are you going to be comfortable with the relationship?

Is the lawyer I am about to select and hire capable of handling my case based on his or her ability and experience? Furthermore, is my lawyer willing to represent me in a timely, competent, and consistent manner, to a satisfactory conclusion of the case? This is a BIGGIE! Remember, earlier discussion was made regarding the lawyers who start out with your case like a "rocket" and slow down to the pace of a "rock."

Do you, as a client, know what the lawyer is going to do for you? Don't worry so much as to how a lawyer does what a lawyer does. That's not your concern. If you know "how," you wouldn't need a lawyer. You wouldn't ask a brain surgeon how a bilateral lobotomy is performed.

Do you know what your legal options are? Does your particular case necessarily have to be filed in court? Will a letter written by the lawyer to the party against whom you are seeking relief solve the problem and avoid a lawsuit? Some lawyers are "quick-triggered," impatient, greedy, insensitive, and want to get on with the "business at hand." Filing a lawsuit makes a statement of declaring an adversary posture on the part of the client. It may not be in your best interest to make a declaration of war. A lawyer makes more money by filing a lawsuit when, often, a letter would have solved the conflict.

When you are being sued, sometimes, a telephone call to the lawyer filing the lawsuit may solve the conflict. However, to be realistic, lawyers wait out the opportunity for compromise since it seldom is accomplished on the front-end of a potential battle when the heat is the hottest between the litigants.

However, don't be too quick to judge. Lawyers know that the results you are seeking by seeing a lawyer must be worth the amount you will be charged in legal fees. A good lawyer recognizes the difference between a worthwhile case and a case that should be handled in the most economical, judicious, and expedient manner possible. Otherwise, you would have resolved the problem yourself.

What does your lawyer think about your case? Is your case worth the legal expense involved? What is the likelihood of you getting the satisfaction you are seeking? How confident does the lawyer feel about your case? What is the lawyer's opinion about whether your case would go to trial or be settled out of court? How much time does your lawyer think your case will take to get what you want?

Remember, lawyers can only guess what's involved when another lawyer shows up on the other side. Involvement, time, difficulty, legal fees, and your apprehension expand proportionally to the number of lawyers who show up to represent the parties from whom you are seeking satisfaction. This idea is true in all aspects of life and not just the legal profession. Does the lawyer with whom you are speaking enter into a written agreement with his clients about what he's going to do for the client and how much such representation will cost?

Honestly, and truthfully, lawyers don't like to hear a client request that the legal representation relationship be described and identified in writing except when they are representing a client in a personal injury claim. Why is this so? In personal injury litigation, a lawyer will not charge an "up-front" cash payment by the client. The lawyer recognizes that a personal injury case is non-quantified and may result is a huge amount of money. On the other hand, a lawyer often "rolls" the dice in attempting to recover a reasonable amount of compensation for the client. Consequently, the lawyer chances that he will be successful in recovery and will "gamble" his time, talent, effort, and energy on being successful. When he takes a personal injury lawsuit, he will enter into an agreement with the client to represent the client on a contingency fee basis. If the lawyer is successful, he will be entitled to a portion of the settlement awarded to the client. This will be discussed in greater detail later.

Lawyers are Lawyers—Not Psychics or Magicians!

There are many professions that have the same difficulty as lawyers in being able to "guesstimate" fees in advance of professional performance. Any one of these professionals engaged in estimating a fee for a client would like to have a proverbial "crystal ball" to take the inexactness and guess out of the exercise. Lawyers never really know exactly how much effort is going to be involved when they take a case, so they are highly reluctant to state unequivocally what the client would genuinely like to know. Only young, inexperienced lawyers and unthinking, older lawyers trap themselves into giving the client an exact expectation of results in a particular case, or set a specific fee for the legal representation. Older, more experienced lawyers know better! There are just too many intervening determinants which potentially influence the time a case will consume before some finality is reached. These same circumstances which affect the estimate of time also can easily affect the approximation of results and the amount of legal fees required from the client before the case is concluded. Admittedly, this all seems to sound logically true in response to why lawyers don't like the idea of entering into a written lawyer-client agreement.

When you were growing up as a youngster, do you ever remember your parents telling you not to play with matches because you could seriously burn yourself? Remember, lawyers are, generally and broadly, intelligent people who recognize and realize that the legal profession, heretofore, has always been cloaked with a mystical air of perplexity, contradiction, and ambiguity. Lawyers have always been perceived as the sources who could unravel this complexity, penetrate this veil, and reach satisfaction for their client for a fee. Many lawyers have hidden their legal sorcery from the client which has consistently given the lawyer a decisive advantage over the weary, uninformed client.

Things are changing. Information is changing things. Now, everyone can acquire the truth on just about everything. If you don't believe this, jump on the internet and surf around for only a part of the evening and you'll be totally overwhelmed by the billions of pages of internet telling you everything from how to make a bomb to where to buy rhinoceros horns. Model lawyer-client agreements represent the formal understanding between the lawyer and the client. Lawyers have, up until now, had their way in almost every way with the client. (See Appendix A)

For All the World to See—Toward a Full Disclosure From Your Lawyer

Marriage vows are not even usually put in writing, so why would a lawyer want to get specific about putting in writing all the details about what and how he is going to represent the client, fully specifying attorney's fees, filing fees, related court costs, law clerk research hourly rates, paralegal expenses, deposition fees, fees for court reporters, charges for transcripts, subpoena fees, and fees for experts? Such an agreement would require the attorney to estimate that these legal expenses would not exceed a specified amount. Potentially, this is going to scare the hell out of the client and the lawyers know this.

This is only the beginning of the nightmare for a lawyer. The list can be extended to include charges for postage, charges for long distance phone calls, travel, investigation expenses, and many other expenses that are made in representing the client—some of which aren't even known or anticipated at the time of the agreement. You are beginning to get the picture. Now, the client has a lawyer talking to the lawyer to be hired, negotiating over the terms and conditions of the lawyer-client agreement. This is only the beginning. The agreement could include client's rights and responsibilities, lawyer's rights and responsibilities, and the procedure to settle any dispute if the client and lawyer get into one concerning fees and/or representation.

No person wants to arm their adversary. At the beginning, the lawyer and the client are never adversaries. They become adversarial when the lawyer doesn't do his or her job in representing the client, can't account for the work for which they have billed, or the client's expectations have not been met at the conclusion of the case. When the client becomes adversary, after entering into a written client-attorney agreement, he or she can thank the attorney for telling him or her (the client) how to make a complaint out against the lawyer since such details are clearly spelled out in the document including the address of the Ethics Commission of the state bar.

Many clients don't give a hoot about facts, circumstances, interventions, and subjectively influenced determinations as a basis for why they lost or didn't get the amount of money they arbitrarily wanted. The reason perceived by the client for losing after the case is concluded is that any failure is all the lawyer's fault. Clients will even accuse the lawyer of malpractice because the client gave the lawyer the name of an irrelevant witness whom the lawyer chose not to call to testify in the case. Clients generally don't care about the reasons for losing. They usually believe they lost their case because their lawyer did not do something that would have produced victory in their case, or the client will often contend that their lawyer got "out-lawyered." Clients seldom find anything wrong with their case. Clients, more likely than not, assume a self-righteousness about their case and are very much unwavering when it comes to anything to the contrary which would tend to lessen their asserted position. If anything goes wrong, it's usually the lawyer's fault. At least, that's the position that, more often than not, is reverberating in the mind of the client.

When clients become dissatisfied with their lawyer during the representation or after the representation, guess who the disgruntled client goes to see? You guessed it! Another lawyer!

This new lawyer, who knows absolutely nothing about the case, then starts digging against the other lawyer. What better place is there to start snooping to learn what that lawyer was supposed to do for the client than the lawyer-client agreement?

You don't have to be a member of Mensa to get the picture. You can be informed about things to do and not do . . .

The philosophy about the practice of law among lawyers is obviously not the same. Some lawyers believe that clients should have all the information possibly available so the client can make intelligent and conscious participative decisions about the case. Others don't agree or subscribe to this philosophical idea and practice law with a *modus operandi* of *caveat emptor* which means "let the buyer (client) beware."

What You See Is What You Get, More or Less . . .

The phase "more or less" is probably one of the most useless expressions in our language. This often-heard tag accompanies an intention to be less specific to the extent of being generic in meaning, signifying little if anything. Lawyers have a tendency to be very generic but you have to listen to their words of qualification to know this. They want to keep the lawyer-client relationship in this posture because such control represents power over the client. Some lawyers are very successful in their practice of the secret that the first order of business and responsibility of a lawyer is to insure that people are prevented from understanding the law. This position has some conspicuous overtones reeking of propriety, possessiveness, protectiveness, and authority. Some lawyers do not think like this. Distinctly, there are many who are not willing to educate the client about the nature of the legal profession dealing with their interest as represented by his or her case. Then, based on what's being said here, if you agree generally with the idea, why would a lawyer want to enter into a written lawyer-client agreement?

There Are Only Two Reasons!

The first reason is because in a large part that's the way personal injury representations are handled between the client and the lawyer. The aspects of fees will be discussed in the next chapter but for now please realize that a personal injury representation by a lawyer in almost all of these cases involves no initial fee from the client. The lawyer in these cases takes the case on a contingency fee basis. This means that the lawyer is not going to ask you for a fee (retainer) to take your case. He or she will take a fee from the amount of money you will receive from the insurance company, the corporation, or the individual(s) against whom you are seeking damages. To approach the insurance company and discuss potential settlement, to enter into negotiations, or to file a lawsuit, the lawyer, to protect their own interest of receiving a fee, initiates the agreement of getting a portion of the recovery in writing with the client. This has become customary in the legal profession between the lawyer and their client. You'll hear more on this later.

The second situation where a lawyer is usually assertive in getting a lawyer-client agreement is when a lawyer's fee billings will be forthcoming over a longer period of time as compared to routine representation. This longer amount of time usually involves another consideration of the amount of out-of-pocket expenses a lawyer has to make to represent the client. An agreement in writing specifying what expenses and fees will be billed, and when, will potentially eliminate any future conflict and will ensure the lawyer of getting paid appropriately and timely.

Is There Anything Routine About the Legal Profession?

The answer is a typical "yes" and "no." Sometimes, the answer is "yes" and sometimes the answer is "no." Sometimes, the answer depends on what is meant in the question by the word "routine." Let's define the word as, "in the usual course of business which may be accomplished with the same consistent standard of treatment on an ongoing basis." This definition will probably not satisfy a dictionary but allows an understanding for our benefit. If a matter is "routine," a lawyer can decide to charge a fixed legal free for the client's representation and not have to vary that fee except when circumstances arise that remove the representation from the routine category.

Lawyers don't like to hear this, and like admitting it even less, but there are some aspects of the law practice and profession which do not require high levels of skill and creative insight. Every lawyer indulges in activities of legal practice that are routinely and competently handled by the lawyer's legal staff which may include legal secretaries and/or paralegals. These "routine areas of the legal profession" may consist of a simple will, a power of attorney, a living will, a bill of sale, all types of deeds, leases on real estate, loan closings, collection letters, releases, eviction notices, promissory notes, and even simple divorces.

Clearly, no lawyer wants you to believe that they are not needed to perform these routine tasks. They are going to charge you the same fee regardless of who prepared the work. An important point is found in the appreciation that regardless of who prepares the routine work in a lawyer's office, the lawyer remains in a position of full and complete responsibility for the contents, accuracy, competency, and legal efficacy of anything prepared in his office. The lawyer is on duty regardless of whether the lawyer did the work or not. That's the point! Lawyers are good at surrounding themselves with highly competent administrative types who are often more attentive and reliable than a lawyer and some of them are much more affable.

Will Your Case Remain Routine or Not?

When another lawyer shows up to represent any party from whom the lawyer's client is seeking some kind of satisfaction, the case loses its routine nature and enters into a new level of representation that may not have not been previously considered and contemplated by the lawyer and the client. Directly, when the case is no longer routine, the lawyer and the client enter into a new relationship where the lawyer will be charging the client on an hourly basis. If you have a routine case, pray that your case remains routine. Remember, involvement expands in time and legal expenses consistent with an appearance of another lawyer and the amount of legal fees that a lawyer charges the client. The amount a client will allow a lawyer to charge him or her is usually relative and dependent on how scared or how angry they are or both.

The Bottom Line Is: Routine Legal Matters No Longer Foot Legal Office Overhead

The bottom line is that there is probably no bottom line. One of the most difficult tasks in talking about the legal profession is in being basic. Even the simplest of ideas and concepts can in rapid fashion erupt into whole episodes of continuing and persistent convolution. In other words, everything, simple or not, can get substantially screwed-up in a short amount of time. This is not to imply or mean in any way that a great amount of law practice is other than boring, mundane, and routine activity surrounding the services demanded by a client.

Notwithstanding that, there are still some simple, routine matters being handled by lawyers. By and large, law practice has drastically changed in the last few decades. There is an escalation of expense in the law office just as you have observed in the general scheme of society. Word processors, law libraries, professional liability insurance, escalating demands of younger lawyers' salaries, legal secretaries, paralegals, and the social expectations lawyers place on themselves have all caused the routine aspects of law practice to become void of routine. Many lawyers no longer indulge in some of the routine matters that served as foundational services contributed by the legal profession some years ago and what many termed as a "necessary evil preserving and serving society in its own inimical way."

Many lawyers exiting law schools these days are hardly considering any evaluation of getting into those areas of the so-called routine practice of law. They are looking for big firms who can pay the big bucks who represent big corporations who are making big revenues from the biggest of consumption on the part of a consuming American economy. Bigness has caught on as a wave in the legal profession. Just like the dying out of the family physician, the legal profession has turned the heads of many practitioners who are aiming for the practice as represented in the opportunity with big businesses or in chasing personal injury lawsuits which aim their wrath at big business or insurance companies which have the resources to make the lawyer's pursuing efforts worthwhile. Lawyers want more, more, and more. Many lawyers do not like admitting that they are in the business of the legal profession to make big bucks.

Routine matters, unfortunately, no longer maintain the personal appeal of a lawyer pursuing bigger and better things. There are still some vestiges of open receptive representation of routine matters in lesser metropolitan and cosmopolitan areas such as rural areas and suburban areas. As all of life escalates, you can expect less and less non-specialization. When you stop to think about the idea for a moment, life has been becoming increasingly specialized since the end of World War II. After that time, there seemed to be the arrival of a new world order and lawyers were certainly going to be an increasing part of it. Right or wrong, whether you want them to be or not, they are and they are here to stay because that's what society wants regardless or what it says. Remember, "Whether a lawyer is a skunk or not depends on whether or not it's your lawyer you are talking about."—BFB

By now, you are beginning to appreciate the culture of lawyers. Watch the word "appreciate!" The implication here is not to imply or have you buy-in to the idea that you agree with or that you like lawyers. The word is simply used here to mean "understand" which, after all, like communication, is also the essence of life.

"Self-Preservation" Is the First Order of Life with Lawyers and Everyone Else

Lawyers, as a group, have been successful in traveling through a process of enculturation, attuning themselves with the knowledge and necessary skills to make a living using that talent. Lawyers can be sensitive toward your interest and needs but are more likely to be more involved in their own. With this point in mind, unmistakably, you want to present yourself to your lawyer in the most encouraging profile and light of which you are capable. Lawyers don't like trouble clients! Lawyers don't like flakes! Lawyers don't like quacks! Lawyers don't like "know-it-alls!" Why should a lawyer take your case when you come across as a "half-baked tuna?" Believe me, regardless of what you are willing to pay a lawyer, if you are a "full-goose bozo" no good lawyer will, for long, want to talk to you and then you will have to resort to some lesser lawyer who will talk to you because they need the money.

Most clients bore the hell out of lawyers unless the lawyer you are talking to just got out of law school and, in that case, he or she is trying to figure out what questions to ask you. The client who bores lawyers the most is the one who thinks and believes that they have to entertain the lawyer by asking him or her dumb questions such as, "Where did you go to law school?" and "What legal fraternity were you in?" All you want is good legal representation at a reasonable fee. A lawyer can pick up the wrong signals from such an irrelevant inquiry.

Self-Help for the Client Doesn't Really Mean "Self-Help"!

Be careful with the "self-help" books. You should read them but don't worship them. Common sense dictates more in dealing with your lawyer than all the books in the world on lawyers and "lawyering." Don't carry your self-help book with you when you go to see your lawyer. Your "legal advisor" book is wonderful but won't help you in your lawyer's office. This is much like taking your "surgery made simple" book to your doctor's office. At best, these books only give you a hint of the legal profession and the activity taking place within its walls. Do not try to be the assistant lawyer representing you in your case! If you have not "been there and done that," then you don't recognize what you see. Don't be your own guinea pig!

Lawyers don't like clients who display their knowledge of how they think their legal problem could and should be solved. Remember, the lawyer has experience and practical insight into what you are dealing with and you only have some fragmented ideas about its nature. Your ideas do not represent the total picture nor do they represent the experience factor of why, when, what, where, who, and how.

Lawyers don't like clients who act suspicious when they talk to a lawyer. Be discreet! Use your common sense! Don't show up in the lawyer's office with a tape recorder to record everything the lawyer tells you. You would not want the same thing to happen to you if someone showed up at your doorstep to only talk about you tearing off the label from your mattress cover. Getting over the line is important in every situation in life!

Don't tell your lawyer that your brother-in-law or your neighbor down the street had a case just like yours and the legal services only cost $300 and the case was over and done with in only two weeks! Don't tell your lawyer that a case just like yours across town was settled out-of-court for $1.3 million! Clients hear "war stories" and believe that their case is exactly like the one in the story and immediately see themselves reaping the same benefits. Remember, there are seldom any two cases alike.

Don't tell your lawyer that you are shopping lawyers. Lawyers want to believe that you came to them because of their legal ability and reputation for being an effectively successful lawyer. To discover that you are merely a bargain shopper is discouraging to a lawyer. It's almost saying, to your wife, "I really want to love you dear, but I honestly just married you for your money."

Now Is the Time to Get an Understanding With Your Lawyer

Get an understanding with your lawyer about your case. Play it by ear as to whether you can get an agreement with your lawyer in writing. Use your intuition, sense of observation, and gut feelings about pushing the issue. Remember, good and honest lawyers know and recognize the uncertainty in every case. Young naive lawyers often don't know the complications of a case and secondly, some don't care as long as they can get you into their corral as a client.

In all of the discussion with your lawyer, you now know what his or her specialization is, what experience he or she has had with your kind of legal problem, his or her usual approach to a problem like yours, his or her reputation and abilities in these kinds of cases, and how he or she plans to handle your case. This represents the overall philosophical feeling a client gets as a first part of dealing with a lawyer. The answers to these questions set the tone for how you feel about having made a decision to hire this lawyer.

The Devil Is Sitting and Waiting in the Details!

You are almost there but you are not there. Your first impressions are important in building trust and confidence in your lawyer. However, perceivably good relationships go awry when parties anticipate, presume, and assume that they are communicating with a common understanding about the communication that both parties never really had. The lawyer knows what he or she expects, and the client knows what he or she expects, but most often they never communicate this to the other. Most conflicts in life do not arise from poor communication but from no communication. We all think the other person understands, and if they don't, we perceive that they should, could, or did.

Do Most Clients Know Their Rights?

Absolutely not! Furthermore, most don't even know what questions to ask! The lawyer will tell you what to expect in your case since the lawyer is slowly building up to talk to you about legal fees in the next chapter. The lawyer is going to expect you to pay the legal fees billed to you and pay a retainer if one is requested from you. Further, the lawyer expects you to unyieldingly cooperate in any manner and at any time you are so requested. This may consist of helping him prepare answers to interrogatories (questions being asked you by the opposing side), prepare a witness list for use in the case, or making yourself available to appear at a deposition (sworn testimony by a witness or a party in the case).

On the Other Hand, What Can You Expect From Your Lawyer?

A good experienced lawyer knows how to manage client expectations. Remember, success is defined as whatever you think it is. Lawyers want to keep a client's expectations realistic in terms of being practical, achievable, economical, and reasonable. If a lawyer allows a client to expect the "moon" knowing that any reasonable probability would dictate a position being accomplished to the contrary, that lawyer is "cooking his own goose." Hopefully, you have chosen a lawyer who has his sense about him to straightforwardly relate to you the realism of what he perceives your case to be in terms of success and the potential for failure. Every case, regardless of what a client believes or perceives, has the same two qualities: success or failure in absolute terms, not absolute success but not total failure, and not absolute failure but not total success. In other words, most cases result in the attainment of a middle position, which translates into the realization that the conclusion of the case is not the best that could have been expected nor the worst. This is the posture most cases find themselves in after long tedious months of preparation, and after there is a serious reckoning of circumstances which dictate that everyone's interest would be best served by settlement of the case.

Some lawyers, much to their chagrin, never talk to their clients about the potential of losing their case. This position is unfortunate for the client and the lawyer. The lawyer is in a similar position of a weather forecaster who always reports that there is a low percentage possibility of bad weather. Not only does the client need to know, the client has a right to know of this failure potential in every case. Manifestly, clients don't really want to hear this so lawyers many times do not tell them.

Communicate with your lawyer about simple things, such as procedures. A question from a client like, "When should I expect to hear from you?" brings to the lawyer's attention that the client is interested in the case and anticipates that the ball will begin to roll immediately. Talk to your lawyer about "progress" in your case and what "time" perimeters may be expected. This area is the greatest of all problems between a lawyer and a client. Clients expect matters to move faster than they do and lawyers often "drag their feet" with the full cooperation of a slow-moving overcrowded judicial system. Once you are in the judicial arena, you can expect to be there for a while unless there is no lawyer on the other side. Then, if your position is unopposed, justice can have a quick turnaround.

Lawyers Know the Procedural Rules . . . You Don't!

"Lawyers have the law, clients have the rights," was a statement my grandfather made at an earlier time in my life when I had very little guess as to what he meant. Now, in the practice of law, clients have been protected by the law in the form of cannons of ethics which attempt to govern the conduct of lawyers and give clients rights when they are represented by lawyers. One that is not commonly known is that clients are entitled to get a copy of everything that takes place in their case. Discuss this with your lawyer and determine if it would be worthwhile for you to get a copy of everything that is generated in your case from both sides. You will have to pay for the copies and this could get expensive since many cases involve large, indulging amounts of paperwork.

Sometimes Your Lawyer Is Only As Diligent As You Are . . .

In many ways that's a horrible thought. You certainly think that way about your physician. Why? The reason may be that when you need to see your physician you usually know it because of a change of condition, pain, or whatever. The client is away from his or her lawyer after they have been hired. The client has no way of knowing what's taking place in the case unless the lawyer writes him or her to advise, or when he or she makes an inquiry.

Remember, you asked for an approximation of the time your case will take and you got a general idea of the activity that will generally take place in a case. Of course, what you heard was an overview far less complicated than what is actually taking place. What you heard probably sounded like no big deal in effort or time. Don't get impatient! You usually won't if you know what's going on in your case.

This area of failing to communicate with a client is one of the lawyer's greatest shortcomings. A lawyer's communicational deficit can be explained but not necessarily justified by the fact that your lawyer probably has many cases similar to yours and when a case reaches a level of acceleration that case must get the lawyer's attention. You need to understand that a case in a lawyer's office takes a considerable amount of time to reach resolution. Every case expands in its time of resolution commensurate with the number of lawyers involved. Lawyers are perceived by clients to drag their feet in getting things done. Unfortunately, this is the nature of the beast. There is a reason for the old saying "the wheels of justice turn slowly." In the mind of the client, they don't often turn at all. Even if lawyers were speedy and expeditious, then the courts would be blamed for the process appearing to be stalled or marred in quicksand. The court dockets are crowded beyond what you can imagine. However, more often than not, the system depends on lawyers working together to settle 95% of all cases that reach the court level. If this were not the case, the system of handling both civil and criminal cases we all know and respect would fail miserably. Whether you appreciate the situation or not, the entire system of justice for civil and criminal cases depends on the process of compromise. This is not easily understood by most clients.

Ask and Ye Shall Receive (Sometimes) . . .

The word "ask" is probably one of the strongest words in the dictionary. The ability to "ask" represents power and demands attention. The client has that power. Don't disregard the use of this power to satisfy your apprehension, wonderment, and "need to know." The lawyer knows that the client is vigilant, concerned, and uneasy when the lawyer gets a "what's going on" call.

A Good Approach to Nudging Your Lawyer . . .

One of the best approaches I have heard is the one where the client calls their lawyer for the first time after the case has been turned over to them: "Hello, (my lawyer), I apologize for disturbing you because I know you are very busy. It's been about 45 days since we last met and talked and I was just wondering if there was anything I need to know." You lawyer will then bring you up-to-date on your case. Now, you should conclude this conversation with this comment: "Thanks for letting me talk with you. I really don't want to bother you but would you be willing just to send me a brief note or call me and let me know what is happening so I won't have to worry you?" The lawyer now knows that you are concerned about your case. You may even want to suggest to the lawyer since you believe they are so busy, that the secretary on occasion could give you a call and keep you advised on "what's happening." (Of course, this advisement is only under the direction of the lawyer.)

Your case may now be reviewed or be moved up to the "front burner." Lawyers are conscious of when a client is worried, concerned, or anxious about his or her case. A lawyer will tune in a little closer when these conditions present themselves. This is on the order of the old adage: "The squeaky wheel gets the grease."

Sometimes, you can't get through to talk to your lawyer. If this is the case, remind the lawyer's secretary that you left word to be called on: (January 1, January 7, January 15 and January 22) and have not received any call back. You will have made your point!

Another suggestion—you may want to also ask your lawyer if there is anything you can do on your case to help. Your idleness and anticipation has probably caused you to feel that more time has been consumed since you engaged your lawyer than what actually has. When a lawyer hears a client wanting to help on his or her case, there is ample notice that the client is on the front edge of wanting the case resolved. This may not speed things along any faster than before, but it may mean that the lawyer will reiterate the time frame of when the case should reach a conclusion.

Most clients think that lawyers, characteristically, have to be prodded. The answer is "yes" and "no." Some do and some don't.

Billy F. Brown

Keep Records of When You Talk to Your lawyer . . .

This idea is not to make an adversarial relationship between you and your lawyer but to keep records for yourself when you are billed by your lawyer. Be reminded that a lawyer usually bills you for the time used in calling or writing you about your case. Such an idea of you being billed every time your lawyer writes you or talks to you on the telephone can be very unpopular with the client and can even create a resentful feeling from the client for having to engage a lawyer to protect their interest.

Irrefutably, there are no guarantees that you can avoid your own feelings of resentment but you can take decisive measures to guard against them. First, you should understand what your expectations are. If you have a poor understanding or no understanding about what you can expect from your lawyer, almost anything that seems the least bit foreign to your customary expectations in dealing with other things will eventually build frustration and resentment toward your lawyer. Most clients view lawyers as "necessary evils" so be in conscious control of your expectations about what your lawyer is going to do in the lawyer/client relationship. You get a basis of what you can expect by talking with your lawyer. Remember, "ASK!" If you don't know, "ASK!" You can only control your expectations based on what you know.

CHAPTER 10

GETTING IN STEP WITH WHAT'S GOING ON

D on't sit around wondering what's happening in your case. Sitting idly by and guessing, trusting and hoping that everything is going splendidly and smoothly in your case is a Pollyanna attitude that will potentially eat into your reasonable state of security about how your case is being handled. In those quiet moments when you are not being bombarded by other things, you will reflect on your "what's going on" inquiry mode and then wonder why your lawyer hasn't called or written to let you know the current status. The more you think about that situation the more you will build resentment and begin to question whether your lawyer is interested in your case. STOP! Quit playing these kinds of games with yourself. Do your part in the relationship with your lawyer. Call or write! This is an important moment in your feeling of well-being in your case. Don't put this off!

The Paper Trail Is Your Refuge and Leverage

Writing your lawyer is recommended because this serves as stronger substantiation and documentation should you need to advise anyone of your lawyer's treatment of your case. Your writing usually gets response from someone in your lawyer's office. You may not hear from your lawyer but under most circumstances you will hear from a "what's going on?" request. W.G.O. in the lawyer's office is the acronym in the lawyer's office for this particular inquiry which is the most frequent of all concerns by the client. Lawyers, also, recognize that clients who take the time and are organized to the point of writing are serious and should be given immediate response. Remember, good and ethical lawyers do not want problems with their own clients. Communication is the key! No matter how many words you read, communication between the lawyer and the client is the most important aspect in your representation. The concept of communication presupposes that the parties have not only established some exchange of information but have reached an understanding of what is transpiring in their relationship on a continuing basis and what each expects from the other.

"All Frustration Is Derived From Disappointment"—BFB

One of the reasons causing you stress, disappointment, and worry is that you expect other people, especially your lawyer, to be as considerate, kind and honest as you are. They probably aren't and probably won't be. Don't misread this! Lawyers are about like everyone else. They are as considerate, kind, and honest as they need to be. This is not to be taken as a general condemnation of the human race but you probably have figured it out. That's just the way the world works and has worked since its beginning. The treatise here is not going to be one on the general state of mankind's condition but is offered only to remind you that you often expect more from other people than you expect from yourself and ever those closest around you.

Be resolved and steadfastly immutable to maintain your cool while your lawyer attempts to represent you. Your case will not be resolved overnight and will probably be resolved in an amount of time greatly in excess than you have previously anticipated for its completion. This is not always a lawyer's fault. There are time delays that are naturally endemic to the legal system. Other lawyers often don't cooperate in expediency. Judges often are frustrated over crowded dockets caused by excessive and frivolous litigation. There is no obvious answer as to why things are as they are. The situation may be the result of no one's fault. This matter can be argued, debated, scrutinized, and studied for the rest of your life with no apparent answer. This comment here has been presented to you so that you will, at least, leave the door open on the legal system and stop totally blaming lawyers for the glut of complications.

There is only one person in the world with whom you can attempt to exercise total control of how he or she thinks. You already know that it is you. You will probably spend the rest of your life trying to do that. Some will have great success, some will experience only minimal results, and others will fall in between. Some will never be aware of how they are doing and there will be others who don't care but continue to want what they want without rhyme, reason, or logic. You are responsible for you.

The point here is to be aware that you are charged with the duty and responsibility of taking care of how you feel, think, and act as evidenced by behavior resulting from your attitude. Don't let any situation of concern build up between you and your lawyer that will change your attitude to anything other than reasonable.

Why Not Work Together with Your Lawyer?

Reasonableness is often based on what you believe it is. You can define this condition by communicating with your lawyer. If you do this, you will be rewarded with greater satisfaction, understanding, and appreciation of what lawyers do for clients. Successful experiences beget successful experiences. The lawyer/ client relationship can be a valuable learning experience. You can greatly assist in that endeavor by being mindful of what you can expect. You can determine this by "ASKING" your lawyer!

CHAPTER 11

PAYING THE PIPER

"How do you explain that everything takes
longer than anyone expected?"—BFB

"A lawyer is a person paid by desperate
people to provide legal excuses for their
own human imperfections usually resulting
in something stupid."—BFB

"One of the greatest problems in life is
getting what you pay for because you are
definitely going to pay for what you get."—BFB

I n most of life's situations some concern for economic impact
is involved. There is probably no greater inquiry regarding
everything and anything than, "What does it cost?" Most
of the things in life we know anything about have a price tag on
them. If they don't, the price is usually determined by simply
asking some responsible party interested in making the sale. This
is the way you mostly live your quantitative lifestyle knowing
what things cost and what you can afford. Most of the people you
know live a life reasonably close to the boundaries of what they
can afford. Hopefully, their lifestyle exists on the inside of those
boundaries and not on the outside! Only after the "quantitative"
aspects of life have been achieved, do people stop and place
emphasis on the "qualitative" life. That's just the way things are.
You are not going to change this operative characteristic about
the process of how we live easily or soon.

Fear results in your life because of perceived risk of the
unknown. Those things which are known to you are prepared
for. Those unknown things are represented by fear and are the

causes of anxiety, stress, worry, and distress. The legal system you have observed in your life time appears as a great mystery often exemplifying an unspecified and undetermined cost at the time of engagement of legal representation. Why? Does this have to be? Unfortunately, the answer is "yes" and "no." This chapter is about lawyers' fees. Whether you like it or not, you are going to pay your lawyer. You are going to pay your lawyer for what he or she does and you are often going to pay for what he or she doesn't do. This is the nature of the beast and you are better off knowing than not knowing.

What Do You Need to Know About a Lawyer's Legal Fees?

Legal fees have a basis for how much or how little they are. Clients seldom fully appreciate the difference because lawyers don't take the time to constructively cover how legal fees are determined. Lawyers are often their own worst enemies in supporting and providing a healthy image in the eyes of the client since most clients only want a "reason why." After all, doesn't the idea of looking for a "reason why" just about touch on the nature of most problems that everyone confronts in life. Most people do, however, seek agreement over understanding of those things unfamiliar to them. You'll have to help yourself in dealing with your agreement but some light may be thrown in the direction of understanding.

How Do Lawyers Determine Fees?

The first thing to realize is that lawyers are not consistent with how much fee is charged regarding the same legal situation. Lawyers are like merchants. Some charge based on their reputation, what they perceive it to be, or what they want it to be. These lawyers charge more for what they do and are usually extremely picky about what cases they are hired for. Some of these lawyers think they are a lot better than they are. Other lawyers charge a generally accepted fee in the area of their law practice. These fees for a routine matter are charged on a flat-rate basis. You just have to recognize that some flat-rate fees are different because all lawyers don't charge the same flat-rate. These fees are charged by the lawyer as a standard fee because they know about how much time will be consumed to the point of conclusion in the representation.

Some are reminded of the old joke about lawyer fees. A guy walks into a lawyer's office and says, "I have just been accused of robbing a bank." The lawyer asks, "Do you have any money to pay a fee?" The client responds, "I have over a hundred grand!" The gleaming lawyer responds, "You will never go to jail with that kind of money!" The lawyer was right. The client went to jail broke. Lawyer fees in the legal profession often get a bad rap. Some are deserved and obviously some are not.

The "Non-Standard" Standard Fee

Regardless of what you perceive as a standard fee, there is no standard fee. Then, there are lawyers who advertise their services with fees which are distinguished as being substantially discounted. You will often find "discounted fees" in legal clinics and by solo practitioners who are working on a "volume business" philosophy or those who are just getting started in a very competitive legal practice. Be cautious about so-called "discounted fees." Sometimes, this fee is charged for those supposed routine matters which only minimally involve the services of a lawyer and are mostly handled by a member of their legal staff.

Remember, a lawyer's time is what he or she is selling. No lawyer really wants to think that his time is worth substantially less than another lawyer's time. Also, be aware that a quoted "discount lawyer's fee" may be for an extremely basic service which may not fit the perimeters of your legal problem. Neither you nor the lawyer will be able to completely discover all the services that will be needed to satisfy you as a client just through having a telephone conversation. Overall, those selling services for lesser legal fees provide a valuable service to those who are concerned with being able to afford legal services. Even so, often there are no short cuts to what you need to effectuate a situation of resolution and complete satisfaction. A "discounted" fee is a basic fee charged for what the lawyer perceives as being totally "routine." You can be reasonably sure that anything that falls outside the boundaries of being routine or extremely ordinary will end up as a part of your legal bill.

A Lawyer's Handling of a Routine Matter

If you have a routine legal matter, shop around unless you have a special loyalty to a lawyer you have hired previously, go to church with, or is a friend. Find out about fees by calling around and asking what the lawyer charges for a routine matter such as a simple will, a power or attorney, a bill of sale, a deed, a simple lease, or an uncontested divorce.

This type of inquiry causes problems of communication for the lawyer and the client. A lawyer may not always get on the telephone to speak to the client because he or she is often not available at the time of the client's telephone call. The lawyer's legal assistant, secretary, or paralegal will not always be able to discern a simple routine and standard legal problem from one that have further involvement with the lawyer's time and services. Thus, when you, as a client, go to the lawyer's office you may expect the fee discussed on the telephone when, in fact, it may be in excess of that amount. A lawyer wants to be paid for his time and most cases exceed in time and services what a lawyer and the client anticipate. Many lawyers are not heavy sticklers on this and will, in spite of enhanced time and effort, live by the fee agreement. However, you and your lawyer should communicate about the eventuality of impending interventions which will escalate the fee agreement.

The appearance and involvement of another lawyer representing any other party of interest is an obvious example. Another example might be when the court would require additional outside sources of determination to protect the welfare of a child in an uncontested adoption. Common sense dictates much of the situation when the standard fee is not applicable. Other situations may not be so obvious. This only emphasizes the important of clear and complete clarity of communication with your lawyer. The word "standard" has almost been discarded and thrown away. There is such considerable variance in legal fees nowadays; you cannot be sure what the standard fee of any legal service is. Unfortunately, in many situations, a fee is charged based on what the traffic will bear. If you are not smart enough to get some comparisons in shopping legal fees, maybe you deserve what you get.

The Most Difficult Fee to Determine

There's an old lawyer joke about St. Peter calling up a young lawyer to heaven. So when this lawyer got to the pearly gates, he complained bitterly that he had been raised from earth prematurely since he was still a young man of only 38-years old. St. Peter then tried to explain to the young lawyer that obviously the young man didn't know how old he was, since St. Peter had added up all the hours the lawyer had billed during his lifetime to determine that the lawyer was at least 102-years old.

That's a horrible story and possibly one of some mild exaggeration about a young lawyer just doing his job as he saw it. Certainly, at a time of ultimate confrontation, you would hope that he is being given the benefit of the doubt.

If there is one specter of the legal profession that causes the greatest concern for the client, it is the aspect of a lawyer's fee. The hourly fee basis for a lawyer's representation is the greatest cause of concern for the client in hiring a lawyer on an hourly fee basis. Clients don't ever seem to know when they are being charged and for what. Lawyers are experts in delivering a statement of fees to a client which all seems to be on the "up and up," since it is substantially supported by dates, times, and alleged activity involved in by the lawyer in behalf of the client. You, as a client, usually don't have a clue about relevance, meaningfulness, or for that matter what is going on in your case that continues to justify your lawyer's billings.

Understanding vs. Agreement in the Reality of Knowing About Lawyers

Undeniably, you will never acquire the "mindset" of a lawyer if you are not a lawyer. You can read all there is to read about what lawyers do, how lawyers practice, and how lawyers think without ever getting there. Many lawyers have the same problems you do about understanding how and why things happen as they do in the law profession. One reason that is often offered for the way things are is that there are many people with different ideas involved in the process and all naturally do not agree with the outcome that's produced from the confronting forces in a legal situation.

What's offered here is not justification, rationalization, or for that matter, explanation for all you will encounter in dealing with the legal profession, its lawyers, and society's attempts of being a nation of laws rather than the whims and dictates of arbitrary individualism. Optimistically, you are being beseeched to appreciate the difference between the conditions of agreeing to what's taking place and understanding what's taking place.

An example to illustrate this point might be that you don't agree with Communism but you understand its nature and what it represents to those who would support those principles of that doctrine's philosophy.

Lawyers think about fees quantitatively. Only those who are sensitive, aware, and concerned with the impact of those who are placed in some financial hardship because they are required to hire a lawyer think qualitatively. Remember, lawyers who charge you by the hour usually expect to be paid, whether their advice is good and causes you to be successful in your pursuits or whether their advice or representation proves to be totally worthless.

What You Should Do About Being Charged By the Hour

When you decide to hire a lawyer by the hour, don't go to sleep at the stick. Don't get billed for the first twenty hours at a hundred dollars an hour, then, decide that since this amount of fee completely eliminates your savings, you should call your lawyer and find out what's going on. Many people live "after the fact!" Their philosophy of life is that nothing's a big deal until it becomes a big deal. Many times and in many situations, it's too late to redeem your stupidity. Find out from your lawyer what you can expect in terms of how many hours he or she believes will be required to bring your case to a satisfactory conclusion.

Who Is Baking the Pie?

A lawyer doesn't do all the work on your case. Never has and never will! Ask your lawyer if the hourly rate you are quoted will be for his or her time or for the time of other law office staff who contribute to your case. Some lawyers will break this out for you in the initial interview. Other lawyers have not thought about that situation, and some lawyers wish you would not have brought it up. A lawyer's time is going to be more expensive than a secretary's or a paralegal's. When you are employing a lawyer on a flat-fee basis, you really shouldn't be concerned about who does the work since the end product should be the same for the fee quoted.

ASK!—The Magic of Asking Your Lawyer

If you don't want to ask, don't grimace when you get what you don't want. Ask your lawyer about their policy of hourly billing for legal services. In some offices, especially larger one, billings to clients only occur once a month. If your case is on the front burner, this could be a whopper. Some other lawyers bill whenever they get the urge and bill consistently when they need the money. Determine your lawyer's policy regarding billing. Also, ask on the front end of the relationship if you are going to be billed for other expenses outside of the hourly legal fees. What about copy, travel, mileage, postage, expert, deposition, and filing fees? Don't get surprised, surprised, or surprised!

Should You Get an Understanding With Your Lawyer in Writing?

Your lawyer has been trained to get most everything in writing. Shouldn't you? First, you don't need a written contract with your lawyer concerning the legal services that are to be performed by your lawyer unless there is some question in your mind about what you think your lawyer thinks he or she is doing. That sounds stupid, doesn't it?

If you think that your lawyer is going to approach the solution to your legal situation in some manner other than what the two of you discussed get your lawyer to send you a "memorandum of agreement" about the case and the fees outlined for your case's completion. This "memorandum of agreement" represents the understanding you may rely on as an understanding between the parties. If you don't understand what your lawyer expressed to you, ask for an explanation or a clarification.

I knew a client once who asked for this "memorandum of agreement" from her lawyer and when she received it, there was a bill for fifty dollars for the preparation of the client's memo. Conspicuously, this relationship did not get off to a roaring start. In fact, it got off to "no start" at all. You are considerably better off knowing on the front-end of a relationship about whom you can trust rather than being disappointed, disheartened, and disenchanted later on. Anyone who has been through the ubiquitous rigors of domestic conflict will certainly attest that they wish they had known earlier what they know now. If your lawyer's behavior doesn't meet your approval in the beginning you can't be realistically hopeful that it will in the end. Cut your losses!! Start over!!

Billy F. Brown

Remember What You Have Learned

Go shopping! Know what other lawyers have advised you about your case and what is involved in terms of time and legal fees. Some may disagree but when you advise a lawyer that you have been shopping, you, as a client, are lessened in the eyes of the lawyer. Lawyers like to think that they are chosen by the client for their talent, skills, reputation, charm, compassion, power, prestige, abilities, or any of the above and not because they were the lowest price. In a bargaining position with your lawyer, you are not completely helpless. You must be treated with respect and as a literate business person. If you are not, you have the choice of seeing another lawyer about your lawyer's conduct, or you may get the state bar association's legal complaints division involved. These threats to your lawyer will often do more harm than good and will certainly scar the relationship. Confront your lawyer and explain to him or her what kind of problem you are having about the progress of the case, legal fees, or the manner in which your case is being handled. The squeaky wheel is the one that usually gets the grease.

One Last Comment on Open-Ended Hourly Fees

If your lawyer does not itemize his billings, ask him to do so. "Your accountant requires that this be done." You don't have to know why your accountant requires this, but by saying this some suspicion may be removed that you are questioning your own lawyer's integrity in billing and being honest with the client.

What If Things Go Bad Between You and Your Lawyer?

There are as many lawyers in life with as many proposed solutions to the problems of clients as there are personalities who practice law. There are some lawyers who fall into a large

144

cluster who always seek to protect their clients regardless of whether the lawyer is adequately paid or not. Of course, you as a client should understand that the "Model Rules of Professional Conduct" (called "Professionalism" in most bar associations) provide that a lawyer who takes a case to represent a client is not off the "hook" because the client has not paid, or does not pay, the lawyer. A lawyer who takes a client's case has a duty to continue representation of the client until usually relieved, dismissed, or pardoned from further representation by a judge.

This ideal scenario for the lawyer being relieved from further representation by the court (judge) is often preempted by the lawyer telling the client that he will no longer be represented by the lawyer. The client's bewilderment often blinds him so severely that he does not realize that all of this is done outside the court's approval. Afterward, the client goes and seeks out a new lawyer who enters an appearance on behalf of his new client.

After this divorce from your lawyer, the situation gets a little dicey. If you have paid your lawyer, are you entitled to any of your money back? Did your previous lawyer earn the amount of fee that you had paid him? Good question! You don't know the answer and will probably ask your new lawyer the same question. Guess what? Your new lawyer will probably not want to get involved over whether your previous lawyer has earned the fee you have paid him. Lawyers squabbling over spent lawyer fees is not a way to begin a relationship with a new lawyer. Unfortunately, more often than not, unless you have mortgaged your house, sold your car, or cleaned out your 401(k) retirement funds, you are probably better off to "let the sleeping dog lie" (for now).

Here's a thought: get through your case and representation by the new lawyer and then after the case is resolved, finished, or tried, go to the state bar association and file a claim under the disputed fee provisions as provided in the state bar association of the state in which you are located. This way you get to have your "say" in the fee dispute and this will not contaminate your relationship with your new lawyer.

A client should realize that it is much easier to fire your lawyer than it is for your lawyer to fire you as a client. Your lawyer has a fiduciary duty to you as the client, but unfortunately, the reciprocity is not the same from the client to the lawyer.

There are a great many lawyers who have spoken about lawyer fees and the rights of clients in this regard. One such lawyer is the Honorable Daniel L. Abrams, who practices law in New York, New York and has given permission to append his great article, "Legal Fees: Ten Things Your Lawyer May Not Want You to Know," as Appendix 4. Daniel has straightforwardly hit the problem squarely on the head. This outstanding Yale law school graduate realizes that lawyers, as well as clients, need to have a clear understanding about the nature, protocol, and rules regarding lawyer fees.

Understanding about lawyer fees is one of most critical aspects in the relationship between a lawyer and his client. Often the understanding about how lawyer fees are set and are expected to be paid is the fragile point in the ongoing representation of the client.

Boons and Windfalls

This is the last part of this treatise on legal fees and is emphatically reserved for the contingency fee. If there is one area of law practice which is more controversial, there is probably no one who could tell you what it is.

First, understand that the contingency fee is a legal fee based on the outcome of a client's case. This should clue you in perceptibly that the spin-off is a successful conclusion of the client's case resulting in the yielding of money from some defendant source which happens to be on the bad end of the law suit. The lawyer is paid out of the proceeds of the recovery for the client. A contingency fee case is typically a claim brought about because of personal injury, wrongful death, product liability, copyright and patent infringements, wrongful employee terminations, sexual harassment, employee discriminations, slander, and libel suits. This is probably not an all-inclusive list but, at least, you get the idea. None of these types of cases are "pushovers." You really need to understand about these types of cases and why lawyers make big bucks in these types of cases. You must appreciate that not all of these cases, even though they fall in the category of contingency cases, are big cases. There are big ones. There are ones that are worth the time and effort. Then, there are those which are "P.I.T.A.s" and are mostly avoided by good lawyers.

Consider That Day

Consider that day already done,
When business is performed just for fun;

Consider that day unusually rare,
When business is conducted just for dare;

Consider that day as improbable or never,
When business is transacted just to be clever;

Consider that day with surprising glee,
When your lawyer doesn't charge you a fee;

Consider you're in heaven on that day,
When your lawyer doesn't make you pay!—BFB

The Contingency Fee Has Its Place

The contingency fee has been blasted by most groups or individuals who are performing under the questionable auspices of self-appointment. Those who claim to be standing guard over the legal profession are attempting to maintain a public vigilance of the legal profession's pursuit of representation of those injured by the personal acts of other humans who are either acting negligently, deliberately, or are failing to properly protect the consuming public in some manner. The argument here is not being made to justify, explain, rationalize, or defend the contingency fee. There is a reason for the contingency fee whether you buy that reason or not. Don't forget that most of us would rather be able to agree with an idea than to understand that idea. Let's try to see what we see . . .

Sometimes "Yes" and Sometimes "No"

There are no exact answers about many of life's complications in terms of solutions. Most everything you and I know are approximations. We live with approximations. If we are going to be happy about life we have to understand and accept approximations. We don't always have to agree with approximations to accept them, or to live with them for that matter.

Sometimes you are appropriately correct in allowing your lawyer to handle your case on a contingency fee and in other cases you can more easily and economically handle it yourself. The question of "when" and "when not" is what most clients go to see a lawyer about. You have to know and understand before you see your lawyer that a lawyer wants a contingency fee agreement only when there is a positive expectation of receiving a fee from their efforts in your case on your behalf. No lawyer wants a loser! When you look up the term "contingency" in a dictionary, you should be surprised to discover that this word is concerned with those circumstances or conditions which are dependent on chance or on the fulfillment of a condition. When you see your lawyer nothing will appear as easy then as it did before.

The Gray World of "Lawyering"

If the world, all the circumstances, situations, outcomes, and events were an exact science, many lawyers would certainly be out of business. The "how-to-do-it" wizards would, if life was an exact science, write all the books and make all the films necessary to tell us everything we needed to know to function in that exact science world. You and I know that's not the way life is and not the way it ever will be. So you have to decide whether you are going to call a lawyer, enter into a contingency fee agreement, and hope to be successful. Anyone's effort of trying to tell you what you should do and not do in terms of entering into an agreement with your lawyer from the pages of a book is playing complete folly.

There Are Some Guidelines

First, most experienced lawyers do want to get involved in a contingency fee contract unless it's worth their time, effort, and money. Often, younger lawyers don't know the difference and will chase an empty covered wagon.

Good, honest, and trustworthy lawyers usually don't want to get involved in a contingency fee contract when the legal situation or circumstances dictate an obvious first approach of solution that the client can often successfully complete on his own. For example, when you were shopping at the mall, the driver of the car next to yours opened his door into the door of your car, caving in the door panel. You got the name of the driver and the name of his insurance company. Do you need to see a lawyer before you talk to the insurance company? Absolutely not! Most insurance companies try their best to make those kinds of adjustments as quickly as possible. Those people often make their fees by the number of claims adjusted. Even if they work inside the insurance company and are not independent adjusters, they want to smooth things over as quickly as possible since they want to satisfy their policyholder and they are often concerned about good public relations. This might even mean trying to get you satisfied in a timely manner so you won't call the state insurance commissioner.

Lawyers don't want to hear from you either on a case like this. Most lawyers want to be nice to you if you call, but will attempt to tell you how to do the settlement yourself. You can't afford to pay a lawyer on a case like this because there is no way you will be refunded your legal fees from the insurance company who is going to pay your claim. They don't have to! Unless there are unusual policy provisions in an insurance policy, an insurance company never pays lawyer fees unless those fees are specifically negotiated in the settlement of the case. This seldom, if ever, happens!

Taking the Scenario a Bit Farther

When the driver in the car next to yours opened the car door, the impact was so hard that the window on the passenger side where you were sitting shattered and lodged glass into the side of your face. The first obvious thing you do is go seek medical care. After a few weeks, you begin to heal. The insurance adjuster has visited you and agreed to fix your car. At that time, the insurance adjuster is advised that you had to seek medical attention for the shattered glass causing damage to your face. The adjuster tells you that the glass shattering was not the insured's fault since all cars are now required to have shatter-proof glass and if there is anyone at fault it would be the automobile manufacturer or the maker of the glass window. However, because of the adjuster's honesty, sense of fairness, and desire to wrap up the entire claim, the adjuster offers you $200 for your injury and agrees to pay the $180 bill for medical care incurred because of the injury. You have noticed what appears to be some potential for scarring on your cheek. You don't know whether this scar will go away in time or be permanent. What should you do? If the glass shattering was not really the insured's fault, then, doesn't it appear that the adjuster is being generous and fair in offering you this amount to sign a release?

What You Don't Know

Isn't life lived dealing mostly with what you don't know? Most of the problems in life arise from not knowing. One of the most common expressions you'll ever hear is, "If I only knew then what I know now, things would be different!"

Get the car fixed! Your wheels are the most important thing you need every day. Tell the adjuster that you are going to wait on the settlement for the medical expenses until later. Don't let an adjuster tell you that he or she has to settle all the claims at one time. That's junk! If you are told that, all you have to do is tell him or her that you are going to take that idea to your lawyer and see if it's true. Trust me! The adjuster will change the tune in a hurry. If you don't want to use the lawyer threat, just tell the adjuster that the insurance commissioner is a personal friend of your brother's and that you are sure that your brother would give the commissioner a call for you. When the blood-red face of the adjuster returns to normal, there will be a new conciliatory attitude and the check will usually be written only for the car damage.

Read the Release

You already have reason to distrust the adjuster, so read the release. Read the release! Make sure that the release specifies only damage for the automobile and NOT "for any and all claims."

Billy F. Brown

What Do You Do Next?

Take some time. Allow your scar time to heal and see whether you are going to be blessed with nature's good healing or whether you are going to have to endure a permanent scar or maybe engage the services of a plastic surgeon. How much time do you have? All states have their own laws governing what is known as "statute of limitations" or "prescription." These laws limit the time in which you may file a claim through a lawsuit. In other words, after so much time has elapsed after the time in which the claim arose or when you were injured, you may be "barred" from pursuing your claim because the claim was not filed in a timely way or within the state's statute of limitations. CHECK WITH YOUR LOCAL BAR ASSOCIATION or GO SEE A LAWYER. Remember, from chapters back, you can call a lawyer and ask about whether they charge for an initial visit.

The Contingency Fee Lawyer

All lawyers like to have an opportunity to discover a good contingency fee case. Therefore, when you call on the telephone you can be assured that no lawyer is going to charge you to listen to your situation which may be the basis for a contingency fee agreement. Some lawyers, especially those who probably perceive themselves to be better than they are, screen their contingency fee appointments to make sure that they are listening to the old proverbial "dog bite" cases. Lawyers know that most clients don't have a clue about what's a good case and one that's not.

Even the lawyer who does not do contingency fee work will listen to a client's tale of woe so that the case can be referred out to a lawyer who does that kind of work. When that happens, as you'll remember, the referring lawyer will be "cut in" for a piece of the action if the case is concluded successfully.

Lawyers want good contingency fee cases that are generally agreed to be those with absolute liability on the part of another

152

party, good injuries resulting from the acts of the party having and bearing the liability, and a substantial amount of insurance or accessible solvency.

What Are Contingency Fee Lawyers Looking for in a Case?

You may live in a quixotic world from Camelot or exist with a utopian perception about life. However, idealistic conception, optimism, and confidence have their grand and glorious place in the vast scheme of things but whistling, yodeling, and singing in the rain won't keep you from getting wet. Lawyers are just as logical about cases as you would be about the many activities over which you may have difficulty deciding whether the cost is worth the benefit. Life is a continuing series of confrontations where people make hard and sometimes fast decisions about "cost/benefit" analysis. Lawyers do not usually go through life with some high sense of endowed mission to right all wrongs and crusade for the common cause of mankind. Some feel this way when they first get out of law school but most lose this sense of unrealistic idealism in short fashion when they discover that, after all, a great part of learning any job or occupation is learning how to make a "living."

Looking for Optimism!

Lawyers look for those characteristics in a contingency fee case that will favor optimistically towards a financial recovery. Remember, no recovery, no fee! There are basically three parts to a successful contingency fee case. The first part, and some lawyers will argue that this part should be second, is that of injury. There are all kinds, degrees, and shapes of injury. The injury requiring medical attention is the most obvious. Lawyers recognize this without reservation or delay. The client who comes into the lawyer's office with his or her leg in a cast sparks a lawyer's whetted appetite. Most contingency fee cases are not of the "most severe" variety. Most fall into the range of bumps, bruises, contusions, and soft-tissue injuries. These are nevertheless important but are just as tough to handle and don't bring home "big bucks" to the lawyer and the client.

Please don't think for a moment that all of these cases are nickel and dime and that lawyers don't work with them. They do! The point being made here is that it substantially behooves the lawyer and the client to know and communicate the difference between the "mortgage-lifter" type of case and the one that pales by comparison. If you were pushed out of the window from the twelfth floor of a building and suffered no injury you would not have a good case. Regardless of the other encouraging characteristics of your case, if you suffered no substantial injury your financial recovery will be minimal.

No lawyer likes nominal or minimal recovery cases. Why? There is still a great amount of work in getting any case in a position for recovery, regardless of whether you are preparing for settlement or preparing for trial. Lawyers never know whether a case will be settled or tried. They have a good idea but sometimes an insurance company adjuster will stonewall the lawyer's efforts in talking and reaching settlement in the case.

This usually happens when the insurance company believes that there is no liability for the claim or there is serious doubt that the client has suffered any injury. Sometimes, a case, regardless of liability or extent of injury, may have some nuisance value. There is always a "cost-of-defense" consideration on the part of the insurance company. A lawyer who repeatedly appears to settle cases for the "cost-of-defense" by the insurance companies will eventually find tough going with insurance companies who will call his bluff.

The second phase of the contingency fee consideration is that of liability on the part of another party for the client's injury or suffering. Regardless of whether you have the most devastating and disabling injury, the most excruciating and prolonged pain and suffering arising out of the injury, you don't have a good case unless there is someone liable for your injury. Unless someone is responsible for causing you injury all considerations of injury, pain, and suffering are for naught. Remember from our previous discussion, the word negligence arises from those circumstances when an injury occurs as a result of a person failing to exercise that degree of care in their behavior that a reasonable and ordinary person would do under those same circumstances. Without negligence on the part of someone, there is no justifiable basis for a contingency fee case with your lawyer.

Lawyers Wearing Blinders

Do lawyers take contingency fee cases when there appears to be no basis of liability? Yes, they do, but often at the time they take the case they have viewed the case with "rose-colored" glasses and have visualized some decent recovery from the efforts required to bring home the case recovery. Most lawyers believe that every case is worth "something" even if there is minimal or no liability. Most insurance companies also believe that every case is worth something even though there is no liability on the part of their insured. Why? As was stated earlier, insurance companies recognize the cost of dealing with a case in terms of legal defense fees and their own time and effort. Because of this, insurance companies will pay "nuisance" value or "cost of defense" to the lawyer and the client making claim for which there is little or no liability. Insurance companies consider this as part of the cost of doing business in this very litigious oriented society. In many cases where the claim is small and there are minimal medical expenses and no liability, the insurance company will not pay any amount to the claimant because the insurance company considers the case unworthy of any lawyer's consideration. Today, most insurance companies are careful to take care of business. They recognize that being fair and attentive to claimants pays handsomely in the long run because such posture obviates the need for an injured party to seek the assistance of a lawyer. Now it's good business for insurance companies to be more considerate and concerned than in the previous days of the "cat-and-mouse" game played between the company and claimants. There is a new sense of relationship and fair-dealing in the claim and adjustment area of settling injury demands.

Lawyers are responsible for having brought forth this new pattern of equity in the casualty insurance business. We can all remember when settling any kind of claim with an insurance company was almost on the order of the "gun fight at the OK corral." There has now been more prevailing peace after years where lawyers have had not only to carry a big stick but be willing to use it. This new user-friendly environment can all be attributed to clients being willing to "pay the piper."

What's the Last Word on Lawyer's Fees?

This is always a good question. Sometimes, you may not get the answer you want, but ask the question anyway. Most often, a lawyer does not know the answer to that question. If a lawyer is charging you by the hour, a lawyer may be able to give you a rough estimate, but a lawyer is never sure how long or how much time will be involved in getting your case resolved.

When a lawyer is going to be paid by the hour, the lawyer will usually ask for a retainer. Your response will probably be, "What's a retainer and what does it mean?" This is another good question not easily answered by the lawyer. Does the retainer mean that any such retainer made by the client will be used as a future deposit to be consumed by the lawyer's hourly charge? The answer is sometimes "yes" and sometimes "no." All answers depend on the personal philosophy of the lawyer regarding the "retainer." Some lawyers consider the "retainer" an engagement or contract fee between the lawyer and the client. The "retainer" can be used by some lawyers as a deposit to be credited against the hourly fee. However, be aware that some lawyers consider the "retainer" fee as non-refundable regardless of how much time the lawyer takes with your case. You have no clue how much time a case is going to take and most of the time, your lawyer doesn't either.

A question that may be on your mind is, "How are lawyer fees set by the lawyer?" More often than not, lawyer fees are arbitrary. Many lawyers use as criteria two considerations in setting the lawyer fee: first, how much time is going to be consumed in representing the client and secondly, how important is the case in terms of what's at stake for the client. When the risk is higher for the client, you can expect the lawyer fees to be more. Complexity, extent of involvement, and exposure to greater levels of risk cause some lawyers to set their fees higher.

This idea about fees is no different than what you would expect if you were going to a brain surgeon as compared to see a medical doctor for the common cold. You would not expect to pay the same fee for each procedure or visit with your doctor.

There are two important points to be made in talking about lawyer fees. First, please realize that in many situations, a lawyer's fee is arbitrary and comes from the mind of the lawyer as he or she assesses your case in terms of time, difficulty, complexity, and whether you are a "problem" client. Secondly, ASK your lawyer about the "retainer" and fees in general. ASK when and how often you will be billed. Get an estimate as to how much your lawyer thinks the total fees will be. This is not a time to be bashful. ASK! ASK! ASK!

Be aware when you visit a lawyer and you are quoted a fee, retainer, or even a gross amount to handle your case, all lawyers are not the same in establishing and setting a fee. When lawyers are busy with other cases, your case may not appear to be one that the lawyer really wants to handle. If that's the case, the lawyer may state a fee that seems high because the lawyer doesn't really want your case. This is not the usual case and most lawyers who don't want your case will either tell you that you do not have a case upon which a reasonable recovery and satisfaction can be acquired, or the lawyer may tell you that he or she is severely overloaded with cases and cannot take on any new cases. Whatever the reason a lawyer gives you not to take your case, thank him or her for the time and continue your search for a lawyer who will take your case. Nevertheless, listen to the lawyer. They may be giving you the best advice you could hear to abandon your pursuit for mental satisfaction for the damage you think you have suffered. Sometimes, when advice is free, clients don't appreciate the candor and honesty being offered them.

Be careful in dealing with your lawyer. Your desperation and overzealousness in being represented by a lawyer may be too obvious. You could be a prime candidate for the type of client who gets charged based on "what the traffic will bear." Thank goodness there are only a few lawyers who may take advantage of a client who is "hot to trot." As a client, cool your jets and use your head in determining if you have a reasonable, practical and sensible understanding with your lawyer about the fees you are expected to pay.

After having read this, just appreciate that lawyer fees are not standard. One lawyer may charge you $5,000 to handle your case. Another may give you a quote of $1200. Which of the two should you choose? Unfortunately, there is no "the answer." You will just have to use your good sense and intuition to make the decision on which lawyer to hire.

CHAPTER 12

DISCRETION AND VALOR

"'Tis better to know that the dance won't last before
you become attracted or addicted to the music . . ."—BFB

"You have an advantage of knowing that you don't know
something than not knowing that you don't know."—BFB

I n spite of good liability, a lawyer still may not want to take
your case because the lawyer recognizes that the financial
recovery will not be worth the effort required.

Every Case is Not a Good Case or Even a Case

Lawyers seldom encounter clients who don't believe that their
case is a good one. The public media has become an icon for
truth and believability in our society and is the quintessential
embodiment of what most people want to behold as their basis
for life's veracity.

The media has not done lawyers any favors. Somehow,
the media's contemporary concern (assuming they had any at
some previous point in time) for relevance has gone awry. You
can now expect media sources of information to direct their
attention to abstruse and extraordinary events, circumstances,
and occurrences in every sector of secular life. The legal arena
has become a "sideshow" of events. People are seemingly being
paid for almost every conceivable consequence of damage in the
wide genre of the marketplace.

A lady in anywhere, USA may get paid mucho megabucks
because she suffered damage when she choked on the paper
wrapper which covered an ice cream "Moon Bar" because she

Billy F. Brown

allegedly did not know that the paper wrapper had to be removed before she ate the ice cream. Of course, the rest of the story would be that the poor ice cream company failed to supply a warning to its label that the paper ice cream wrapper had to be removed before the ice cream was eaten. The warning, according to the lawyer who would have filed the lawsuit, should have stated: WARNING: REMOVE THIS PAPER WRAPPING BEFORE EATING. FAILURE TO DO SO MAY RESULT IN SEVERE DAMAGE TO YOUR HEALTH, SUCH AS CHOKING, NAUSEA, DIARRHEA, AND OTHER RELATED CONDITIONS OR INJURIES.

And the beat goes on . . . You can guess at all kinds of scenarios which will produce the lawsuits that are filed in the courts these days. This could include drinking lighter fluid, charcoal grill fire starter, motor oil, car wax, anti-freeze, drain cleaner, and on and on. The real question is, "Should anyone this stupid be paid any money?" Many lawyers think so!

Everyone seems to hear about those horrible cases which often can't be explained by the courts, judges, lawmakers, or the lawyers. Clients hear about those cases and believe that their "off-the-wall" case is even better than that one. The legal system has provided an arena which appears like a "wheel of fortune," where many are spinning the wheel with a sense of megalomania looking for the big deal. There are lawyers who'll spin the wheel with the clients by being creative advocates, entering legal arenas where none have dared before. Sometimes, they are successful. Many times, they aren't. Some lawyers have a philosophy that "if you throw enough junk against the wall some of it will stick." Lawyers have never been accused of not being daring and resourceful.

The Real Problem With Lawyers and the "No-Account" Case

Some lawyers will and some lawyers won't. Some lawyers do and some lawyers don't. Some lawyers will tell you the truth and give you their honest opinion. Others won't. There is not a lawyer alive or dead for that matter, who hasn't had the opportunity to be approached by a potential client with a "bummer" case. They come from potential clients the lawyer has never heard of or seen before, from friends and neighbors next door, from relatives and kin-folks who watched you become a lawyer, from other lawyers who have confidence in you and want to share in a referral fee, and even from your spouse, who has referred a friend to you so you can take their case. When these potential clients come to you as a lawyer with what appears to be a "bozo" case, tremendous pressure is placed on the lawyer to amicably, cordially, sensitively, and respectfully extricate himself from engaging in a lawyer-client relationship with this case. These cases are like getting "gum on your shoe."

A lawyer can casually fall victim to investigating into the case knowing, all too well, that they would not take the case if the client paid him or her. A lawyer has to remember that most potential clients don't have a clue about what is a good case, and one that's not so good or just outright bad.

For A Brief Moment

Every lawyer likes to hear, for a brief moment, those words that are often expressed by a potential client, "I have heard that you are a good lawyer and that you can win my case." Without any doubt and immediately, a lawyer should be put on notice that the worst is yet to come. The client means well but has probably already shopped several lawyers with their purported and alleged case. Seasoned lawyers are wary to such overtures on the part of clients and only hear the sweetness of the sung praises initially. After that, a wise and experienced lawyer uses their creativity and "having been there" to move you on to another lawyer who won't know the difference.

Most Potential Clients Are Not Ready

Potential clients are much like inventors in that they fall in love with their ideas. Clients do not want to hear that they do not have a good case. Most lawyers do not want to tell potential clients that they don't have a good case. Now, this is the delicate part. Lawyers want clients to come back to them for repeat business in the future. Thus, the lawyer is presented with a dilemma. The lawyer poses a question in their own mind: "If I tell this client that I don't think that he has a case in which I would be interested, or that he doesn't have a case, will this client return with any future cases or legal problems he may have?" Most lawyers would conclude that the potential client would perceive the "not so favorable" answer as being consistent with the conclusion that "the lawyer must not be such a good lawyer after all." Most lawyers know that people think like they think, feel like they feel, and act like they act, regardless of the facts, circumstances, and any evidence to the contrary that they should not. Lawyers are often found trying to explain to a potential client why he or she doesn't have a good case. This usually results in further deepening of the wound.

Many potential clients don't perceive explanations, nor do they want to hear them. They generally just want what they want.

Lawyers Are Busy People

The easiest way, not necessarily easy, for a lawyer to get away from an unwanted case is to be "tied-up" with other cases that won't allow him or her to give your case the immediate attention it needs. This is usually "bunk!" If you walk into a lawyer's office with one eye after the other had been shredded in an automobile accident, and the car in which you were riding as a passenger was struck from behind by an 18-wheeler, do you honestly believe that the lawyer with whom you are talking would be too busy to take your case? Remember, lawyers refer out cases to other lawyers when a case demands more than their skills, expertise, or their ability to fund the pre-trial preparation, will provide. A trial test of how the lawyer with whom you are talking feels about your case will be made by simply asking the lawyer to refer your case to another lawyer who can handle it. If that lawyer does not refer your case out to another lawyer, you probably need no further explanation of what that lawyer thinks of your case. Sometimes, the old experienced lawyer will refer you to a young "up-start" who has not ever taken off his or her "rose-colored" glasses. This is often a method of "passing the buck" used by lawyers who don't want your case.

This can be dangerous for a lawyer who hopes you will come back when you have another legal matter. A referring lawyer is always at the mercy of the referred lawyer, just like one physician referring you to another physician. Both referring professionals are generally held, in the minds of the client and the patient, to the standards of professional care and service of that rendered by the referred professional. A referral can be a double-edged sword for the referring professional.

The Last Part to a Successful Contingency Fee Case

Now, after having been exposed briefly to the issues of injury and liability, the third part is a make or break part of the overall consideration. You might have the greatest and most grotesque injury imaginable, and absolute unmitigated liability, and yet have nothing. You have a case but you have nothing.

This seems about as dramatically involved as life gets. This third area of the legal arena is probably the most misunderstood one of all the considerations as to what makes a good contingency fee case for the client and the lawyer.

The third area is that of defendant solvency. In other words, after the lawyer works with his heart and soul and spends lots of money to bring home your case recovery, are there sufficient resources from which to collect the amount of financial recovery which is in the form of a verdict rendering an amount of money in favor of the claimant who has been termed a plaintiff in the lawsuit? This is a crucial threshold question. This question hardly ever goes away. Even at the start of a case there may be ample evidence that there is plenty money from which to be paid if the case is successful.

What to Look for

You know that big multi-conglomerate corporations are the wealthiest entities in modern society. Often, we all fail to realize that these same gigantean, colossal creations have correspondingly monstrous, massive, and immense debt. Some are here today and gone tomorrow. If you don't believe this, ask those in the airline, automobile, and manufacturing industries. You may find some solace in knowing that you are going after an ostensibly rich corporation but you will be in better straits if you can determine and discover that the party against who you are seeking damages has substantial liability insurance coverage for the injury you are seeking recovery.

An Empty Pot Is an Empty Pot

This point of finding defendant solvency in the form of some type of liability insurance coverage is absolutely essential. There is, however, some confidence justified in going after the "biggie" corporations, which have net worths in the billions of dollars. Settlement is often times more difficult since they appear nameless in authority and are operated by committee acting through various sublevels of execution. On the upside, in spite of the corporation's hugeness, it nevertheless protects itself with liability insurance for the various forms of potential liability.

If you the party against whom you are seeking damages (known as the "defendant"), doesn't have adequate liability insurance or the personal viability of resources, you are essentially looking at "empty pot." An "empty pot" is an "empty pot." No lawyer or client wants an "empty pot." The "empty pot" idea represents nothing as opposed to something. You can't get anything if there is nothing there.

How Can You Know?

Most of the time, a lawyer knows or can discover what's there. In most situations, lawyers tell lawyers that there is liability insurance coverage. They don't always relate immediately how much there is, but they will confess that there is insurance coverage. Another clue and your lawyer will know: certain lawyers in any locality always, and almost exclusively, represent insurance liability companies. When certain lawyers show up in a case, you can sometimes be reasonably assured that it is the "A Insurance Company" or the "B Insurance Company."

Another Avenue for Receiving the Reward of Pursuit

You've indulged some years of patience, forbearing, consternation, and doubt, just waiting for your case to reach its final destination. Now, since you have been awarded a judgment, you are logically waiting for the money. If you discover that the big corporation on which you relied for money has gone "belly-up" in bankruptcy and there is no liability insurance coverage you are probably "S.O.L." This "Sure Out of Luck" finality is never consoling, even if this position brings an end to the many years of toil and turmoil. This "S.O.L." can be a factor in any case after receiving a final financial verdict. Even when you have sued an individual and have received a money award for damages you may encounter, if there is no insurance, the personal filing of bankruptcy by the defendant blows away everything you think you have gained. If the individual defendant does not file bankruptcy, you may find that the only way to receive any money from the defendant is by seizing any property he may own which doesn't have a lien on it or by garnishing his wages if he works for an employer. Each state has laws that govern the terms and procedures for such attempts at satisfying a judgment. None of these attempts at satisfying a judgment even hold a candle to the fiery incentive that substantial liability insurance provides.

A Lawyer Weighs All of the Above

There are few gifts in the business of law practice. On rare occasion, a lawyer may encounter a fresh, new "out of the box" insurance adjuster who titillates his sensibilities beyond reality. On the distaff side of such luck, new insurance adjusters aren't given much settlement authority so the windfall is a meager one. Most of what a lawyer makes is well-earned. The worst nightmare for the lawyer and the client is to chase an "empty covered wagon" and not know that it's empty at the time they are chasing it. Lawyers who have been around awhile are careful in not indulging the sport of "empty covered wagon" chasing. For those who have not been around that long, they may not have learned their lesson yet. Even as a client, you need to know about the realistic aspects of recovering a verdict. Every lawyer looks for liability insurance. If there is none, your case will be seriously and, most often, severely impaired in its favorable prospects for recovery.

A lawyer does not stop at the injury and liability factors as the final assessment criteria for evaluating a contingency fee case. Every aspect of a case being considered by a lawyer is a vital part of its whole appeal. No one factor makes for a good case. The factors of injury, liability, and solvency of the defendant that have been evaluated here are more appealing and alluring to the contingency fee lawyer when these components are reasonably and ideally balanced.

There Is Seldom the Ideal in Anything

Would life be so wonderful if anything and everything was ideal? The answer would probably be "no" since everyone would become bored and start tinkering with the ideal to reconfigure it towards making it better. No case is hardly ever ideal to the lawyer. Sometimes, you have great and absolute liability without injury. Sometimes, you have massive catastrophic injury without liability. Sometimes, you have fantastic liability and equally profound injury without a hope of a solvent defendant. The answer in the legal profession of what's really desired would be the ideal of great liability, great injury, and great amounts of liability insurance coverage. Unfortunately, this is seldom the case. So, what a contingency fee lawyer usually hopes to find is balance in these three areas. Most lawyers jump with glee when this appears on their doorsteps. However, there are others who would not jump under any conditions. Just as in life, lawyers are no different, to each their own.

Is an Agreement in Writing With a Lawyer Essential?

You, as a client, may not need an agreement in writing with a lawyer but a lawyer needs a written agreement with you. As discussed, lawyers are bound by rules which are fair and equitable for the client. If you don't like what your lawyer is doing, you may present your complaint to a "Division for Bar Complaints" under the State Bar Association in the state where your lawyer is licensed to practice law. This association investigates the facts, circumstances, and the situation once the submitted written complaint is made by a client against their lawyer. The State Bar's Disciplinary Committee, after reviewing the "where" and "wherefore" of the complaint, may decide that the lawyer is on solid ground in his behavior or position, or may decide to disbar, suspend, publicly reprimand, privately reprimand, or informally admonish the lawyer for his conduct.

A lawyer's interest in your case is going to be based around whether that lawyer believes that he or she can be successful for you. Putting this in writing is protecting himself or herself by specifying your agreement to pay them when they get a recovery for you. To get you to give the contingency fee lawyer the case, the lawyer wants you to know that if he is not successful in recovering on your case, you will owe the lawyer nothing. You, as a client, want this in writing as much as the lawyer does.

The Conditions on Which a Lawyer Will Take Your Case

A lawyer in a contingency fee case is going to take your case based on the belief that the case is sufficiently meritorious for recovery of a decent lawyer's fee and an amount that would reasonably satisfy you, the client. Traditionally, the Courts and Bar Associations have approved the contingency fee contract between the lawyer and the client based on the premise that when a lawyer takes a contingency fee case, there is a risk of the lawyer losing and not getting a fee. So, in exchange for the risk of loss, the lawyer is paid a percentage of the proceeds of the recovery in the case. The percentage of interest in the case for the lawyer handling it is usually set between 25% and 50%. Sometimes, a lawyer will only charge 25% as a contingency fee if the case can be settled without filing a lawsuit, and when there is little, if any, question of injuries and liability.

The Higher the Risk, The Higher the Fee

The second level of contingency fee case is that of 33 1/3% of settlement proceeds. This is usually the standard fee and is the one that most clients know about. This contingency case is one that, as a rule, presents itself as more work for the lawyer in terms of gathering medical information, investigating the situation and site of the injury, and involves considerable time while the client reaches maximum medical recovery. A lawyer in a contingency fee case must convince an insurance adjuster, an opposing lawyer, the court, or the jury that the person or company causing the injury failed to follow and abide by an accepted standard of care of how a reasonable person would have acted in the same situation and under those circumstances that accompany the event. Then, those injuries must be measurable or determinable to the extent that they are significant, and not trivial, making the lawyer's time and effort worthwhile. Lastly, the negligence of the person or company must have a substantial causal relationship as to the reason for the client's injury.

More Than Meets the Eye

All of these areas must be established by the contingency fee lawyer before any financial recovery will be made. To the client, this ordinarily looks easier than it is. In most cases of the contingency fee, the lawyer well earns his or her fee. There are some windfalls where there is a minimal amount of effort required to get the case resolved, but it is generally the exception.

Up We Go

The next level of contingency fee is the one which renders to the lawyer an amount of 40% of any settlement proceeds or amount recovered. Most "Attorney's Retainer and Fee Agreements" provide that at any time a lawsuit is filed, the amount of the contingency fees raises to an amount of 40% of recovery. The reasoning for this escalation of fee is logical. The lawyer at this point has prepared his or her presentation for settlement and, for one or a number of reasons, settlement has not been reached. It's now time for your lawyer to "put up" or "shut up." In other words, your case has failed in its first phase of negotiation with the opposing side (routinely an insurance adjuster). Filing a law suit is a "big" deal and much discussion will follow about its overall implications.

The Most Extraordinary Case

There is a case which presents itself in the arena of law practice, and justifies a contingency fee of 40%. The character of this particular case is the one that is not typical, routine, or customary. This case is distinguished by high risk for the lawyer in terms of potential for recovery because of seriously questionable liability, problems of a causal relationship between the injury and the alleged causation, or, perhaps, the exceptional nature of the expensive posture in preparing the case for litigation. In other words, this case represents great potential failure. Lawyers who take on the "big" cases roll the dice. The potential for prodigious fees must expend immense amounts for experts, accident site simulations, accident re-constructionists, countless depositions, and often, these lawyers end up splitting their fees with other lawyers who have had some experience in the area of litigation being pursued.

The "Big" Boys Play Hard

You have probably heard the old cliché that, "He who has the gold makes the rules." Because of our judicial system, that has not been the rule in so far as consumer rights and advocacy has gone. Some would say otherwise because the small, minimally injured consumer has little chance of recourse against the behemoth industrial giants who dominate commerce in our society. In a great sense, those who plead for the small consumer and small claimant in society are partially correct in alleging that many of the lesser needs for redress are going unacknowledged and unfulfilled because of the push forward towards bigger claims making large and more complex litigation. In turn, those lawyers who indulge in the large claims take home the larger piece of bacon. This allurement is attractive to most lawyers and now the illusion of grandiose conquest looms as a focal point of intensity for many practitioners.

Corporate success has not been produced by casual, easy-going "do-gooder" attitudes from its leadership. Much of their success has been honed from a no-nonsense philosophy of doing business. If you believe that just because you think you have a lawsuit that they are going to roll-over and play dead, you best go to the refrigerator, get a glass of milk, have a cookie, and go back and finish your "Alice in Wonderland" movie you must be watching. No longer is a lawsuit perceived as having a bombastic impact, or received as horrendous devastation as it once was. Now, lawsuits are routine and are simply turned over to a battalion of lawyers already on the payroll for just such purpose. Their only job is to blow the claimant's lawyer out of the water at "whatever" cost, take no prisoners and shoot the wounded. Litigation against big, impersonalized, colossal corporations may take years to bring even to a point of resolution—good or bad. A lawyer who assumes a role as David against a Goliath deserves a 40% contingency fee since he will certainly, in most cases, go far beyond earning it.

The Written Agreement—The Lawyer's Retainer & Fee Agreement

"A rose by any other name is still a rose." "A lawyer by any other name is still a lawyer." A contingency fee contract by any other name works just as well as an understanding between the parties as any. What you call it doesn't matter. What's in it does. Most people don't read anything except the headlines of their newspaper. Most people don't even read the articles under the headlines. What makes you believe that people will read a standard form contract with a lawyer?

The Standard Form—There's Really No Such Animal

Many people are deterred from inspection or reading anything when the document has the appearance of being a printed form. For some reason, a printed form is considered to be sacred. There are gross misconceptions that the words on a printed form are etched in stone—they can't be changed. This is folly! A printed form is only what those who prepared the form agree to. What about what you want to agree to? You could go get your printed form, bring it to the meeting, and look just as official and efficacious as anyone else. Get the idea out of your mind that the printed form can't be changed and that this is the agreement you must sign as an agreement between the parties. Lawyers are no different than anyone else when it comes to wanting you to agree with and do what they want you to do. Think about it! You really don't want anyone disagreeing with you either, do you? So, let's take a look at what's in the "Lawyer's Retainer and Fee Agreement."

Look at What an Agreement Means and Not Just What It Says

"What you don't know won't hurt you, "as the old adage goes. Well, that's a big lie! You may never feel the pain since it may kill you. Don't get distressed about being afraid of entering into an agreement with your lawyer. Just knowing what you should expect and should promote in your own self-interest is a great deal different than just knowing what you should expect.

What's not in a written agreement is often more important than what's in the agreement. Most of the time, people think and write in terms of the big picture, and in doing so leave out those necessary details which actually bring meaning, color, and harmony to the ongoing beauty of the picture. In writing out an agreement, the meaning or lack of meaning is construed strongest against the person preparing the agreement. In other words, if you prepare an agreement and the terms and conditions are not well-defined, the person preparing the agreement will be held most responsible for any misunderstanding. This, however, will not relieve you of being responsible for being agreeable to the terms and conditions of the agreement. Such responsibility only reflects slightly in the favor of the one who did not prepare the agreement. Forget all this legal-type talk and understand what should be in the agreement with your lawyer!

Misunderstanding is misunderstanding. Don't get trapped into agreeing that "the agreement says what it says." We have even been confused in the past by ex-presidents explaining what sex wasn't and attempting to help us understand by expressions of "what is is." Don't buy in to rhetoric and mumbo-jumbo. The important part is that you understand what's been agreed upon between the lawyer and the client.

An Example May Be the Best Explanation

In **Appendix A,** an example has been provided of a typical agreement given by a lawyer to his client to sign when the lawyer has agreed to represent the client in a contingency fee case. Some of the paragraphs are reasonably routine and some only appear to be routine. Below is an evaluation of the agreement considering each paragraph in order:

Initial Un-numbered Paragraph—THIS AGREEMENT:

This paragraph names the client, the lawyer or law firm, and the date. NEVER, NEVER, EVER, allow this to be left blank. You probably think that anyone would be crazy to leave blanks in a contract of agreement. People do it every day. They don't think it's important.

Make sure that the contract is executed in duplicate so you and the lawyer can have an original. After you have completely filled in the introductory paragraph and signed the agreement, get an original of the contract and take it with you. Don't have one mailed to you. Be professional! Don't accept the idea that one will be mailed to you. Just simply suggest that you prefer to take your original with you. Why be so persistent about an original of the completed contract? Lawyers often put things aside and move on to other things. Getting you your duplicate original of the contract just may not be such a high priority. So what? Later, when you are trying to establish the date you entered into a contract with your lawyer, you'll need the contract to see the date. That date could be important later to remind your lawyer about the levels of progress you were promised in your case, or to establish the date your lawyer got your case when you discover that your lawyer failed to protect your interest within the time allowed under the law for filing your case.

1. STATEMENT & SUBJECT OF EMPLOYMENT:

You know why you are entering into an agreement with your lawyer and your lawyer knows why they are entering into an agreement with you. So, what's the problem? There is no problem unless you are going to be involved with other legal matters which are ancillary to your direct claim, and which are dealt with or discussed at the onset of your case.

For example, if your spouse was killed in an automobile case, there will customarily be a legal requirement in your jurisdiction of opening up a decedent's estate. In some jurisdictions, the heirs of the decedent must have court approval before proceeding with a claim for wrongful death in behalf of the estate. Also, if there are minor children as heirs, there is a requirement that the minor children have a *guardian ad litem* (an unbiased, impartial neutral person who is an officer of the court appointed by the court) to represent their beneficial interest in any matters that might inure to their benefit. These are just a few items that may present themselves in the course of proceeding with the claim for death or damages.

The point of this is not to tell you what must be done to move forward with the claim but to raise the question of whether your lawyer is going to represent you in these ancillary matters and, if so, will there be additional fees? If so, will they be taken from the potential recovery? If there is no recovery, will you still owe the fees? Caveat: Most lawyers do these things as complementary to the claim for damages and do not charge legal fees for such matters, except for filing fees, and even that is discretionary with your lawyer. The only emphasis here is "Don't get surprised!" If you know what to expect, you can prepare for it.

2. ASSOCIATE COUNSEL:

When you first hear about this paragraph as a client you are glad that you can have the benefit of the best in the profession at no additional cost or expense to you. That's true. However, a lawyer generally knows what he knows in terms of what areas of representation he is routinely familiar with. So, ask your lawyer whether there is any anticipation about bringing in another lawyer on the case. Too many times, a lawyer brings in another lawyer on your case only after discovering that he's in over his head, or realizing that your case is not as good as was initially evaluated and he needs help bringing it "home" or sharing the risk. Caveat: Ask to be advised if another lawyer is being considered as coming aboard on your case. Ask that you be given permission clearing approval for associating other lawyers. Wouldn't it be cute if your lawyer associates a lawyer you had previously decided not to hire or the lawyer who represented your spouse in a divorce against you? Don't lose control of your case by remaining uninformed about what's happening. Remember: you are the client, you have the gold!

3. COSTS & OTHER EXPENSES:

This area of the lawyer/client agreement in the contingency fee case is probably the one of greatest concern for the client. The paragraph seems harmless enough, but the client doesn't appreciate the circumstances that can cause those subliminal potentialities of this short paragraph to create undue stress and disappointment. The client in the initial interview with the lawyer appreciates that the lawyer, in order to win the client's case, must incur expenses for depositions, experts, and other such things. There are two approaches to take in questioning this paragraph.

First, to what extent will expenses be incurred and what will determine their relevance to the client's case?

Second, and foremost, when and by whom will these expenses be paid? Obviously, you need to know the nature of expenses that will be incurred in your case. You can easily anticipate direct expenses in your case such as medical reports, your doctor's fee for deposition (you may not have known that your doctor is going to charge a fee for testifying about the medical treatment that was rendered in your behalf), deposition costs, transcripts, long distance telephone calls, photocopying, filing fees, travel expenses, and expert fees. There are numerous others which you can easily anticipate to be reasonably necessary and logical as a part of your case. Other expenses may become a close call.

For example, your lawyer has one of his paralegals doing research on your case at $35 per hour, your lawyer uses the firm's in-house investigator to do work on your case at $25 per hour, and the list could go on. So where should the line be drawn? Does this make a difference? Absolutely! Every expense in a case in either going to be paid by the client or the lawyer. With most expenses in a case, lawyers are required to pay their bills when they are presented. Deductively, you can understand how a lawyer can get into trouble with expenses on a case since the case may ongoing for a considerable period of time.

In theory, a client is responsible for any expenses in a case that are incurred by the lawyer in preparing his or her case. In reality, if the lawyer had to depend on the client in paying for all the expenses, the case would never get "off the ground." For that reason, lawyers, in some cases, get into hock over the matter of expenses.

The party being sued or against whom the claim is made will never consider what expenses have been incurred by the lawyer and the client in their settlement offer. In fact, the defendant doesn't care. In many cases, a lawyer is working feverishly to get in a position to get their expenses back when a case is not going so well. This happens more frequently that any non-lawyer would expect.

Now, the business of understanding the real thrust of this paragraph is found in the last sentence, "In the event the lawyer pays any such amounts, client agrees that the lawyer may be reimbursed from any gross recovery received." Lawyers intend for this to mean that those expenses incurred in the client's case will come first from the gross proceeds of the recovery. An example best illustrates this. If the client's case is settled for $35,000, and if expenses in the case have been incurred by the lawyer in the amount of $5,000, a settlement would reflect the following net proceeds to the client:

Gross Proceeds from Recovery.....................$35,000

Less: Expenses incurred...............................$ 5,000

Net Proceeds..$30,000

Less: Contingency Fee (33 1/3%).................$10,000

Net Proceeds to Client.................................$20,000

A client can quickly see that expenses make a substantial difference in the disbursement to the client.

Down below in paragraph five, the aspect of the importance of timing as to when the contingency fee is removed from the recovery will be more fully discussed.

Some lawyers have earned a flawed reputation for taking their fee from the gross proceeds first and then taking out the case expenses. Thank goodness there are not many who would do this. Here's how that looks:

Gross Proceeds from Recovery $35,000

Less: Contingency Fee (33 1/3%) $11,666

Proceeds Remaining $23,334

Less: Expenses incurred .... $ 5,000

Net Proceeds to Client $18,334

A client who does understand how a recovered settlement is to be allocated and divided is at the mercy and discretion of the divider of funds.

Another repetitive problem that confounds and compounds the complexity of the settlement understanding, which is seldom addressed in the "Lawyer's Retainer and Fee Agreements," is that of medical expenses which have been advanced to the client and now must be reimbursed to the insurance company under their subrogation rights. Some understanding should be made between a lawyer and a client about how this should be handled. Neither the lawyer nor the client are excited about making sure that the medical insurance is repaid because it takes money from the settlement proceeds which would otherwise go the client and the lawyer.

Discuss with your lawyer at the onset of a case whether you should sign an agreement reimbursing your medical carrier. Some medical insurance companies seek reimbursement and others don't depending on the contract terms of the policy. When you first meet and sign a retainer agreement in your lawyer's office, advise your lawyer when you have signed a subrogation agreement with your medical insurance carrier.

The medical insurance reimbursement situation is a tricky ordeal for the client and the lawyer. In most situations, the lawyer can negotiate towards reduction of the amount of subrogation demanded by the medical carrier. Regardless of whether the amount is reduced or not, having to deal with this as another expense in the settlement is a real "bite on the bullet."

Here is a suggestion: As opposed to having it covered off the top of the settlement as a case expense, or having such amount come straight from the client's portion of the proceeds, let each of the parties pay a proportional amount in relationship to the interest they each have in the gross proceeds of the case. In other words, in a typical case the lawyer will be responsible for 33 1/3% of the amount and the client would be responsible for the balance. Otherwise, the client could argue that the entire medical reimbursement be taken from the top of the settlement as a case expense. On the other hand, the lawyer could argue that such medical care was provided for the client and that the entire reimbursement should be taken from the client's portion of the proceeds. There is never a case of pure and absolute equity in dealing with reimbursement since neither the lawyer nor the client has further benefit from paying the reimbursement. Caveat: Discuss this openly with your lawyer. Don't delay discussing this potential concern on the representation from your lawyer that, "We'll discuss that if and when it comes up." For your own confidence and peace of mind you need to know what your understanding is. Remember: "Communication is a meeting of understanding between parties."

4. LAWYER'S LIEN:

This paragraph is probably a bluff and a control effort more than any thing else. This language seemingly leads the client to believe that regardless of any circumstances the client is "stuck" with the lawyer holding his or her hand out for payment. Then, reasonably, the client would ask, "How can I afford to pay two lawyers out of my potential case settlement recovery should I decide to fire my present lawyer?" Then, the client sighs in disgust, "I guess I'll just keep the lawyer I've got!"

A lawyer's lien is about a lawyer getting some of their money back if you decide to fire them and go get another lawyer.

Most clients don't know that they can fire their lawyer. (This does not have to be in the retainer agreement between the client and the lawyer. If you want to fire your lawyer you have a right to do so.)

Maybe, every client has seen on T.V. when a judge would not let a lawyer off of the client's case. This is, by far, an exception and when two people have reached a point of not wanting to work together "all the king's horses and all the king's men" can't make it happen. You can fire your lawyer without worrying about that lawyer getting all of the portion set aside for the contingency fee. If that lawyer has done all the work, and produced the settlement recovery, that may be a different story. (More on "firing your lawyer in just a minute . . .)

Every state has a Fee Disputes Division of the State Bar Association. If you have a problem, this is the most reasonable and logical forum to assist in the resolution of the conflict.

The effect of this paragraph is to protect the lawyer from double-dealing and dipping into funds that rightfully belong to the client. Believe it or not, there are some situations where this may happen out of confusion and unclear communications. After your case is over and has been successfully concluded, there a great feeling between the client and lawyer when both believe there was fairness and equity in the final results of recovery. Ideally, this is what the lawyer and client desire after many years of working to reach this point.

Young lawyers generally charge less, and lawyers not so young charge more. Paid for talent . . . not for time . . . the time lawyer is gradually being withered away into the archives except for civil defense attorneys. The younger the lawyer, the less the fee. Reputation is more important than ability in getting clients.

A lawyer's license is sometimes considered "a license to steal" by the public as well as by the lawyer himself. But believe that no lawyer ever considers himself or herself to be a thief. Any channeling of funds away from its rightful habitat is momentary redirection for the purpose of pursuing a justifiable cause if it's only for maintaining survival of the lawyer. Rationalization is a heavy tool of the lawyer used as a serious coping device to separate the confrontation between "what is" and what's configured as a reasonable basis of justification for doing what you have to do or what you have done.

Trust funds are not the lawyer's funds. They are funds entrusted to the lawyer for the benefit of the client. These funds sometimes have a tendency to leak or escape away from their place of habitat but do so always with the intention of them being fully replaced, recaptured, or returned in plenty of time for their rightful distribution. Illusion often precedes reality.

Lawyers love "easy money" but who doesn't? A case being considered by a lawyer for representation represents either "easy money" or "hard money." "Easy money" is considered to be a "bird in the hand." "Hard money" is money that may have some considerable risk with whether or not you will be paid. "Easy money" case representations by the lawyer can take the form of what most lawyers call "office practice" lawyers. These lawyers are often involved in real estate, LLCs, corporations, commercial transactions, financial law, copyright, trademark, healthcare law, public law and policy, government contracts, business law, and estate practice. No lawyer who works in these areas of practice would probably ever agree that this is "easy money" because it is not "easy money" *per se*. There are many lawyers who would tell you that if they get paid easily without having to badger the client to pay that would be considered "easy money."

"Hard money" takes a situation involving greater risk for the attorney getting paid for their legal representation. These cases readily appear in the lawyer's inventory of cases as those which are contingent. Contingency means the lawyer will be paid only when the case is successful for the benefit of the client. Otherwise, the lawyer, as well as the client, goes home empty-handed. However, don't lose sight that the lawyer has already spent a barrel of money on the case attempting to prepare it for trial by going through depositions, hiring experts, reconstructing accident scenes, and countless other expenses not including their time and contribution. A lawyer walking away from an unsuccessful case results in a substantially lessened financial position than when he took the case. This case preparation and in its impending process may have taken as much as two-to-five years.

To get this "empty hand" result is as equally devastating to the lawyer as to the client in some ways. The lawyer is not only out money, time, and effort but has to face an unsatisfied client and deal with the frustration that accompanies such a position. There is not easy solace for either the lawyer or the client.

Lawyers who take cases on contingency are given a bad rap by many as being money hungry, ambulance chasing, greedy parasites of the legal profession. This careless regard is far from ever being considered for any credence about who lawyers are and what lawyers do.

If you don't know the environment, venue, nature, situation, and circumstance of where and why lawyers do what they do, you should consider refraining from your distain of bias and jaded assessments about lawyers. Walk a few steps in their shoes and your attitude, perspective, and appreciation would change immediately.

Understand what lawyers do and why they do what they do before you place a sword in your hand and reach for your shield. Become informed before you lash out just based on your own self-designed, emotionally induced, and ill-formed opinion.

That's just reality and a fact of life in the daily decisions in the life of lawyers and their potential clients.

5. CONTINGENCY FEE PROVISIONS:

Much of the contingency fee was discussed under "Cost & Other Expenses" above. The point to remember here is that fees are negotiable before you sign a "Retainer and Fee Agreement" with a lawyer. Again, watch what is being said in the agreement, as well as understand the meaning of what's being said.

In this paragraph, please note that "said contingency fee shall be based upon a gross recovery." Does this mean that the lawyer's fees will come directly off the top of the settlement? Well, that's what the agreement says! Clients seldom understand what an agreement says or means. Does this mean that the lawyer is going to take his or her fee off the top of the settlement before the lawyer's expenses are paid and before any of the settlement proceeds are committed to reimbursement under a medical subrogation claim? This could be the meaning, but most lawyers want the client to come out the situation of settlement with a fair and equitable share of the proceeds. Even so, don't be lulled to sleep by this remark. Some lawyers take their fees right off the top just like the agreement says.

Some lawyers use this "right-off-the-top" clause to negotiate with the client when conflict arises over what was a legitimate expense of the case and what wasn't. The lawyer habitually wins these kinds of arguments. If such a provision is in the agreement you are asked to sign, discuss the relevance of this in the agreement when you know that customarily case expenses are taken out first before the lawyer imposes the contingency fee formula to the proceeds of the settlement.

This is **MOST IMPORTANT!** Remember, lawyers are skilled artisans of tautology. In other words, they are highly capable of saying the same thing in different ways using different words to convey the idea. Don't get into a discussion with your lawyer about what a particular phrase means in the "Lawyer's Retainer and Fee Agreement." A lawyer's jargon will leave you at the lesser post of understanding. Here's the RULE: If what is written does not convey what you perceive to be the meaning of the communication, change what is stated in the written communication. Make it make sense to you! If what you read is not understood or does not make sense, ASK QUESTIONS! A lawyer 99.9% of the time is being straight-up with you. If you don't understand, it is your fault. A lawyer is not a mind reader so don't pretend that he is one.

There is a favorite phrase in most legal documents that purports to cancel, negate, abrogate, disclaim, nullify, neuter, and disarm any spoken words said by the parties leading up to the signing of the written agreement which would tend to contradict the written agreement in any manner. Clients should be aware of the phrase in written legal documents which states that "anything not herein written shall be to the contrary and notwithstanding." This parlance of the legal profession is oft overlooked as having the impact of significance that it has. Clients need to believe that what a written agreement with their lawyer says is what the lawyer can enforce with the client.

Clients want to believe what they think they heard their lawyer say. But remember what the client hears is regularly not what's being said by the lawyer. Clients and the rest of the world bring to the table their own perceptions, misperceptions, apprehensions, misapprehensions, motivations, attitudes, needs, and belief systems which influence the way they see and hear everything. Being foretold is analogous to being forewarned. Human misunderstandings arise from failures in communications. Protect yourself from future misunderstandings with your lawyer by communicating about those areas of the contingency fee agreement you don't agree with or don't understand. Your silence will be construed as acquiescence. Don't play the role of being reluctantly acquiescent. Later, you'll wish you hadn't!

6. POWER OF ATTORNEY:

Most people know what a "Power of Attorney" is and what it purports to do. What most people don't realize is that the "Power of Attorney" is primarily a document of convenience when the party giving the "power" is unable because of some conditions, other than health, to conveniently able to perform the task to which the "power" alludes. A standard "Power of Attorney" presupposes that the person being given the entrustment of "power" shall act in the capacity of the grantor as though the grantor were there performing the act for himself. If a person is incapacitated by reason of health, or deceased, a "Power of Attorney" according to the standard perception is null and void and is of no effect. Indisputably, when you grant a "Power of Attorney" you must have the capacity. Once you lose that capacity, the "Power of Attorney" also disappears. Why would you want to give your lawyer a "Power of Attorney?"

There are some good reasons to do so but most of the reasons are bad ones. Your mind's wheels are probably already beginning to turn. Why should you give your lawyer a "Power of Attorney?" Are you leaving town? Do you not want to be bothered? True enough, there is much in handling your case that you do not really want to get involved in unless you are a total "busybody" who must know every time your lawyer files a pleading for you. So let your lawyer have the "power" to sign pleadings for you after the case has started. But agree with your lawyer that you will be allowed to read the lawsuit before it is filed and sign it if that is appropriate in your jurisdiction. A lawyer should also want the client to sign or agree to the lawsuit being filed since that would cover all the bases for the lawyer and the client.

Would you want your lawyer to dismiss your lawsuit without telling you? Absolute not! A "Power of Attorney" would bestow that right on your lawyer. One of the feared and perilous areas of conflict between the client and lawyer is that of the critical time of settlement. When the opposite side makes an offer of settlement to your lawyer, do you want him or her to have the power to accept settlement without your permission? Absolutely not! Would you like for your lawyer to sign something releasing the other party from any liability for your injuries and damages? I don't think so! Lawyers have even decided that this sweeping provision of "power" gives them the right to endorse and deposit settlement proceeds into their trust account.

This transfer of "power" from the client to the lawyer gets many lawyers in trouble when they abandon the laws of "reason" and "respect." In these situations, lawyers perceive that they are in complete and absolute control over the client's case. A lesson can be learned here for the lawyer and the client. The case is the client's case. Regardless of the position given to the lawyer, the client should always be the one who has the last "word" about the case's disposition. The lawyer should be the "worker bee" and allow the client the ultimate call in making the decisions in the case once the lawyer has properly and thoroughly presented the options to the client.

When you meet with your lawyer initially and you are asked to sign the "Retainer and Fee Agreement," read and determine what authority you are giving your lawyer. Know your rights and responsibilities in the case. Don't put your case on automatic pilot in your mind. Be involved! Be willing to participate! When you do, you'll know what's happening in your case.

7. SCOPE OF SERVICES:

If you know about a situation or position, you should not later be in a posture to complain. Lawyers want to make sure you know that no appeal is provided for in the "Fee and Retainer Agreement." In a case that is tried in court, you can expect typically that one side will lose. In those situations where there is no loser, there is no winner either because the jury could not make the appropriate decision under the law for either side. That kind of case is either retried, settled, or abandoned by the parties.

In the "Winner v. Loser" case there is always one side which has the right to appeal the case. Just because you have won, you cannot always begin to count your money. Appeals take time, effort, and are expensive. The lawyer may have a vested interest in your appeal because of the contingency interest in your case. To provide for such an eventuality, lawyers sometimes place in their contingency fee agreement (as in paragraph five above) a provision that should the case be appealed, the contingency fee would be raised to an amount of 50%. They also include an understanding of whether the client, or the lawyer, would pay the appeal costs, which would include such things as the cost of the transcript, the appeal filing fee, and a bond, in some cases. This is a serious matter of consideration in every case for the lawyer and the client. This should be spelled out in the agreement because most clients assume that the appeal is included in the representation of the client at no additional cost or percentage in the contingency fee contract. Should your case be lost in court, your lawyer will discuss appeal with you most of the time. If he does discuss the appeal of your case with you, you discuss it with him. Just be aware that if you lose, you do have a right to appeal to a higher court but it's not free and is not included in your earlier representation unless previously agreed upon.

The other issue that may arise in the "Scope of Services," having been addressed earlier, is that of other services that may arise out of the basic representation in the contingency fee case and not be contemplated by the lawyer as a part of the agreed upon representation which serves as the basis for the contingency fee contract. In your initial contact with your lawyer, get this out front. Ask the lawyer what other matters are anticipated in the overall picture of representation. If there are other areas of concern projected, talk to your lawyer about including them as a part of the representation in your contingency fee case. You would be surprised how many lawyers will work for you on these other matters just to get your contingency fee case. If you don't ask, you'll never know whether your lawyer would have helped you or not. Then, if you don't ask, you can expect a surprise later on. If you like unwanted surprises, don't ask!

8.   FAVORABLE OUTCOME NOT GUARANTEED:

You know that already! But it just has to be said. In your dealings with your lawyer, you either like, dislike, or are indifferent to your lawyer. In your initial meeting, you were impressed with something about the way he or she communicated with you. Most of us form our opinions about other people based on how they communicate with us. A lawyer is perceived no differently.

People buy the mood, charisma, charm, and emotions exuded by those with whom we come in contact. Sometimes, that aura abounds with a rapport of trust; sometimes, with a feeling of power; sometimes, with a sense of authority; and sometimes, with the awe of knowledge. Regardless of how a client reads his or her lawyer, that lawyer is believed to be the "deliverer," the "redeemer," or the "solution" to the client's problem. Lawyers don't have to guarantee, lawyers don't have to promise, lawyers don't have to be client-assuring, nor do lawyers have to predict outcomes for the client. The client buys what the client sees in those qualities he or she likes about the lawyer.

This paragraph is a reminder for the client, should such be necessary, that as to the conclusion of the case, the lawyer has not promised or guaranteed anything whatsoever. You must, as a client, recognize that there are never any problems in the beginning of a relationship. All problems of whatever kind or description arise in the middle or at the end of relationship. At the beginning the language of the lawyer's "Retainer and Fee Agreement" will not be so important. Only after trouble erupts in the relationship or failure of the case will the language become significant. Then, as most of us can easily recognize, it's too late to criticize and just as worthless to agonize about what you didn't read in your agreement with your lawyer.

Evidently, many people don't pay attention to what they read anyway. When they read anything that strikes their keenness of mind and interest and are brought to a point of concern, they can be rerouted by just being advised that the agreement is "simply a standard printed form and you have nothing to worry about." The client drops his interest of inquiry and slides back into the reposed recesses of believing that what he has perceived his lawyer to be is what he is going to get.

Isn't the marketing and packaging of whatever human beings buy the reason they buy, as opposed to what they buy being the reason for what they buy? Isn't the package often more attractive and more alluring than the product? Isn't this idea of buying the package, rather than the product, almost the way of the world today? Buy what you buy and not what you want to buy. Know what you are buying and not what your lawyer wants you to buy. Don't look for guarantees or promises. If you get them you are hereby put on notice that the lawyer with whom you are speaking is dealing with you from a basis of weakness and insecurity arising from his or her self-assessed deficits in reputation, confidence, skills, and ability—or all of them. The legal profession is a no-guarantee business.

9. COOPERATION BY CLIENT:

Lawyers use this clause to remind the client that the client may often be needed in the case, but the clause is also designed to empower a lawyer, in choosing to get off of a case, with the necessary arsenal to do so. Sometimes, for whatever reason, a lawyer wants to be cut loose from the representation in a case. The reasons are legion. Clients move, leave town, change addresses, go to jail, go insane, and even die without the lawyer knowing about such events.

Lawyers should keep up with their clients as well as clients should keep up with their lawyers. There is nothing worse for a lawyer than to spend a large amount of money attempting to prepare for a case when later in the case, the client cannot be found. Clients have a strong tendency to believe that lawyers don't need their assistance on the case. In many ways, lawyers are glaringly at fault in this misconception. If lawyers would maintain better contact with a client, the client would patently be more aware of the case and would feel a part of the process, if for no other reason than to be available for the lawyer to keep him or her informed. Remember: a missing client is a lawyer's nightmare and one that will have to be overtly explained to the court and the opposing side eventually. A lawyer's desperate hope is that the client will give some regard to his responsibilities of seeing the case through to the end. Clients need to remember that if it were not for them, the case would never have existed.

This problem can be avoided by lawyers keeping their clients involved in the case through the client's efforts in discovering witnesses, reading and attending depositions, and performing other matters like making copies, filing, and organizing files. This seems like a wonderful answer but it's not. Clients who get too familiar with what a lawyer is doing become overzealous, obsessive, and critical about the way a case is being conducted by a lawyer. A little information is a dangerous thing so clients become "P.I.T.A.s" When they do, more often than not, the music stops and the dance is over. The client and the lawyer can no longer coexist on the same case. The lawyer says "goodbye" to the client or vice versa. If the case is a megabuck one, the client must bite on the preverbal bullet to endure it to the end. This is a real example of reluctant acquiescence. If the lawyer is going to be substantially paid for it, they can routinely and unreservedly handle the abuse.

10. SUBSTITUTION OR DISCHARGE OF LAWYER:

On first glance, the client would not expect this paragraph to appear in a document prepared by a lawyer. Before you decide that this is all in favor of the client, you should look very keenly at what's being said to understand that this paragraph is very self-serving for the lawyer. The client, according to this section of the agreement, can *"terminate the services of the lawyer at any time for good reason"* (emphasis added). The client never has a good reason in the eyes of the lawyer—and never will—for a lawyer's discharge.

Lawyers recognize that lawyers get fired. Just like medical doctors, athletes, school teachers, politicians, and newscasters, lawyers sometimes get fired. Conventionally, every lawyer knows that clients fire lawyers so the lawyer is behooved to place in an agreement the terms and conditions that would protect the lawyer for time, effort, energy, and expenses expended up to the point of firing. The term "good cause" is usually placed in the retainer to remind the client that the lawyer must be fired for a good sensible reason and not for frivolous ones.

However, please note that many lawyers do not place any reference to firing in the representation contract between the lawyer and the client. If the client learns that he may fire his lawyer, good for him. Otherwise, the client should stay in the dark on this and "let the sleeping dog lie." Probably, no lawyer in his right mind would want to continue representing a client who wanted to fire him. The disgruntled lawyer will have probably already talked to another lawyer. At that point, the lawyer with the dissatisfied client should be on "pins and needles" since the client is on the edge of wanting to make sure the lawyer lives a life of grief with a seething client from that day forward. The job is difficult enough representing a client without adding any acrimony, contrived ill-will, or mean-spiritedness from the client. Almost every lawyer has to take his licks in this area of client disgruntlement at least once during his reign of law practice. Sometimes, a lawyer is much better to just cut his losses with the case, as opposed to pressing forward while an unhappy client and some anonymous lawyer is looking over his shoulder at every move he makes.

When, in fact, a lawyer is fired, the matters of compensation for work performed will be based and expressed by "the reasonable value of their services based upon the hours expended on behalf of client, the legal and financial complexity of the matter, and the experience, reputation and ability of the lawyer, together with all expenses incurred by lawyer at the time of the termination." What does this all mean?

First, no lawyer really wants to hear this, but all lawyers can be fired at any time and for "no reason." However, this may not be true in a criminal case where the judge has some discretion in allowing the defense lawyer to simply exit the case leaving the defendant in care of a new lawyer. More often than not, the judge will make sure the reasons for dismissing the lawyer are worthy, such as the uncooperativeness of the defendant. If the judge decides that a lawyer has to continue with the criminal case and if the defendant is found guilty in court, the lawyer can reasonably expect to see an appeal by the defendant based on the unworthiness and incompetency of the lawyer in representing the defendant. Most defendants who have been found guilty believe they have nothing to lose in throwing stones at their lawyer.

Does the client need a reason to fire his or her lawyer? The unfortunate answer is "no." The answer is the same as the answer in a state where an employee is employed "at will" and where, void of a contract, may be fired "at will" for no reason. In a civil case, the client might have a reason but "no reason" refers to the fact that the client does not have to have a motive, or justify or explain that reason to anyone—not even the lawyer being fired. This seems harsh and hard against the lawyer being fired but this is the nature of the legal process and the historical culture which supports the integrity of the client's wishes in legal representation.

The other part of this paragraph attempts to address the fairness and equity of how a lawyer will be paid for his or her time, effort, and expenses incurred in behalf of the client's case. Generally and categorically, there is only slight, if any, fairness and equity rendered to the "fired" lawyer.

A lawyer representing a client in a contingency fee agreement does so more than just to be compensated for their hourly contribution in efforts to the case. They, again and again, pour their heart and soul into trying to make a case successful. This untiring effort cannot be equated into hours and minutes or any matter of time. The lawyer's creativity, motivation, intensity, experience, knowledge, skills, and ability all come to the front in make a successful case. By firing a lawyer, you have just pulled the "rug from under their feet." There is no way the lawyer can be adequately compensated financially or psychologically, as he or she is depending on the contingency effect of the fee to generate compensation in the case. Lawyers who practice law around contingency fee cases don't think in terms of hourly fees or on any other level that would potentially compensate them when they are removed from a case by the client. The judicial system respects that clients can and may do things like firing their lawyer for their own reasons but clients must understand and recognize that this is not as beneficial to the client as it might first appear. There is a "double-edged" sword effect just waiting to befall the client.

If you as a client don't hear anything else, hear this. **This is important**: Don't fire your lawyer until another one has agreed to take your case. Remember, most clients think that they have the world's greatest case. This misperception by the client is present in probably 80% or more of all cases. Most clients believe that lawyers will line up to take their case. They are wrong. No lawyer likes to follow or trail behind another lawyer unless the bucks in the case are worth the trip. Taking on a client's case after another lawyer has already worked on it is like eating stale bread. You don't want to unless you have to and then when you do the experience is not nearly as rewarding as when things were fresh.

Lawyers are suspicious by nature. When you, as a client, are out in the street looking for a new lawyer the first question the new lawyer is going to ask himself or herself is, "What's wrong with you?" As discussed earlier, clients often do things for the wrong reasons, regularly expect those things they are not entitled to, and want more than they deserve or can get. Getting everyone on the same page is never easy, regardless of who is singing or the occasion. New potential lawyers look at everything. They do not want to carry another lawyer's burdens or garbage. Many lawyers will never pick up another lawyer's case because of the many conceivably concealed landmines that may exist in the case. Their philosophy is that there are just too many cases in the arena to pick up a hand-grenade that has had the pin pulled. Much like Forrest Gump and his box of chocolates: "You just don't know what you are going to get." A case that has been fumbled, bumbled, jumbled, and convoluted by another lawyer is a botched case. What lawyer in his right mind would want to unravel the mess?

Is it hopeless? Can a client find a lawyer to take the case? Absolutely! Lawyers are no different than most people. Perception is in the eye of the beholder and your perception is your reality. In life, if you don't like what you see just keep looking. If things don't get any better then you have to change the way you see things because the problem is you.

At one time in the history of the legal profession, a lawyer was perceived to be the paragon of all power, control, and influence.

No one would dare cross a lawyer. Nowadays, lawyers are hunting down lawyers. You can find a lawyer to hunt down your lawyer without too much trouble. However, the nature of the beast dictates that your case had best be worth the lawyer's effort in going after another lawyer.

But first, before you go in search of a "lawyer gunslinger," if you have any problem with your lawyer regarding any concern, then confront, talk, and communicate first to your lawyer to get the problem resolved. Realize that your lawyer wants to resolve any problems that come between their representation and the understanding of the client.

If the problem is not resolved to your satisfaction, talk to another lawyer. But, remember to tell the lawyer you go see that you have a lawyer and are having problems in communicating and understanding certain aspects of his or her representation. This new consulting lawyer can be of great assistance and may give you some help. You should, nonetheless, realize that the consulting lawyer you are speaking with is not normally going to get into the case and tell you what you exactly want to hear. Most lawyers are not going to give you such tactical ammunition for you to go back and blast your retained lawyer. The legal profession just doesn't work that way. Lawyers recognize that life makes a noticeable circle and nearly every turn comes back around. Those who don't understand this idea will eventually discover that it is a fact of life. The lion's share of lawyers, even though they may not like a particular lawyer, are careful not to trash or lay blame on another lawyer in a locality where they may encounter this lawyer in the day-to-day practice of law. More often than not the consulting lawyer will attempt to consol the client and suggest methods of reconciliation with the retained lawyer.

Most lawyers do not want to criticize another lawyer because the world evolves, and many lawyers get their turn to pay back the unwanted woes of another lawyer looking over their shoulders, second-guessing from now being involved in the case. Unless you have a "high-bucks" case, you will have considerable difficulty picking up another lawyer to patch up the work of the first lawyer or pick up the pieces of the puzzle and put it back together. It is like a contractor being fired from a job. Any new contractor who is hired to finish the work has no idea what went into the foundation and whether the project has been constructed with the integrity required to meet acceptable standards. The same is true with one lawyer taking over another lawyer's case. If there aren't big bucks involved, there is no lawyer who wants to get involved. No medical doctor wants to take over another doctor's botched patient. Does it happen? Yes, there are those brave souls who will indulge into the unknown.

The absolute last thing a lawyer contacted by a disgruntled client wants is for the client to return to the retained lawyer and be quoted. The client, more often than not, will hear what the client wants to hear and will seldom approximate what was said. Lawyers are careful when dealing with clients looking to dump their lawyer.

There are some exceptions. There are those buzzard-like scavenger lawyers who practice "scavenging" other lawyers' cases, and who often lie in wait for the first sign of conflict between a lawyer and their client. Don't be misled. There are some who lie in wait and there are others who are very proactive and make opportunities where none really exist. This lawyer damages and taints the legal profession. If these lawyers are seen for what they are, no sensible, clear thinking client would succumb to the level of this scum-sucking lawyer. What you see with this lawyer is what you get!

Lawyers come in all colors, sizes, and shapes with different perceptions, motivations, attitudes, values, and experiences that cause them individually to see things different than other lawyers. That's the reason a client can get a new lawyer. Just hopefully, the client has a meritorious case and the new lawyer fully sees a substantial fee worth his time out of it. If the client has no meaningful case but was represented by a lawyer who had no experience in recognizing that fact, the client is going to have severe difficulty finding a new lawyer until he or she can find another equally naive lawyer like the first. Some clients give up looking for another lawyer in an attempt to fire their first one. This should tell the client something about his case and may explain to the client why his first lawyer was not more interested in the case.

Most lawyers have great and extreme difficulty in telling clients both when they are considering the case, and after they have taken it, that the client doesn't have a substantial or meritorious case. A junk case is a junk case. Some lawyers will handle junk cases for clients. They are fee-oriented and not service-oriented. These lawyers get the client's fee for a case which has practically no imaginable probability of solution or satisfaction for the client. The client, sooner or later, goes away disgusted, disappointed, angry, bitter, and with less money than when they hired the lawyer. They'll get beyond their experience with the legal profession but they won't forget.

11. WITHDRAWAL OF LAWYER:

What's good for the client is good for the lawyer. If the client can fire their lawyer, the lawyer can withdraw from representing the client. Lawyers don't fire clients because they never hired them, so lawyers "withdraw" from representation of the client. The defined underlying basis for withdrawal is the client's failure to cooperate, as was discussed in paragraph 9 above.

The second part of this section deals with the client being "bogus" about some material fact or some underlying and supporting fact or circumstance relied upon by the lawyer as a basis or highly relevant in processing of the client's case. Some clients make misstatements about things they think they know but don't.

Some clients know the difference between what they know and don't know and lie about what they know. When a lawyer discovers that a client has "exaggerated" a position which was earlier considered to be the "truth," a lawyer has to consciously weigh the relative value of that position in terms of how the case is affected. This presentation is not going to tumble with those debates over what a lawyer is to do in such situations. That is a matter that must remain glued to the overall context of such situations and not be judged far in advance of the realistic concern or whether that information is used or not to influence the truth.

Lawyers despise clients who lie about their case, which serves as basis for a lawyer accepting or rejecting the case. Lawyers know that clients have had actual experience with cases and some have read books like *What Your Lawyer May Not Want You to Know* and other such similar treatises on the legal profession. When clients read these books, it does two things. First, clients become informed and educated about what to expect from a lawyer and, as a result, lawyers become more attuned to what clients are expecting, which results in better lawyer/client relationships.

The second reason is not as beneficial as the first because there are those clients who manipulatively attempt to take advantage of information they can acquire. In so doing, these clients bend, force, and configure whatever's necessary to make their case fit within the legal perimeters they anticipate a lawyer is looking for in deciding whether or not to take the case. These are "trouble" clients and lawyers are more discriminating than ever before about their client's case and the accompanying client's integrity before they jump on board. The client who misleads, fabricates, or lies is a dangerous client for the lawyer. If this client will utter whatever's necessary to make his case, he'll do the same thing about the lawyer presenting it. It's generally accepted that people who lie about one thing will lie about other things.

The last section of this paragraph concerning the withdrawal of the lawyer is really the purist one. This position is not based on what the client did or didn't do or what the client said untruthfully or not. Sometimes, in life, you just have to call it like you see it. That's not to say that everyone will see it the way you see it, but that's the way you see it.

If after full, complete, and extensive investigation, a lawyer determines a case can not be successfully concluded, the decision should be rendered to withdraw from the client's representation.

This is one of the toughest decisions a lawyer has to make. There is no worse discovery in law practice than hearing of a case you refused on the front end or one you, as a lawyer, withdrew from, settling for millions of dollars. If this is not something that rocks your boat of self-confidence, your boat probably won't get rocked.

Sometimes, the question in a case may not be one of liability but of the cost/benefit analysis. Law practice in many ways is no different than any other business. Would you advertise an amount of $2,000 to get a return on the advertisement of only $500? Not likely! Lawyers face some similar dilemmas. If a case had absolute liability and considering that with the damages experienced by the client, the case could only expect to gross $1,200, would a lawyer take the case if the case would require 40 hours of the lawyer's time? Probably not!

As a businessperson, a lawyer knows that overhead in his or her office requires an exact amount per hour. The lawyer must be aware that regardless of whether he wants to take the case or not, there are overriding considerations that dictate that a cost/benefit analysis takes priority. Young lawyers don't give regard or respect to this idea and commonly take "whatever" comes through the door. Some do so with the idea of "panning for gold" and believe that these clients will come back to them when they get the "big one." Some will and some won't. Lawyers who grimaced about taking a client's case in city court, when that same client later got run down by an 18-wheeler, have to overhear the client exclaiming, "We would have liked to go back to see that city court lawyer but we were just sure that city court cases were the only kind of cases he handled."

Many lawyers now recognize that you can break your back in law practice and never create any loyalty from your clients. Clients have their own ideas about what type of lawyer a lawyer is and, irrespective of what that lawyer does, the opinion will not change.

Lawyers are under pressure to make a decision early in the case about whether a client's claim has merit. The longer a lawyer waits, the more that lawyer comes under scrutiny of another. There is a short time before a case must be filed and once the time for filing it has expired, no new lawyer is going to jump into the new case. Ethical lawyers give a client plenty of time to seek a new lawyer. Other lawyers are an appropriate subject for scrutiny by a disciplinary section of the state bar association.

The Final Analysis

If you knew as much as your lawyer, you wouldn't need your lawyer. Ergo, why pretend? You can get a great bit more out of life, time after time, by being humble than you can by being arrogant and a know-it-all. Let your lawyer be Queen or King. Play the Jimmy Stewart part. Remember, he used to say, "Sir, I'm sorry you'll just have to forgive me. I just don't understand!" Lawyers don't really want you to believe that they want to be Queen or King, but most lawyers want to be in control. If that means King or Queen, so be it. Ask if you don't understand! The most powerful three letters you have in your life, besides G-O-D, is the power to A-S-K.

"I have Read, Understood, and Agreed"

This is probably the biggest lie you'll ever tell. In fact, most people don't even read the "Lawyer's Retainer and Fee Agreement" until they disagree with something in the case that the lawyer is doing, or disagree with the settlement provisions once the proceeds from the case hit the table. When you understand anything, the sting of disagreement is lessened. Most people in life are cruising through looking for those things they agree with. They often fight or reject those things they disagree with. With your lawyer, first seek understanding and not agreement. Understanding promotes trust and confidence. Disagreement begets conflict and doubt. The time for understanding is on the front end of anything.

Unfortunately, many buy signals and perceptions on the front end have nothing to do with understanding. How do you try to understand? You do this through communication. How do you communicate? You do this by asking your lawyer.

The End Is Near but the Melody Lingers On

You have been to school on the bittersweet experience of "Paying the Piper" and "The Nature of the Beast." You have experienced the winding, bumpy, uphill trail leading to the conclusion of your case. Most of the time, you don't want or won't want to go back and do it over for "love or money." You'll hope that this will be a "once in a lifetime" experience. Many times, if you had to do it over, you wouldn't do it. You now recognize some of the reasons why the legal process and its lawyers receive criticism. Some of it is earned and justified. Some of it is not.

The experience surrounding the event of "Paying the Piper" and learning about "The Nature of the Beast" is an educational one. Sometimes, an education may be negative and, at other times, the education may be positive. Hopefully, you have had a positive one. If not, maybe you have learned enough to transform your next encounter with the legal system into a favorably optimistic experience. Only you know what you have encountered in the experience although all who have ventured into the system have indulged in some common characteristics they may reluctantly share.

Many have spoken in response to the demand for a change of the system. None have seemingly provided any better solutions than what we now have. Those faint plaintive cries for reform do little for adding any new justice to where we are. Like most movements for reform, all efforts at change tend to go backwards rather than forward. The basic inquiry that may be posed in closing is whether "dueling to solve human differences" or the "dictatorial mandates of individual tyranny" surpasses and rises above "Paying the Piper" and "The Nature of the Beast." My guess is that it does. Everyone has to discover some solace for themselves in any system with which they deal.

Understanding is the bridge for peace and not agreement. If we are all waiting for agreement, then, we have unwittingly without any realistic hope of victory waged war on "The Nature of the Beast."

Law Practice as an Exact Science

Do lawyers ever apologize? The good ones do. Do medical doctors ever apologize? The good ones do.

You have to remember that law practice, like medical practice, is not an exact science, no more than life is an exact science. We do not live in a mechanistic, robotic world that has been flawlessly engineered by mankind in its improvement efforts since the dawning of modern man. We have come a long, long way from the beginning, but as long as we are able to individually think as human beings, we will always have differences in thoughts, feelings, and how we act. This discretionary individualized lifestyle of thinking and doing is what we have attempted to maintain as a part of our heritage and for those who follow behind. As long as there are human beings, there will always be a capacity for differences in ideas, philosophies, patterns, and lifestyles. Diversity is what life is about, and with diversity there is opportunity for expansion, growth, and development in every conceivable facet, plateau, and scope in our existence. Along with this, there will always be conflicts. These conflicts can be dealt with by reason, logic, good sense, and a good means of resolving that which cannot be solved on its own. Hopefully, our system of laws and its applications represent the greatest progression of meaning, understanding, sensitivity, and care for each of us as human beings as can possibly be made.

Many Stages of the Thinking Process

A client should recognize that a lawyer goes through several phases of the thought process when working with a client.

On the front end of the relationship, a lawyer attempts to learn about the client's case by listening to the client's version of what he or she thinks the situation is. A lawyer listens to gain an *insight* into what the case is about. At this point, there is consideration about what is real, what is intended, and what is expected. A lawyer then formulates through his thinking processes to produce a vision of *foresight.* From this position, he develops a strategy of going forward, processing, and preparing the necessary procedures and approach to making it happen. The process of executing the foresight phase is the most time-consuming and laborious the lawyer and client will have to indulge. Sometimes, a solution will come quickly and relatively easy, but most of the time, much more time will be required than that estimated by the lawyer. For the client, the time seems much longer than it is. For the lawyer, there is never enough time to work the client's case because the lawyer has many other cases making the same demands for time.

The Nature of Representation

A big factor in controlling and being in charge of the time it takes to reach a successful and satisfactory conclusion for the client is whether or not a lawyer shows up to represent any other party involved in the case.

Lawyers represent clients regardless of whether you or anyone else thinks they should or not. That's their job. That's the way they make a living. That's the way they are trained to think, act, and do. That's the nature of their business. That's their commitment of oath, allegiance, duty, loyalty, and honor in doing so. Whether you like it or not, a lawyer is doing his duty in representing his client even when you think the lawyer's client is wrong, lying, dishonest, untrustworthy, or guilty.

The testing of a lawyer's *foresight* comes into question when a lawyer representing another party in the situation comes into play. This is where a lawyer considers "what we plan to do," what the adversary party does, and what is anticipated to take place.

When another lawyer appears in a case, the results (or outcome of the case) become less certain than before. When a lawyer does not appear to represent another party in any conflict, there is considerably less compromise required to settle the problem being dealt with. Up to the point that a lawyer shows up, there is a sense of reasonable predictability. Lawyers who enter a case representing an adverse party create uncertainty for the lawyer and the client.

As has said here, lawyers cannot eliminate risk (assuming that risk is not getting what you want) but they can reduce uncertainty by the approach of compromise. Compromise assures all parties that they may not get the whole pie, as they thought they would, but at least they can a piece of the pie.

The last phase of the thought process on the part of the lawyer about a client's case is the *hindsight* phase. This is where the thought processes are concentrated on what should have taken place, what we wanted, and what we wish we had done.

Woulda, Shoulda, and Coulda

This stage of thinking has questionable value along the lines of *woulda, shoulda,* and *coulda.* After the facts are known, and the final resolution is in hand, all the second-guessers come ashore with their two-cents offering advice long after the gate has been closed and everything in the stable is asleep. This phase is of little value except for the lawyer to learn what should have been done and to make sure there is an etched memory made of the situation and circumstances for later reference, should the same situation reoccur in his or her law practice.

Lawyers are smart when they make a mistake and recognize the situation, avoiding the making of the same mistake again. They are wise when they learn from other people's mistakes and avoid making that same mistake.

Lawyers often incur the wrath of those who shoot with hindsight thinking they know more than the lawyer who was involved with and represented the client in the arena where the action was. These lawyers show up after the fact with pedantic attitudes never having "been there and done that." They are the ones who, regardless of being right or wrong, are never in doubt. Lawyers can be cynics, critics, and downright nasty to one another. This will probably never change because of the adversarial environment in which they live, but there should be basic civility toward one another since they all are in an indispensible ecosystem, working toward a similar pursuit of the maintenance of order and the preservation of humanity.

Thankfully, most lawyers are civil and ostensibly respectful to one another.

CHAPTER 13

FROM HERE TO ETERNITY . . . THE BEGINNING OF THE REST OF THE STORY

"You may think you know what's
about to happen in most situations
but you don't because your illusions
most often precede your personal
reality."—BFB

"If given a choice about something,
most of us would later chose something
different than what we choose because we
had little or no idea what the choice entailed
when we made it."—BFB

"If you knew then what you would later
learn, you would not be in a position to
discover later what you didn't know then."—BFB

Your lawyer knows many things that you don't know at this point in your relationship. There is absolutely no way for your lawyer to fully explain, relate, or illustrate what you are about to embark upon. Representation carries with it a vast array of activities that frankly are almost incomprehensible to a person who is not a lawyer.

However, the point should also be made that lawyers don't know the exact outcome you are seeking in your legal representation. Lawyers can only project, predict, and relate what they foresee happening based on their knowledge and experience in such matters. Experience is more important than knowledge since knowledge is most idealistically based on those unique and particular circumstances which give rise to a conclusion at that specific time. Knowledge is supposed to be field-tested, battle-tested, and the subject of consistency when encountered again. Hopefully, those conclusions, if made consistently enough, become knowledge. A lawyer's experience means that he or she has been there and done that. That's what experience is. A lawyer's business is called a practice because a lawyer's work is not an exact science. Therefore, a lawyer has an opportunity to learn, study, and acquire a set of reference points in his or her involvement that aids in the evaluation, analysis, and application of what is in the best interest of the client.

A medical doctor is fundamentally involved in diagnosis, application, and prognosis. A lawyer goes through the same process of involvement when learning of a client's legal concerns. Some problems are easier than others and become routine for the lawyer and/or the physician. So, your legal problem may be one that's easily resolved, almost on an objective level, or it may one that is much more complex and/or perplexing. on a subjective level. Subjective level problems are those that have difficult prognosis and a speculative conclusion. The outcome is never certain in the mind of the lawyer. Many areas of law practice are highly and extremely predictable. Lawyers who practice in the estate work areas can reasonably foretell the client what to expect. The same goes for real estate and, most of the time, even in the divorce areas of law practice.

The Factor of Intervention

Unpredictability is relative to another lawyer showing up to represent an interested party. Complications in the resolution of a client's case are always influenced by whether another lawyer is involved in the solution to the situation. Lawyers who become involved in a case have a sworn duty to represent their client and will do so consistent with how well they are paid. Lawyers don't like to hear this since they are duty bound to represent their clients regardless of how well they are paid or even if they are not paid. On the other side of this idealism is the reality that human nature dictates that equity prevails either consciously or unconsciously throughout life. *Quid pro quo* is one of the most fundamental principles of life and has been so since the beginning of time. This has not had to be explained to anyone. Such is a part of the mechanism of the life process. Experience matters. You do not want some new lawyer to O.J.T. (on the job training) with your case, if it is other than a routine case, no more than getting a new doctor to perform your brain surgery.

Would you rather have someone represent you who has been there or someone who has merely read about it? A great many lawyers have gotten their first time experience on their own without the assistance of a fellow lawyer who had been there before. Perhaps the client survived and probably some didn't. Good lawyers learn from other lawyers. Would you look forward to surgery being performed by a heart surgeon undertaking his first surgical heart by-pass operation, without even having seen such an operation? You would probably take your chance in not having the operation at all.

This discussion is not intended to mean or imply that the legal arena is as consistently critical as the medical community. Many lawyers are accused of being dilatory in working for their clients because they are, in many situations, unsure of what they are doing. This may be true, obviously, in some situations but not most. Lawyers eventually learn what to do in most of the situations they encounter. This does not mean that they always deliver to the extent of their knowledge and experience. Lawyers are not the exception to the "knowledge, experience, and delivery rule." Everyone, including medical doctors, contractors, and everybody else, falls short in doing the very absolute best they can do in every endeavor. This "less than the best" in every situation is part of the human condition and is endemic to human nature. There are some professions, occupations, and skills which are more visible and more scrutinized than others. Lawyers are probably second-guessed the most only ahead of physicians. People often think they know more about what lawyers do and should do than any other professional service. Lawyers have to contend with this perception on a continuous basis because of what has transpired in our national media.

Never has there been such a time of what appears to be openness in communications from first-hand viewing from the front row of a courtroom to the live scene of a military conflict in some remote part of the world. The world is full of media "spin-doctors" who seriously influence the shaping of opinions of the masses. From comedians and sitcom stars to talk-show hosts, the masses are being bombarded with characterizations of what's politically incorrect to what ascendant icons should be honored as part of our scared heritage. The media communicators are delivering powerful political, economic, and social messages about what's "hot" and what's "not" in the way we all live and think. What you think about your lawyer may have been seriously and successfully influenced by what some others have said and what they think. Hopefully, you are responsible for how you think and how you feel but most of us are not aware of when we are being influenced by sources outside of ourselves and when we are not.

This chapter begins to talk about the beginning of the rest of the story . . .

The Fairy Tale vs. The Horror Story

Have you ever thought about it? Had you rather listen to a Fairy Tale or a Horror Story? Most people had rather hear a fairy tale. However, there are those macabre few who would like a horror story. Lawyers candidly don't ever try to scare the daylights out of anyone when they talk about representing them as a client. That's probably just not a good way to get a client. Hence, lawyers talk about possibilities, probabilities, "maybe," and "might." The lawyer talks in broad generalizations and presents a big picture overview of things to come. A lawyer seldom talks about some of the necessary things and events which will occur during the course of your case such as depositions, interrogatories, experts, background investigations, and delays. Lawyers don't usually talk about the anxiety, frustrations, and doubts which come with almost every case. Your lawyer wants you to buy the relationship. Your lawyer wants you to feel that you have made the right choice in selecting a lawyer for your case. For now, your searching and worrying about what to do is in your lawyer's hands. A load has been removed from your shoulders. You have a feeling of peace and joy in your life and believe you'll be able get back to own reality. People don't like having to make a decision about something they really know very little about. In your mind you want to take a deep breath, try to relax, take a reprieve, and allow your lawyer to handle your case.

Fairy Tales Are Just What They Are

Wouldn't life be just wonderful if it worked just like we designed it? Life doesn't work totally in accordance with any expectations and assuredly never will but we all keep attempting to design our destiny anyway we can.

Most of the time, the onset of reality is slow, gradual, creeping, incremental, and subtle. From the onset of aging, cancer, or the loss of your hair, nothing seems to happen just overnight. When you leave your lawyer's office, you leave with the impression that the problem you left in the hands of your lawyer is really a great deal less complicated than it is and that your problem's solution will take a lot less time than it will. Clothed with this misconception, you wait for the quick, easy, and ideal solution to your legal problem from your lawyer.

As a youngster, you were probably told, "What you don't know won't hurt you!" Well, that's a big lie! You may not worry about what you don't know for a while. When you suspect that your expectations aren't being met, you begin to accelerate the reality of what you anticipated based on those expectations and look inquisitively for the appropriate repository of your projected blame. Such a response is essentially an individual's "cause-and-effect relationship" mechanism being placed into operation. The manifested product may be blame but the rationalized process is based on the scientific foundation of "cause-and-effect" (a.k.a. "An Input-Output Resultant Theorem").

Clients are generally good about waiting for a reasonable amount of time to find out about "What's Going On" in their case. Why? There is reason to believe that clients don't really feel a need to talk to their lawyer. Why?

Clients think in terms of conclusions and results. Lawyers think initially about a case in terms of generalizations and the overall nature of the case. The way the lawyer thinks at the time of meeting the client, and the way the client thinks after meeting with the lawyer, is often incompatible, not on the same page, and not in the same book of how and where the case is going. This concern leads to a discussion of when, how, and what causes poor communications between the lawyer and the client.

Often the Problem Is Perceived to Be Larger Than the Solution

As a matter of fact, more often than not, a solution is often more complicated, more difficult, and much more involved than the problem. The problem is often more easily dealt with by not solving the problem than those problems created by the attempted solution. This is one of the most difficult areas of a lawyer's relationship with the client to contend with.

My Lawyer Is a Superhero

Clients sucker lawyers into thinking that lawyers are superheroes. The term "my lawyer" to many people brings on the feeling of hope and promise against the woes and oppressions of life. Lawyers get caught up in this adulation and think they can be all things to all people, sometimes failing to realize they can't.

Lawyers think and work on a common business idea that the purpose of law practice is to get and keep a client. Don't take this literally! Lawyers, when they get a client and do work for the client, want that client to return later for future business should the client have any. This keeps a lawyer's inventory of clientele at a level where the lawyer can sustain an active practice without the need for attracting new clients. Old clients really only represent a base of clients and the lawyer is always looking for lucrative new representations for those who don't come back or don't have new business. This is called "growth" in the business world. Many lawyers think continuously about keeping the clients they have seen before. This is as much a problem, at times, as is getting a new client. Remember, a superhero is a superhero! There's a bumper sticker that says it all: "My Lawyer Can Beat Up Your Lawyer!"

Lawyers Are Gladiators

Lawyers want to help their clients. Clients want to be helped by their lawyers. So what's the problem? The problem is evolution. Most clients don" distinguish between levels of cases. A case is a case to a client. Regardless of whether a neighbor's dog is barking constantly late into the night, or whether the client has been slandered at work by the janitor, every case is a case. Clients want some redress regardless of what grievance exists to cause them some worry, pain, inconvenience, or discomfort. They don't care about the magnitude of the case. They turn to their lawyer, their superhero, their gladiator as a person and place of final resolve.

Damned If You Do and Damned If You Don't!

Life, according to the modern philosophers, should be lived in relationship to other people in a win/win posture. Lawyers live in a world that finds this posture to be uncommonly rare if meagerly existent at all. Lawyers learn quickly when they began the practice of law that clients want what they want regardless of what has to be done to affect solution, regardless of how much it costs and how nonsensical the solution makes in terms of any cost/benefit analysis of the overall situation. Yes, ladies and gentlemen, boys and girls, clients are frequently and sometimes infrequently "boneheads." You are probably surprised about this and if you are you may be protecting the species with denial.

What's a "Bonehead" Situation?

You, by now, after having read this far, probably can think of many situations which might be called "boneheaded." Here are some potential examples:

- You purchased a concert ticket for $15.00 and when you got there no seats were available since someone else was sitting in your seat.
- You found a fly in your soup at your favorite local restaurant before you started to eat.
- You want to sue the manufacturer of car wax because it's not as easy to wipe off as you saw on TV.
- You want to sue an abdominal exercise machine marketer because you have only lost two inches in your waist in a month.

The list could go on and on.

The "Bonehead" Case

There are usually one of three qualities that make a "bonehead" case. Only one of the conditions is necessary but one or more may be present. First, there is the circumstance that only minimal or negligible damages are experienced, at best, by the client. Secondly, there is little, if any, chance of recovery because of a lack of proof, duty to the client by the wrongdoer, or solvency of the defendant. Thirdly, all the elements of a case may be present but because evaluation of the cost/benefit value (i.e., you would spend $500 to get a return of $200) the case is not one that should be reasonably, practically, or justifiably pursued by a lawyer.

Lawyers who let clients be in charge of determining what's a "good" or a "bad" case can expect to end up in trouble with the client. A lawyer just can't deliver the expectations of the client without some personal sacrifice to their office, other clients, and the personal donation of their time. Eventually, a lawyer must deal with the inequity present in the cost/benefit evaluation of the case. Lawyers end the pursuit without getting what the client wants and then telling the client that nothing more can be done with the case. The lawyer then appears generous with the client by telling the client that no fee or no further fee will be charged. The fact that a client was not charged or charged a very small fee makes no difference. The lawyer is routinely labeled unfavorably by the client and, more times than not, the client will not return to this same lawyer for future representation. However, there are those lawyers who follow any pattern necessary to satisfy the client.

Regardless of What It Is

Lawyers in response to "bonehead" situations are regularly called into action to be their "gladiator" selves to produce the desired results. Guess what! The lawyer now takes on the characterization of the nature of the situation. The lawyer now takes on the aura of "bonehead." Clients don't get accused of doing stupid things—lawyers do! Think about it! Clients don't know anything or, at least, they aren't given any credit for knowing anything. All the blame goes to the lawyer. Thus, the lawyer assumes the role of the "bonehead."

When a lawyer tries to apply common sense and logic with a client about a "bonehead" situation, they are, from time to time, successful but are not regularly and consistently successful. There's not a lawyer dead or alive who hasn't taken a case he wishes he hadn't, or knew at the time he took it that he shouldn't.

The Easy Way Out, or Is There One?

Lawyers want to be superheroes. Even the "Intellectual" lawyer wants to be a superhero. He or she may not want to acknowledge that fact but the idea is a fact of life. This desire to be the epitome of what a client wants a lawyer to be makes lawyers vulnerable to following the whims and dictates of clients beyond the far rim of reason and logic on many occasions. So, what do lawyers do? They try to do the least thing in attempting to get some part of the client's expectations. Lawyers try to use the influence of their title, position, and clout. Sometimes, a loud roar gets as much attention and action as you would get if you did otherwise. Expect your lawyer to write a letter to the party from whom you are seeking relief expressing your severe distress, torment, and tribulation resulting from the grievance. Remember, lawyers are word-slingers! A bark will often work as well as a bite! What if that doesn't work?

A good lawyer who is concerned about keeping a good relationship with his client tells the client exactly how and what the situation is. A "junk" case by any other name, using any kind of logic, and regardless of whose case it is, is still a "junk" case in the legal arena. Suing a restaurant for an apology for not allowing you to eat without wearing a coat and tie is not worthy of consideration in the judicial system. A lawyer has a duty to protect the client from stupidity or the "bonehead" status. All lawyers don't think this way. Some lawyers believe that "if a client is willing to pay, the lawyer is willing to play." Maybe that's the reason some lawyers have the reputation for being willing to do almost anything.

Whether some lawyers want to admit it or not, some clients are insatiably dedicated and directed toward self-destruction. Regardless of what their lawyer tells them, they still maintain a position of "full torpedoes ahead." A lawyer often finds themselves in a "catch-22." If they don't deal with the client's obsessive, irrational, and unreasonable whims, the lawyer could lose a long-standing client, a good friend, and/or future representation of this client. Some lawyers stand their ground and tell the client that they are "acting like an idiot." Others hope they will go home, sleep it off, and forget about the idea. Others, however, often have to bite the bullet to appease their client.

The case of the litigation that was filed about a business establishment is a good example. The client had dinner reservations at a high-end, nationally reputed, and recognized restaurant. When the client arrived, the restaurant was jammed and the entire restaurant was behind in serving its patrons by at least an hour. The client was given an accommodating table and free drinks to wait for his reservation. After a few drinks that caused the client to "think" (feel) more clearly about the situation, he decided to speak to the owner/head chef. Of course, the chef was deeply embedded in food preparation, attempting to shorten the wait time, and did not respond to the client's request. The client and his spouse decided they had waited long enough and stormed out of the restaurant making a few remarks that were not complimentary to the restaurant.

What possibly could he sue for? For the breached time of the reservation? For the restaurant's failure to comply timely with the reservation appointment and the subsequent breach of the alleged contract? He could even sue for mental anguish and suffering. No, believe or not, he sued the restaurant and its owner for an apology. After the debacle, he wrote and called the chef/owner asking for an apology and got no response. Again, he reached an all-time passion for revenge because he felt rebuked. The suit was filed but the client never got his day in court because he had a heart attack and died.

Lawyers Should Remember That Clients Think Differently

Remember, clients are clients who do things for their own reasons. This reinforces the old truism that "clients think like they think, feel like they feel, and act like they act, regardless of who thinks they should or should not."

Lawyers get in trouble telling their clients that they will begin on a case the lawyer does not believe in. If a lawyer does not believe in a client's cause, there is continuous reluctance to make the case successful. Half-heartedly, the case is eventually concluded in failure to the chagrin of the client and the loss of a client by the lawyer. Lawyers must draw a line in sand and understand what they will and won't do and communicate this to the client. Most of the time, there is seldom a question in the lawyer's mind about which cases they should and should not accept. The only persistent problem is in following his or her logical and reasonable intuition of what they know they should do when confronted with the primary concern for satisfying the often whimsical and capricious desires of the client. Lawyers recognize, in most lawyer/client relationships, that the client is looking for someone to champion his cause and return a victory. A victory has no universal standards. Some clients are not looking for money or relief but vengeance. The motive of vengeance is the most expensive indulgence a client can ever expect to pursue.

Is an Honest, Truthful, and Straight-Forward Lawyer an Oxymoron?

At least, that seems to be the perception. There are lawyers who will tell it like it is and there are those who won't. So, why are you surprised about lawyers when most professional people fall into the same dilemma of attempting to weigh the difference between the outright telling of a client what the professional really thinks and feels and what the client wants to hear?

If you went to a medical doctor and were told by the doctor that you could not be helped, what would you do? Obviously, if you were intensely concerned about your complaint, you would seek out another doctor. The same response is given to lawyers and other professionals who give people advice and render an opinion about the feasibility of doing a particular project. Somehow, human nature dictates that if you don't get what you want you'll keep looking.

The Successful Lawyer/Client Relationship

No relationship in life is ideal. There is no such animal. But, notwithstanding that relationships are not made in heaven, you can appreciate what's necessary to have a healthy and reasonably successful relationship.

The First Thing

First, be honest with your lawyer. Don't go through some tiresome process of experiencing a learning curve by attempting to discover what you need to tell a lawyer in order to get him to take your case. Some clients get extremely knowledgeable about their legal circumstances by shopping lawyers. Clients eventually discover which "buttons" to push to excite a lawyer. The downside of this kind of farce is that the facts usually do not support the client's illusion of recovery and the lawyer's time is wasted until the faulty foundation on which the case is assessed is discovered. At that point of realization, the lawyer recognizes that the client doesn't have a case and the client has wasted valuable time and effort for "nothing." The lawyer and client sever their relationship and generally that client will never return to that same lawyer, believing that the lawyer was fully aware of the client's deception. Some clients believe that lawyers can do anything. Lawyers can do many things that seem impossible but changing facts is one of the more difficult tasks. Lawyers, at best, can only "repackage" what they get.

The Second Thing

Second, you need to know what to expect from your lawyer. If you expect the moon and get only a small piece of cheese you will not be happy and only disappointed. Your expectations must also be reasonable. There are two components of what you expect in your lawyer's representation. The first component of expectation is "quality" representation which consists of courtesy, politeness, promptness, competency, diligence, and many other attributes. What you expect also depends substantially on your own philosophy of life which is displayed in your own personality. The second aspect of expectation in your representation is that of "quantity." Quantity is a part of everything we do in life. "Quantity" is a quality that should be understood in the lawyer/client relationship.

The Representation of Quantity in Your Life

"Quantity" represents how you will be satisfied with what your lawyer does for you. From the time you are placed in the world you begin learning about quantity. Quality is important and should never be belittled or minimized, but quantity ultimately determines our satisfaction. Most of your expectations are based on quantity. Once quantity is achieved in anything your perceptions are that you can then buy, realize, or achieve quality. Most, when they think of quantity, think of money. Can my lawyer deliver the "quantity?" Is my lawyer strong enough to bring me satisfaction with "quantity?" A "quality" lawyer can be a good friend and a wonderful ally but can the lawyer deliver the "quantity" of my expectations to produce the satisfaction I am seeking? Can you see how a difference in your expectations of "quality" and "quantity" can influence the lawyer/client relationship?

The Third Thing

The third component is your personal commitment to do your part in the lawyer/client relationship. Stay in touch with your lawyer. Cooperate, respond, and show due diligence about your case. This in many situations is perceived best by the lawyer in your faithfully paying the case's administrative fees and the lawyer's fees when requested in a timely manner. Also, advise your lawyer when you remember facts that were not earlier related in your initial and subsequent discussions. Help your lawyer help you.

The Fourth Thing

The fourth component necessary for the best lawyer/client relationship is to understand your lawyer. Lawyers operate in a very complex arena of life. Most clients would like to believe that life and the theater of law practice operate in a more exacting fashion than they do. Most clients would like to believe that the law clearly discerns "right" from "wrong," "justice" from "injustice," and "fairness" from "unfairness." Unfortunately, the system of justice is not singularly focused on the pure content of things as most things, in and of themselves, hold the opportunity for purely objective assessment. Ideas and things given individual attention as items of content, experience different values when placed in the relationship of other ideas and things. Most of life is perceived as having realistic meaning in the "context" of things. This "context" scheme of things is where life takes place in relationship to all other things.

Is a hammer a "dangerous weapon?" Your first impression might say "no" because you were thinking of using the tool to build a beautiful cathedral. If you had to consider the hammer as an instrument used to kill a person, would those circumstances cause you to consider the hammer in a new "context" of situational circumstances? Seldom is anything, in and of itself, totally bad. Only when a fact or circumstance is placed in its setting of totality can such a situation be evaluated. This evaluation is not usually objective but subjective. What does "subjective" signify? The answer could easily be "many things to different people." What you see is what you see. One of life's great ironies is that I can't tell you what you see. I can only tell you what you should see. Probably, the best description of subjectivity is that which lies in the "eye of the beholder."

The system of law, just as life itself, is not objective but subjective. What may be right or wrong in one situation might not be perceived the same in another very similar situation. Lawyers have to sort out the "subjective" from the "objective" world in representing their clients. There are very few "absolutes" in the lawyer's world any more. There are very few questions that can be answered with a "yes" or a "no." The answer always seems to be somewhere in the middle. This even further confuses what the world of "old-fashioned" referred to as the truth. The truth in the legal system seems now to be what most of those who have any influence in the system believe.

You, as a client, must begin to appreciate the difficult arena in which a lawyer operates before you can have the highest respect, empathy, and rapport with your lawyer.

Multiple Tasks, Multiple Demands, and Multiple Roles

Lawyers are expected to know almost everything. Much to the surprise and shock of many, they don't. Some lawyers don't even know that they don't know everything. In your initial and later conversations with your lawyer, you will attempt to learn as much as possible about what your lawyer thinks about your case. The lawyer, on the other hand, is trying to learn as much about your case as possible before giving you an opinion concerning its merits. Most clients want a lawyer to be an exact as possible. Lawyers, as a rule, are trying to stay as far away as possible from being specific, exact, direct, clear-cut, explicit, definite, precise, and unambiguous. That's the reason a lawyer's first expression might be vague or highly generalized about his or her impression of your case. A lawyer realizes that no one knows what facts will be developed in your case. The client's version is only one part of the story. Some other parts of the unfolding saga will be learned later and some will never be known.

What makes the beginning of a good lawyer/client relationship is for the lawyer to tell a client when he or she does not feel competent or confident in dealing with the problem at hand. The position of confession concerning a lawyer's lack of competence or confidence about your case is very difficult for a lawyer.

The more skilled lawyers handle their uncertainty with the adroitness of a gem-cutter and still retain the client's confidence. Others, not as experienced, or skilled, or both, won't tell a client how they really feel and consequently, take the case in the expectation of trying to make "something happen."

The Smartest Lawyer

The smartest lawyer is the one who knows what he or she doesn't know. This lawyer is capable of rendering very valuable service to a client by either researching to discover the answer to a client's problem or referring the case to someone with greater qualifications to handle the problem. Remember, most lawyers want to be "all things" to a client and any show of weakness dispels that status and positional aura.

Know the Difference

A client should recognize a lawyer's jargon. Legal lingo is kin to a doctor's shop talk. Only those skilled in picking up the distinction of comparisons will be able to meaningfully and correctly perceive what's being said. For instance, the words "probability" and "possibility" become very important in listening to your lawyer. Everything is a "possibility" but many less things are a "probability." When your lawyer starts talking about "possibilities," you can figure that your lawyer is less sure about the outcome than if discussion was being made about "probabilities." Each of these words is customarily qualified around contingent circumstances and events happening or certain facts being ascertained by reasonable accessibility after further involvement in the case.

The Fifth

There is a fifth component in promoting a wholesome relationship with your lawyer. This component is a virtue. This component is a godly quality. This component separates maturity from immaturity, men from boys, and women from girls. The virtue is patience. Michelangelo remarked, "Genius is eternal patience." No one can give patience to you. You can't buy patience. You must learn patience. You learn patience by understanding and knowing that any time a process of completion of anything involves many parties, you can expect delays, roadblocks, and inertia. The legal process is extremely burdened with these obstacles. You must realize that whenever you are pushing your lawyer to "hurry up," a lawyer on other side is being urged to "slow down," delay, postpone, roadblock, and impede your lawyer's efforts.

Be patient with your lawyer. Honor and respect the barriers your lawyer is having to overcome to acquire your satisfaction. Remember, if there were not other people attempting to block you from what you want, you would not need your lawyer. A lawyer's work is not easy. Regardless of the nature of your situation, there are other people involved who have competing or conflictive interest and want to stop you from asserting your position. This is why you need your lawyer.

Understanding Is Deeper Than It Looks

Many of the processes of life, as well as the legal environs, are much like the "iceberg principle." There is always more than meets the eye. Supposedly, one can only see about 1/10 of an iceberg peering above the level of the water. The province of the legal terrain is much the same. Clients want immediate answers and solutions. Neither is ever immediately forthcoming. Every activity in a lawyer's life, as he or she tirelessly works for their client, is a "process." Seldom is any accomplishment a one-step involvement. Work to understand your lawyer and what lawyers do and you'll promote a better relationship between you and your lawyer. Remember, the key to resolution of any concern, conflict, or doubt is to communicate directly regarding your feelings. Most problems in communication arise because of a failure to communicate and not communication itself. When people confront communicational problems they are, under most circumstances, routinely solved. These times when communications are open and are used to clarify values and understandings, you will be able to see the iceberg below the level of the water. The real problems in communication arise from those that are not known, not visible, not addressed, or acknowledged.

Remember, both parties in the communicational process between a lawyer and a client are responsible for the clarity and the quality of the communication. To blame your lawyer for failing to communicate is pure folly. Assume an equal responsibility for good communication between you and your lawyer and you'll enjoy the highest ideal of a quality relationship.

The best part is that, more than likely, you will assist your lawyer in helping you get what you want. Remember, everyone in life is listening to the same radio station. That station is WII-FM! You have been listening to it all your life. Do you recognize the call letters of the station? You should because it's What Is In It For Me! You should recognize this station since you have been listening to it every day of your life since you have been in the world. As long as you are on earth you will continue and consistently listen to this station. This is just the way we are!

CHAPTER 14

THE SEARCH FOR THE TRUTH

"There is a difference between those who would not recognize the truth if they saw it and those who would not acknowledge the truth if they did."—BFB

"There are so many people already confused, why further confuse them with the truth?"—BFB

"A lawyer's chief aim in life seems to be in perpetuating the act of lawyering."—BFB

T ruth has often been associated with reality. Truth is supposed to be connected to the actual condition of a situation. So in life, the truth should be in conformity with fact.

Philosophically, a case could probably be made that truth and justice should be one and the same. When a person enters a courtroom to give testimony, they are asked to pledge or solemnly swear "to tell the truth, the whole truth, and nothing but the truth, so help you God." Witnesses being asked to take an oath to tell the truth give the impression that justice in some manner must be centered on the truth. No treatise on lawyers, the judicial system, and a system of laws would be complete without discussing the most obvious and most glaring weakness in the entire scheme— that of "finding the truth." Unfortunately, the system's entire basis of integrity lies in the cluster of its greatest deficiency—that the truth is not found by applying a simple objective standard. Getting to the truth has always been the system's greatest challenge and most important component. What's happened in our judicial system is the same thing that has happened across the behavioral norms of our society. See if you agree with this assessment.

Scatter, Expand, Convolute, and Clutter. Just the Beginning

Most systems in life have an inherent tendency to expand, to grow, to evolve and self-perpetuate. Rules, laws, regulations, and customs continue to be enlarged beyond any reasonable capacity for toleration, endurance, or total comprehension. Our system of jurisprudence has also been victimized by the ongoing evolution.

You Can't Go Back, But Take a Look Anyway

There are many profound questions plaguing our society regarding how to sustain a system of laws with the gradual but accelerating advocacy of social justice and equality. Similar questions have probably imposed themselves in all societies at some time. One would think and reason that at least one generation would be able to put a handle on some simple solution of balancing law and social justice which could be transcended to the next generation. At best, that supposition has only appeared as folly and fantasy. Why? There are possibly as many answers as there are those who would ask the question. One proposition has been offered which attempts to justify or rationalize that all societies are in a continuous state of evolution. Each society seems to adopt new values since they are not content with the "old" ones. New generations seek individualism, and in pursuit to establish new values, new behavioral and cultural norms are formed. These patterns of behavior over time are eventually recognized in our system of protection through the law.

There are those who would like to turn back the clock but would probably agree only on some things. Most would probably not want to give up the TV remote control clicker which controls mega channels with "nothing to watch," the Internet which has expanded to over 60-million pages of immediate access, the speed of most things or even the fast-food boon. Sports and entertainment icons are heralded and chosen as heroes as opposed to political, moral, and spiritual leaders. Kids see their parents less than they see their school chums and teachers at school. Those on the political "right" say that government is doing too much for society and those on the "left" say it's not enough.

A fierce battle is taking place between the rights of the accused and the rights of the victim. The accused appears to be winning. To be in style, to be popular, and to be in power, you have to emerge as a part and supporter of the masses. Individualism is no longer rewarded as gallantry. Churches are struggling to exist. Most citizens are discouraged from being ambitious but are rooted wherever they are hoping to survive without participating in massive sociological and cultural adjustments called "changes." The "X" generation has no hope. The "Y" generation, because of their inside track on being born with a computer in their hand and exploring every aspect of technology, may have a better chance. Generation "X" perceives that most positions of status and contribution have been preempted by those ahead of them trying to maintain their status quo. There is obviously a quiet struggle between the "haves" and the "have nots." Many of the "have nots" believe the government should fill the gap. In all of this, one would have to look hard, far, and wide to discover any efforts to better the place from where we have come to where we are going as a society.

More Is Not Always Better but a Little More Is Not Enough

Lawyers have played a major role in the ongoing energy of modern evolution. Modern evolution is not necessarily noted and observed in the manner by which revolution is characterized. Evolution is not anarchy, skullduggery, or wretchedness. Evolution is a silent process stimulated by the quest for continuous changes in existing rights, systems, and values.

Lawyers have been a driving force in a new society that seeks to expand, modify, and force its way for the satisfaction of individuals, and not society, irrespective of cost, the quest for the truth, or the overall good of society.

What Is the Truth?

Many lawyers would suggest the answer to this question, logically, as well as obviously, as depending on which side the lawyer is on. This suggestion probably meets what the general public thinks of lawyers and begs the question, "Where do lawyers 'fit-in' in the search for the truth in the judicial process?" Do lawyers have a duty to search for the truth? Do lawyers have a duty to tell the truth? There are countless treatises and literally millions of words attempting to answer these questions without satisfactory resolve.

You cannot find a wholesome or credible treatise anywhere that suggests that lawyers should lie. However, you should appreciate that there is a difference between "lying" and "telling the truth." Lying implies a deliberateness toward not relating the truth by expressing contrary to that which is known. "Telling the truth" implies a duty to relate, offer, and express that which you know to be true. Can you see the difference? A lawyer may know that his client is guilty of wrong-doing but a lawyer is duty bound to the client not to express that truth because of the confidentiality relationship between a lawyer and a client. On the other hand, a lawyer is likewise duty bound not to allow his client to lie if the lawyer knows the truth. The line between these ideas of "lying" and "not telling the truth" understandably confuses most people about what happens in a lawyer's life.

One question can be approached with a practical and straightforward answer. Lawyers are prohibited by their rules of ethics, called the "Cannons of Ethics," from lying to the court or their clients, as well as allowing their clients to lie to the court. These rules dealing with lawyers have evolved historically based on the experience of the judicial system as one which promotes integrity and honesty in the legal system.

Not a Single Word About Truth

Every lawyer who enters the legal profession raises his or her hand and makes an oath swearing to uphold the duties and responsibilities of being a lawyer. A typical lawyer's oath is to uphold the integrity and honor of the legal profession; to foster and encourage respect for the law, courts, and judges; to honor, respect, and observe the state's Code of Conduct of Professional Responsibility; to act, perform, and serve as member of the legal profession dedicated to public service; to conduct themselves in a manner which would reflect credit on the legal profession; to instill and inspire the confidence, honor, respect, and trust of their clients and the public; and to seek and strive to avoid not only professional impropriety but even the appearance of impropriety; and to uphold the law.

There is not a single word mentioned in the entire oath about a lawyer's relationship to the truth.

A Lawyer's Relationship to the Truth

Lawyers are not supposed to knowingly lie or knowingly allow their clients to lie. However, this proposition raises some very interesting concerns and questions. Most people are prone to tell the truth and do not have to determine what a lie is. There are others who have a broad base of rationalizing around what a lie is. Some are not at all sure what a lie is. There are some who believe that lying is on the far, totally opposite end of where the truth is. People who live in great reverence for the truth believe a lie is any expression other than the truth. What do you think the truth is?

If you are a salesperson and have relevant information the potential customer does not have concerning a product or service, do you have an obligation to relate any adverse information about them to the consumer? Isn't the first question you have to answer, "How relevant is the information you have?" Don't

229

salespeople decide what's fair, right, and justified in dealing with a customer?

Lawyers get caught up in the same maze of obscurity which works mainly to their advantage. Cloudy, fuzzy, vague, and ambiguous meanings are lawyers' friends.

Remember, lawyers are wordsmiths and if given an opportunity, they will use their skill to great advantage in representing their clients. The English language has the largest vocabulary of all the world's languages and dialects. Many words attempt to convey the same or similar meanings. Through usage, application, and custom, many words have acquired meaning other than what was originally intended. A quick review of a thesaurus would convince you of that point. Lawyers use a multiplicity of words to engage in the art and skill of cross-examination of a witness. A witness can be made to look like a truth teller, a liar, or just simply incompetent. A lawyer's job is to represent his client. To do so might require a lawyer to engage in a dialogue with a witness attempting to extract the lawyer's version of the truth and not necessarily what the witness thinks the truth is.

Candidly, a lawyer has no relationship with the truth, except not to intentionally shield or rearrange it. If the truth comes out, happens, or whatever, so be it. Truth is incidental to a lawyer's representation of his client. The lawyer's job is to WIN! Anything to the contrary is a crock and, of course, notwithstanding!

Most of us have gone to school on what happens with lawyers who get mesmerized with their own artistry of words. How could anyone forget that former President Clinton spun the folks of the world around about his obtuse definition of what he thought "sex" was? Let's not even think about indulging in a discussion of what anyone thinks "love" is. Burt Lancaster in the "The Rainmaker" said, "Love is the morning and evening star," which is probably as good a definition as any other depending on how you feel and how you think.

Is Truth As Elusive As Some Would Pretend It Is? Is Truth Merely That Which Lies in the Eye of the Beholder?

Clients pay lawyers to win. Lawyers must work diligently to honor that entrustment of confidence and employment. Lawyers do not seek the truth. They seek to WIN! In spite of this insatiable quest to win, a lawyer must nevertheless honor those rules under the Code of Conduct of Professional Responsibility requiring him to make certain disclosures about the truth. Obviously, one of the prime goals of a lawyer is never, never ever knowingly lie. What a lawyer knows and does not tell often comes under severe scrutiny by a judge. Usually there is considerable difficulty proving that a non-disclosing lawyer knew information he had a duty to disclose.

When Does A Lawyer Have to Tell the Truth?

There is a substantial difference between whether a lawyer is required to "search for the truth" and the position of a lawyer being required to "tell the truth." Lawyers in civil cases are allowed to ask "relevant" questions of the opposing side. The purpose of these questions is to "discover" as much information about the plaintiff or the defendant as possible, which might be used as an advantage against that party. These questions are called "interrogatories" and are usually submitted by each party in a civil lawsuit since interrogatories are not allowed in criminal cases.

The real point of asking these questions to the opposing side is to get information from the party's position in relationship to a particular fact. You probably remember O. J. Simpson's answer in a deposition when he was asked if he had ever worn Bruno Magli shoes. He answered that he had never worn them and later at the trial had to confront pictures showing him wearing this type of shoe. Somewhere between his statement at the deposition and his subsequent confrontation of the pictures at the trial is the truth. Interrogatories and depositions are opportunities for the lawyers on the other side of your lawsuit to trap you into saying something which would be against the best interest of your case. In other words, these are devices that seek to lay a trap to catch you in a "lie." Good lawyers diligently rehearse their clients before the client has to give their deposition.

When asked, a lawyer has to tell the truth as long as the answer does not violate his client's rights and is not a matter of what the courts have termed "work-product." Work-product is that product being produced by a lawyer for his client in the interest of the client's case. In other words, lawyers may keep some secrets from being disclosed but not everything. Your opponent in a lawsuit has the right to know what witnesses you are going to call, those you might call, what exhibits you plan to place in evidence, what experts you plan to have testify, and what they are expected to say, as well as many other inquiries which may be relevant in presentation of the case to the court and jury. The rules of both civil and criminal procedure have evolved substantially away from the old "trial by ambush" days when everything was basically kept a secret and you were often scoured, booed, glued, screwed, and tattooed by what you didn't know and your client didn't tell you. The judicial system has attempted in large part to allay these concerns. However, "ambush" is still a threat when your client testifies from the witness stand and lies. If he testifies that he is not able to bowl, water ski, walk, or run, any evidence may be produced by the opposite side to show facts to the contrary. Often, clients are hoisted on their own petard. The client's lawyer is about as helpless as preventing a lunar eclipse when this happens.

Lawyers get themselves and their clients in deep "dung" when they do not tell the truth when asked. If a lawyer knows his or her client will lie if the client is placed on the stand, the lawyer should not allow the client to testify. Of course, lawyers have the prerogative to believe their clients unless the client is obviously lying. Then, what's so obvious to one is not so obvious to another and here we go again on what's a reasonable interpretation of that which is being interpreted. And so it goes . . .

Ask and the Truth Shall Set You Free

There is much controversy over the nature of truth. If a lawyer knows facts which are adverse to his client's case, no one could argue, really, that he has an obligation to make those facts known. On the other hand, there are those who would argue that the lawyer would be hiding facts and would be participating in a cover-up tantamount to lying. If that were the case and a lawyer would be required to "tell all," the lawyer/client confidential relationship would go out the window. If there was no lawyer/client confidentiality privilege, lawyers would be in a position of adversity with their clients and would subsequently be rendered totally ineffective in protecting the client's rights. There would be a total breakdown of the judicial system, law and order, and all integrity anyone could possibly repose in the overall system. Certain inalienable rights are absolutely necessary for a lawyer/client relationship. Otherwise, the system would be totally inoperative.

Do Lawyers Lie?

Some lawyers believe there is a great difference between not telling the truth and lying. Lawyers, like politicians, are masters at not answering direct questions. Have you noticed politicians or lawyers when confronted by questions beginning with "will," "could," "should," "can," "do," or "would" never answer with a simple "yes" or "no." In response, they engagingly pontificate from a macro perspective about the vast perplexities that the question entails and never seem to even touch the edge of the question. The response is usually unintelligible. Then, the editorial plaudits, aka "spin-doctors," make soup from the strewn carcass.

Skilled responses to the "yes" or "no" question are almost always in avoidance of a direct answer and the characterization of the question. A direct answer invites alienation, disenfranchisement, polarization, or contriteness on the part of someone. Peace at the price of being vague, non-committal, imprecise, and wish-washy is what is usually called for in confrontational environments. The lawyer with his client operates much in same way. The hard questions have hard answers. Does the lawyer really want the client to know about the real difficulty in getting what the client wants? At least, the lawyer does not want the client to know on the front end of the relationship. Otherwise, the client may say, "Before I spend all this money on my lawyer, I might as well forget the whole thing and take my pain." Sometimes, if a lawyer tells a client what the lawyer really thinks, the client will often wonder what they are paying a lawyer for. On the other hand, a lawyer at the beginning of a client relationship may not honestly know what the prognosis of the client's position is until further study and investigation have been concluded. Lawyers may use this same sense of rationalization when dealing with the court, jury, and other lawyers in representing their clients.

Life Is Context, Not Content

The legal process is supposed to represent "life" with its opportunity for justice, equity, fairness, and impartiality. What do these words mean? They mean what you want them to mean. What is Love? What is Peace? What is Justice? What is Equity? What is Fairness? What is Impartiality? And finally, what is Truth? Don't you believe that each of those qualities are what you say they are? There is no standardized and accepted definition for any of them. Of course, they are in a dictionary, but do you recognize each of them when they are observed where they occur? Much of what's done in the legal community revolves around attempting to decide what is right, fair, and just under particular circumstances. Thus, we learn that the content structure of life only goes so far. The balance of what really takes place is a contextual matter resting on the when, what, where, why, who, and how of each factual situation.

The system of courts, justice, lawyers, and the law have a basis for their existence based generally on the United States Constitution, the legislative laws passed in furtherance of it, each state constitution, and those laws passed in support of it. These laws are specific, yet, many are hard to explain, define, and apply. These laws are as close to being "content" in nature as you can get. They are intended to be easily understood and interpreted. Most fall short of their goal. When lawyers, politicians, and other interest holders get finished with their own ideas as to what is meant by the various laws passed, many are confused and find fault with legislative efforts to be exact, descriptive, and clear in their proposed meanings. The point is that little in life has much value outside of its contextual environment. Knowledge of contextual surroundings is one of the most important understandings one can give to the variation of meanings placed on words, laws, and their applications. Lawyers understand the nature of life in its contextual mode. A murder cannot be condoned or forgiven. However, when circumstances are expressed relating to this happening out of a long history of spousal abuse, compassion may alter your perceptions from how you first viewed the killing. The contextual nature of life is where reality is.

The context part of life is the broadest part. When you look at a narrow dimension of just the facts (the content) without putting them in the broader scheme of their environment (the context) you can never have a true picture of the created reality. Lawyers help people explore the context of life where you will discover ideas, things, values, and meaning not hitherto revealed. Lawyers believe the truth lies in the context of situations not merely in the simple content of the event. You must know by now that lawyers don't lie. They indulge in an interpretive agenda of discovery on the outer edge of content evaluation. A lawyer can really believe what he or she believes. What did you honestly see? Some people see different things when they view a car. Do you see a vehicle?

An automobile? Or transportation? Is a truck a vehicle? Is a truck an automobile? If a truck is not an automobile, then, why are trucks and cars both vehicles? Yet, one is an automobile and other is not?

The point is not to play games but to allude to the nature of language and its subjectivity. Language is only subjective because of our need to place words and their meanings in relationship to other words and meanings. This interaction of relationships between words accounts for the contextual nature of life and lawyering. Lawyers are much maligned for their adventure-proneness into the outer limits of perception when dealing with their clients, the courts, and witnesses. Lawyers are looking for their own truth which fits the needs of their client. Often, an inquiry into the perceptions being expressed by testimony from a witness becomes a cat-and-mouse-game with victory being had by the most cunning. Some witnesses have had their memories reconstructed with the able assistance of their lawyer. The ordinary events of life don't signal their arrival by a bell clanging. Witnesses are being probed, prodded, pushed, and questioned about minute details by the lawyer on cross-examination for his client.

And When the Tale Is Told . . .

Lawyers don't knowingly lie but they don't search for the truth within the confines of how you mean the question. Let's back off a bit. Indisputably, some lawyers do lie. Those who would be compelled to lie do not lie consistently. When they do lie it's ordinarily to get their buttocks out of trouble (C.Y.A.—"Cover your assets" or "cover your anatomy").

Ask yourself the question, "Have I ever known anyone to tell the truth when telling a lie would have been to their advantage?" There are some self-righteous readers out there who are probably answering "yes" without thinking. If you are one of those, how big would the advantage have to be to make that person lie?

The story goes that everyone has their price. In an ideal world, everyone is honest and tells the truth. If you want to live and survive in this world of fantasy be sure and live alone. Lawyers know they live in a real world and explore every part of it in search for their truth. A client wants aggressive, competent, and dedicated representation. In the commercial battlefield of legal competition, lawyers are meeting the demands of trying to satisfy their clients.

Give Lawyers Their Due:

Within the judicial and procedural rules,
Within the boundaries of reasonably fair play,
Within some spirit of reflecting credit on the legal profession,
Within his self-serving efforts to minimally cooperate with fellow lawyers,
Within some subliminal determination to exercise a duty to uphold the integrity
and honor of the legal profession, and
Within close avoidance of professional impropriety,
A lawyer will do whatever it takes to WIN!
Isn't that what you, the client, want?
If not, call the milkman or the postman next time you need a lawyer.

A Matter of Denial

Obviously, law practice is different from the practice of medicine, dentistry, or engineering. No two lawyers would describe the practice of law the same while in medicine, dentistry, and engineering there would be gross similarities in the practice, application, and execution of their specialties.

The variety and scope of law practice is diverse. No two lawyers think alike and could easily agree on what law practice is all about. Politicians have the same or at least a similar problem. What politicians do and their purpose is often misconstrued and misperceived by their constituency and politicians themselves. What's the real difference between how politicians and lawyers function and other professionals such as medical doctors, dentists, and engineers? Have you ever considered that there are differences?

Think about this for a moment. Medical doctors, dentists, and engineers have an advantage in their professions. They are frequently given a problem that can readily and more quickly be defined than a lawyer. These professionals rely on their clients and/or patients to give them objective conditions with which they are expected to make a diagnosis, develop a prognosis, and apply some method of application to resolve or solve the immediate problem.

Of course, this is easily recognizable as being extremely too simplistic, unrealistic, and superficial. Truly, there is considerably more depth to their involvement and professional protocol than depicted here. The medical doctor, dentist, and engineer have the advantage of "objective" standardizing. There are established professional rules and science that medical doctors, dentists, and engineers follow to measure, gauge, evaluate, analyze and assess the data they are presented. Any one of these professionals has an objective basis for determining the procedure, application, plan, and treatment of the problem to arrive at an expected solution.

Admittedly, there are some subjective symptoms from the patient involved with a medical doctor but these symptoms are often validated by other methodologies used by the physician. Physicians have methodologies of "case management" protocol as a guide for when and what they do in relationship to their patient.

However, no attempt at in-depth analysis is necessary to make the distinction between what they do and what a lawyer does.

The Practice of Law Is Different

By now, you are seeing the point. The profession of practicing law does not have the advantage of consistently relying on objective data in making an overall assessment of a client's case.

You already know that lawyers don't have such an advantage of extremely well-defined law and carefully honed language to guide them in their endeavor of representing their clients.

If a lawyer's client robs a store with a water pistol, was the store robbed with a dangerous weapon? The criminal statute does not say that a "water pistol" is a dangerous weapon or if you possess it you are considered "armed." Hence, if a court has not ruled that a "water pistol" can be construed as an "armed" or "dangerous weapon," a lawyer must work diligently to convince the court that the "water pistol" was not a "weapon" in terms of what the criminal statute intended.

Lawyers don't have the "hard and fast" rules of science on their side. Engineers have the law of gravity and the law of the hypotenuse triangle on their side. Medical doctors and dentists have the law of molecular structure in their corner. Lawyers have the arena of the human mind with its aura of infinite possibilities firmly entrenched in the lawyers' domain.

Lawyers have a guideline that the law is based on the intent and best possible description of what is being said by legislators using the most precise language possible as the meaning for what the law represents. This concept often goes awry as in the "water pistol" example above.

You can take this discussion almost any direction you choose, from what a former president of the United States, and also a lawyer, who fuzzed up the definition of "sex" by declaring that the sexual relationship he had with a female associate was not "sex" to the massive description and definition of the Affordable Care Act.

What's What

Lawyers have always had considerable difficulty deciding "what's what" in representing their clients. This is not a revelation, a prediction, or recognition of new phenomenon. This is the way the legal profession and its innate law practice has always been.

Law practice is not science nor could it ever be made out to be such because of the diversity, variety, variances, and incongruities of humans and their accompanying conflicts. Conflicts among humans arise because of differences in minds and the disparities between how people think, feel, perceive, act, and believe. The subjectivity of law practice is alive, well, revalidated, and refortified every moment of every gleaming day when humans interact with each other bringing forth their own vision of the world in which all of us are expected to live.

Lawyers are multi-faceted in their thinking. Their mission in life is to think. However, they are extremely all purpose-oriented depending on what's happening to their client. Lawyers wake up every day to a world that is more:

* Subjective than objective
* Contextual than content
* Ambiguous than concrete
* Processed than routine
* Abstract than tangible
* Interpretative than clearly defined
* Pliable than rigid
* Alterable than unalterable
* Impressionistic than regimented
* Perceptional than traditional
* Adaptive than instinctive
* Creative than structured
* Thinking than feeling
* Multi-faceted than singular-faceted
* Multi-dimensional than singular-dimensional
* Complex than simple

- Multi-tasked than singular-tasked
- Extroverted than introverted
- Dominant than docile
- Social than antisocial
- Intellectual than dull
- Flexible than inflexible
- Opinionated than not opinionated

The list could be propagated even further but notice the one thing that each of the compared characterizations has in common: Each of these dimensions of quality and behavior are manifestations of the human mind. A lawyer must be geared to deal with people every day who carry around a complex mindset consisting of values, ideas, and thinking that causes them to be like they are. Each client in the world sees the world from the platform on which they are standing. They each think like they think, feel like they feel, and act like they act regardless of who deems that they should or should not. A lawyer's job is much, much more than anyone who has not trod in a lawyer's shoes would or could ever comprehend.

Down the road after a few years of law practice, there are many lawyers who wonder why they did not choose to become a medical doctor, dentist, an engineer, or even a truck driver.

The Nature of a Lawyer

Lawyers are "object" and purpose-oriented, relative to and depending on what's happening to their client. There is, more often than not, no exact or specified protocol, science, or methodology in how they will respond to a particular situation except to follow the procedures, rules, and structure of the legal profession. The approach, theory, and personal interpretation of what a solution should be remains entirely subjective to the wisdom, experience, and discretion of each individual lawyer. There is latitude, subjectivity, and individualization in what lawyers do but there are no "hard and fast" rules on how to get it done. "What" to do is the threshold question for every lawyer. Other professionals may encounter "threshold" questions in their field but they have been trained much more objectively in answering them than lawyers have.

Lawyers see things, situations, and involvement from a much broader perspective than other professions. The practice of medicine, dentistry, or engineering has a base of measurement by which these professionals practice. In law, no such standard exists. Do lawyers get "second-guessed" by other lawyers? Absolutely! Many lawyers who are not at the helm of a case always think they know how a case should be dealt with more so than the lawyer responsible for the disposition of the case. This is not unusual and follows the same patterns of "hindsight" seen in almost every facet of society and life.

Lawyers are often subjected to whimsical discretions of judges and even juries who often do not see the same interpretations, circumstances, perspectives, and situations as offered in a lawyer's position of advocacy for his or her client. A lawyer's job is typically centered on efforts to place circumstances and the U.F.A.C. (underlying facts and circumstances) of a case in the most favorable perception possible for the client. Lawyers are at the mercy of influences and positions of authority beyond their control and are intensely hopeful they can gain favor through logic, reason, compassion, and understanding, but they know that the lawyer opposite has the same objectives of persuasion using a different set of reasons to gain approval and be convincing.

Some lawyers believe they have to defend what happens in law practice because often the outcome of a case or situation is incongruous with what the lawyer and client expects. This disparity between "expectations" and "results" causes some lawyers to deny the subjectivity of the law practice process. The world looks for reasonable explanations for why things are the way they are. Sometimes, there are just no good answers.

A judge's discretion in rulings, decision making, and renderings is based on his experiences and, hopefully, his knowledge of the law. However, any application of the law by the judge or a jury is founded and premised on a "finding of fact." Facts, as we all know, are manifestations in the "eye of the beholder." Facts are not always obvious because of the context in which they exist.

Black vs. White vs. Gray

Lawyers often have the dubious task of making what appears to be "black and white" the color "gray." Most lawyers do not like to think of this idea as their task as a lawyer. In fact, most lawyers would "deny" this idea as being superficial and not representative of a "search for the truth" to establish or promote justice. A lawyer's job is to test the foundation of facts upon which truth should be based.

On the side of what lawyers do, consider that all positions of physical assessment, until challenged, represent themselves as "facts." Many "facts" that arrive void of unchallenged scrutiny remain as such regardless of how untenable they are or may be.

Once upon a time, many considered the earth to be flat and/or square before this position was challenged. Because this position was challenged, we now know the truth.

Assumptions give rise to untruths but they remain and retain their nature until shown otherwise. Any assumption in the practice of law will never lie dormant and quietly unchallenged. The nature of a lawyer and the culture of law practice dictates—if not demands—that any foundation for belief be critically shaken if any person's liberty, equity, or any kind of justice depends on such position. This is simply what lawyers do. It's their nature!

This challenge as to what might or might not be true is what lawyers do as a part of their purpose.

CHAPTER 15

RULES, RULES, AND MORE RULES . . .

W*hat Your Lawyer May Not Want You to Know!* and its author would be extremely remiss if there was not some attempt to address one of the most complicated and ambiguous matters in the practice of law.

Surprisingly, this subject is not the law, or the way it manifests itself into the system of justice, order, civility, equity, and discipline of the profession. No, it's all about behavior. That part of the human organism is usually evidenced by what humans say through communication and how they behave in relationship to one another. People generally communicate in the manner in which they behave. Others have said that we all behave in the manner in which we communicate. Which is correct? Maybe it doesn't matter as long as we understand that behavior and communication are inseparable, concurrent, and manifest themselves as one entity. Many years went by before there was any effort given to the "standardization" and modeling of a lawyer's behavior. Now, there is an effort to unify behavior within the bounds of the "Model Rules of Professional Conduct."

The Model Rules of Professional Conduct

Consequentially, the behavior of lawyers is measured by a promulgation of rules called the "Model Rules of Professional Conduct." This very lengthy compilation of rules for lawyers' behavior toward clients, the public, and other lawyers consists of 336 pages outlining how lawyers are supposed, proposed, and intended to act as professionals.

These rules have tediously evolved over a period of time since 1977 in an effort to define, illustrate, and clarify how lawyers should conduct themselves in the practice of law. These rules can be studied and evaluated by going to the American Bar Association website at www.americanbar.org.When you go to this site, click on "Resources for Lawyers." This will produce a list of subjects for you to examine. Under "Ethics and Professionalism," click on "Model Rules of Professional Conduct." On the next page under the category of "State Adoption of Model Rules," you will see "Links to State Ethic Rules." When you click on "Links to State Ethics Rules," you will see your state listed as having adopted the "Model Rules of Professional Conduct." There you will have all the rules and "comments" on each of the rules.

The "Model Rules of Professional Conduct" is a resource for lawyers and clients on the order of a Bible of information for lawyer ethics. These "Rules," with some slight variations, have been adopted in 50 jurisdictions. Federal, state, and local courts in all jurisdictions look to the "Rules" for guidance in resolving lawyer malpractice cases, disciplinary actions, disqualification issues, sanctions, and questions of conflict that may arise in the daily practice of lawyers dealing with courts, clients, and other lawyers.

Each of the "Rules" is accompanied by "Comments" that explain each "Rule's" purpose and provide suggestions for its practical application. The "Rules" will help you identify proper conduct in many different situations, review those instances where discretionary action is possible, and define the nature of the relationship between you and your clients, other lawyers, and the courts.

The "Conduct" rules pertaining and applying to the lawyer/client relationship are contained in the "Rules" down to rule 1.8. Here is how the entire list of "Conduct" rules appear:

INDEX FOR THE MODEL RULES OF PROFESSIONAL CONDUCT

Table of Contents

Rules

Client-Lawyer Relationship

Counselor

Advocate

Transactions with Persons Other Than Clients

Law Firms and Associations

Public Service

Information About Legal Services

Maintaining the Integrity of the Profession

An Incredible Undertaking

This is an incredible amount for everyone to remember, learn, or read. No lawyer knows all of these "Rules of Model Conduct." In fact, these rules frequently evolve over time so they can be understood and be used more practically in governing the relationships of lawyers. When you find your state ethics rules, you may be surprised learn that there is a part of the presentation of each rule which alludes to "comments." These "comments" have been made over time to help clarify what the rule means and how it exists in application. You may be asking the question as to why this would be necessary since the rule is succinctly stated for its use and understanding. That's just the point! Lawyers are not always sure what the meaning of meaning is. You and I can easily disagree as to what the familiar terms of reasonable, simple, and fair are supposed to mean. Beauty and meaning of almost everything is in the eye of the beholder.

Many words we use in life are intended to express meaning to levels of quality such as liberty, freedom, fairness, beauty, diligence, and reasonableness. What those words mean to you may be completely and diametrically opposed to what someone else thinks they mean.

The history of the human race, mankind, civilization, or whatever you want to call it, has had its major conflicts over the use and misuse of language. Nothing has changed in the last two thousand years and the prospects for change in the better use of language is considerably less than optimistic. Consequently, we all must struggle to deal with the ambiguity, vagueness, and uncertainty in our use of language. As our world becomes more diverse, our lives through language also become more diverse.

A Blessing or a Curse

The use of language can be an ally, a curse, or a blessing. Once you appreciate the variances in the use of language, you are better equipped to deal with understandings and misunderstandings that are derived from our attempted use of common language. The pain involved in the continued misuse of language as a vehicle to get what we want will continue as we become more diversified across our world culture. The only hope we have to make our lives better and avoid conflict is to be more conscious of the consequences of our malapropism. Language can be a sword or a shield. This has always been the case, since mankind uttered the first words. A natural position of behooving would be for each of us to make an endeavor to be more critical in carving out every word before we let it fall.

CHAPTER 16

A FEW IDEAS ABOUT LAWYERS (CONCLUDING REMARKS)

"What you think you know may
not be any basis for believing
that you do."—BFB

"Some lawyers are like dogs;
some know when to bark and
others do not."—BFB

"Lawyers are guardians of the
people against unreasonable
and arbitrary behavior; some
of the time, unfortunately, this
behavior comes from your lawyer."—BFB

From where you sit, how do you view lawyers? Many have paradoxical good and bad feelings depending on the circumstances. Attitudes about lawyers seem to be good if your lawyer is doing what you expect him or her to do. A general attitude concerning lawyers, when you are not being represented by one, leans more on being critical of the legal profession. This cynicism appears to evolve around some aspect of "excess." Either lawyers are excessively greedy, excessively dilatory, excessively arrogant, or excessively untrustworthy. People have a tendency to be critical about things they don't understand. Consequently, most people don't understand lawyers and what lawyers do.

Lawyers Do Have Some Idiosyncrasies

Idyllically, lawyers should be just like everyone else. They're not! All lawyers have a philosophy of life which is totally incomparable to yours. You do not engage in a direct, adversarial, and confrontational relationship for a living. You get some of that but on a less frequent basis and are able to pick your spots where you allow this kind of tension to enter your life. Lawyers seldom get a choice. They don't normally pick the clients who come to their door. They usually have little choice over case delays. To understand a lawyer, you must have some appreciation of what a lawyer does, how a lawyer thinks, how a lawyer acts, and why they do what they do.

There Are No Easy Answers

When questions appear to be easily answered, the answers are not always the correct ones. Most questions asked about lawyers have no easy answers. What some clients believe about their lawyer is not all, or even reasonably close, to what the lawyer thinks about himself. Just as there are as many different personalities as there are people, there are as many different types of lawyers as there are lawyers. Every lawyer has their own philosophy of how they should operate and conduct business in the legal profession.

Most often, a great divergence of opinion between lawyers is over when a lawyer's conduct can be reasonably construed as effective representation. Some lawyers deplore the conduct of other lawyers. Some lawyers play and perform strictly inside the rules. There are others who push outside the lines as much as possible. Then, there are others who have little, if any, regard for where the line is.

Some Common Ideas About Lawyers

Some lawyers don't believe in telling the client too much about the case to avoid the potential concern of the client thinking he can solve his own case.

Some lawyers never want their clients to perceive the legal aspects of representation as easy, simple, or quick. A lawyer's ego often demands that he look intelligent, powerful, and wise.

Many lawyers believe in displaying an air of mystique while trying to convince the client that the lawyer can solve the problem competently and effectively. After listening to their lawyer, many clients believe that their legal problem is much more complicated than it is.

Some lawyers believe in expressing to the client a prognosis of desired outcome. This is always based on some reasonable probability and conditioned on the occurrence of a number of contingencies, all of which are beyond the control of the lawyer or the client.

Some lawyers believe clients do not care if a lawyer is honest or not as long as the lawyer is honest with them.

Some lawyers believe the legal profession operates in an arena of inexactness, uncertainty, and minimal predictability. The more a lawyer fails to advise and remind a client about the incalculability of payoffs, the closer a lawyer comes in failing to meet a client's expectations of a specific end result.

Some lawyers believe they can not reasonably and fairly predict the outcome of many legal situations any better than 50/50 and that clients don't want to be told of such average chances of success. Some lawyers try to counterbalance reality for an even chance of recovery or overstate to the client their true feelings concerning the potential of the case. The most serious question confronting a lawyer is at what point he tells the client that his or her case is a "crap shoot."

Some lawyers believe and recognize the value of "home cooking" as the strongest influence a client can have on his or her side. Some cases lend themselves to "home cooking." Others don't. A good lawyer knows when it's available. Often "home cooking" is better than having a good case.

Some lawyers highly value postponement in confronting a legal issue as the strongest position of defense available for a client. Some lawyers believe the longer and more times a case or legal issue is postponed, there is a lessening of interest in pursuit of the issue by the one who is seeking satisfaction. People eventually wear out and lose their interest! Some lawyers believe in the idea of all interest in anything dissipating and weakening over time. Eventually clients simply get tired of the chase and will settle for less than what they originally expected.

Some lawyers realize, mainly after the fact, they should have never taken certain types of cases and represented certain troublesome clients. The illusion of "big bucks" most often precedes the reality of getting less.

Some lawyers take "loser" cases and clients they don't like in a time of temporary weakness because of the unrealistic hope of being able to quickly "make a buck."

Some lawyers appreciate the reality of "any money earned quickly is not well-earned." There is seldom a "quick buck."

Some lawyers believe that many lawyers, in order to get away from an undesirable client or a "loser" case or both, would give the client his or her money back in a "heartbeat," if it were possible to do so without exposing the lawyer to the critical query of another lawyer concerning what he did or did not do on the case. (Remember, lawyers are always concerned about "C.Y.A.")

Some lawyers believe when you get a "loser" personal injury case, there is considerable difficulty getting another lawyer to take the case. Therefore, they look for a young, inexperienced, "green-horn" lawyer fresh out of law school to pass the case on to who hopefully won't know the difference between a good and a bad case.

Some Lawyer Tips to Think About:

- Lawyers are considerably different than what you think they are.
- Lawyers are likely to be how you see them than what they tell you they are.
- Most people find great mystery in what they don't understand and find little mystery in what they don't agree to.
- What a lawyer is speaks so loudly you cannot usually hear what they are trying to say.
- The tragedy of humanity is the treatment of mankind which should not be aggravated or perpetuated when you are represented by a lawyer.
- The life of a lawyer is dealing with conflict between humans each believing they are correct.
- Do not fight with your lawyer; regardless of who you are, unless you are a lawyer, you are unprepared and unarmed.
- The safest position in any conflict is non-involvement.
- When a lawyer is confronted with an opportunity to honestly express his or her love in life, most of the time it's toward himself or herself.
- If there were no conflicts in life, there would only be a few lawyers to console those who only thought they had a legal problem.
- Many lawyers work for bragging rights.
- Lawyers should be allowed to toot their own horn but not loudly or too often.
- Lawyer's Embellishment Justification Theory: Most lawyers' stories are so boring that otherwise no one would want to listen.
- Lawyers see clients these days who when asked, "Who do you want to sue?" candidly respond, "It really doesn't matter!"

- Legal advice is much like cough syrup; it only works when you take it.
- Lawyers who are arrogant are almost always consistently arrogant; however, when they are not, they are cordially condescending.
- Many clients fail to tell their lawyers everything on the theory of justification—the lawyer already knows.
- The reason many lawyers are like they are is that they spend most of their time trying to be right since that's what their clients are paying for.
- To most lawyers, being right means winning their case.
- Final Resolution Theory: The more you pursue a long-sought goal without accomplishing it, the more you will be inclined to eventually accept whatever you can get. (Most lawyers know this!)
- People should employ lawyers because of their own ignorance and not because of their stupidity.
- One of the most important conditions for lawyers in life is having someone else to blame for the poor outcome in representing a client. (Remember, it's always someone else's fault!)
- The Lawyer's Credit Creed: Take credit for good results regardless of what reason they exist. Blame anyone else who had any relationship with the case if the representation results in a poor outcome.
- Lawyers who are rude, ugly, impatient, and inconsiderate have discovered this kind of behavior to be more natural than being otherwise.
- The Lawyer's Dilemma: Had I rather be loved by some or feared by everyone?
- Whether a lawyer is a skunk or not depends on whose lawyer you are talking about.

The list could go on and without any doubt you can think of many ideas and expressions about lawyers which would be appropriate as advice, a quip, or a quote concerning the most controversial profession ever. Unless you have begun to understand the legal profession and the nature of lawyers, these clear admonitions will have little meaning. Understanding lawyers and the legal profession is your hope of bridging the gap of inequality between you and the skills of your lawyer.

The Story Is Far From Over . . .

What you have learned in this book about lawyers and the legal profession represents only a scintilla of what can be learned by clients. Often lawyers don't understand their own profession because lawyers are not taught how to practice law in law schools. Such a statement is inflammatory to law schools and you can understand why. Most assuredly, no one could learn how to practice law by going to law school for three years. Relate this same situation to the medical profession. Doctors, after medical school, go through periods of residency and internship during which they actually begin the practice of medicine under the watchful eye of a supervisor. During these years they begin to learn about the practice of medicine. Getting the technical information in a profession does not qualify you to practice that profession. Of course, you may acquire a license to engage in the profession but often that's a far cry from being qualified.

A law school spends three years teaching a student how to think, problem solve, and analyze while being exposed to the broad culture of the history of law. Law professors should not be slighted with this sweeping assessment. In some courses, you learn rules of procedure and some specific information about some written areas of the law. But for most of the journey through law school, you learn broad and general theories of the law. When you get out in the law practice arena, you quickly learn that application is the key to survival.

Notwithstanding that, you may leave school a brilliant scholar, but you will have only a meager grasp of how to practice law. This should not be a surprise to a client and is certainly no surprise to lawyers. Because of a lawyer's exposure to the academic side of the legal profession, you should not be fooled into believing that a young starting lawyer is severely handicapped when entering the practice of law.

A Lawyer's Learning Curve

Lawyers, on the whole, are quick learners. They are, by and large, bright intelligent people who have an ability to quickly grasp information and apply that data to situations. Lawyers are adaptable. They have learned something in law school because of their training under a baptism of fire, confrontation, and tension, defending themselves for three years as to whether they were worthy of graduating. A lawyer must continuously qualify to stay in law school and to graduate.

Law schools take a great amount of pride in their product. Law schools make every effort to establish academic, ethical, and moral standards which are applied consistently to weed out those unworthy. Some slip through, but they slip through in every profession. The test and trial of the marketplace takes care of those most of the time. Sometimes, it doesn't and those who meet minimal standards of skill, ethics, or morality operate with their inherent deficiencies to stink up the reputation of lawyers. This element wreaks havoc in the profession. They are usually small in number but cause the most problems. Good, ethical lawyers have to deal with them and sometimes fire is fought with fire.

You may get the picture of lawyers being mass produced, to the extent that there's a lawyer for approximately every 330 people in the United States. Lawyers are feverishly fighting for survival because of competition, excess litigation, and pure hard adversity with clients and other lawyers. This competitiveness has promoted an aggressive litigious environment. Older lawyers are experiencing a new paradigm in their law practice. The new lawyers are drawing their swords early in the scheme of conflict and are not prepared to take any prisoners. Win/win seems no longer to be an agenda item. Victory is viciously pursued until the resolve has reached an indisputable position rendering a Winner and a Loser.

Admittedly, this all sounds hard and unrealistic, but each individual in the system has a sense of survival that often dictates extremism and aggressiveness to produce the desired requirement of survival. Otherwise, an advocate may go unnoticed and unacknowledged by clients as well as other lawyers. You can appreciate this characterization by asking yourself, "If I had a serious legal problem, would I hire a lawyer who would do whatever was necessary to win even if it meant breaking the rules?" or "Would I hire a lawyer who worked only within the rules of fair play?"

More and more lawyers are being pressured to win. Some are willing to win at great risk of moving across the line of fair play. A similar analogy could be used where in some parts of the world there are too many dogs and not enough food.

Where You Have Been and the Rest of the Story

For a brief time you have been on a ride through "Lawyerville," USA, taking a look at how lawyers act, a little of what they do, and an overview philosophy of the legal profession. Many holes have remained unfilled. Many roads were not traveled. Many sites were not seen. Honestly, there was just too much to see on the first trip. In fact, you only got to visit, meet, and hire your lawyer. You never actually got out of his office. You really aren't sure what to expect from this point, are you? There is much more you need to hear and see since this could be the ride of your life.

At this point, you have discovered *What Your Lawyer May Not Want You to Know*. You may now have a variety of ideas that may be helpful to you in working with your lawyer. You are better informed than before you started the journey through "Lawyerville." There are some things you still need to know concerning your lawyer and what he is doing in your case.

Meanwhile, you will be made only one promise. You will not be left on the roadside wondering what you need to know next. *More of What Your Lawyer May Not Want You to Know*, Book II, is on the way.

Until that time, use this book as your safety net with your lawyer. The presence of this book under your arm, in your hand, or just a casual reference to it will allow your lawyer to appreciate you as an informed client. As a result of your information, your lawyer knows that you have been "foretold" which serves as a "forewarning" to him that you know your rights, duties, and responsibilities as a client. You now have knowledge of what to expect in the lawyer/client partnership and your lawyer's acknowledging your understanding will lead and promote a lawyer's efforts in meeting your expectations as a client.

Appendix A

T he word "typical" is largely a contradiction since there
are so many various forms and multiple uses of different
wordings. But for your use, study, and reference the
agreement below is offered as a "typical" agreement. Please use
this agreement as the comparative reference in evaluating what
an agreement should include as suggested in Chapter 12, "Paying
the Piper."

Lawyer's Retainer and Fee Agreement

THIS AGREEMENT is made on this the ____ day of _____,
19____ by and between _____ herein after designated
as the CLIENT and (Larry Legal Lawyer) hereinafter designated
as the LAWYER. This agreement of employment between the
CLIENT and the LAWYER shall include the following terms and
conditions, to wit:

1. STATEMENT & SUBJECT OF EMPLOYMENT: The CLIENT,
    in consideration of services to be rendered by the LAWYER
    for the CLIENT, hires, retains, and employs the LAWYER to
    represent him/her as their LAWYER in connection with the
    situation involving:

_____

_____

2. ASSOCIATE OTHER LAWYERS: The CLIENT understands
    and agrees the LAWYER may, in his/her sole discretion,
    associate, hire, and employ other lawyers in representing the

CLIENT to assist in the pursuit, prosecution, and processing of the CLIENT'S claim at no additional expense to the CLIENT other than what is contained in paragraphs 3 and 5 below.

3. COSTS & OTHER EXPENSES: The CLIENT understands and agrees that the LAWYER may, in his/her sole discretion, employ experts, investigators, and incur expenses, for and in behalf of the CLIENT, such as photocopying, transcripts, depositions, telephone calls, filing fees, service of process fees, and travel expenses. In the event, the LAWYER pays such amounts, the CLIENT agrees that the LAWYER may be reimbursed from any gross recovery received from the CLIENT'S case. The LAWYER may request for the CLIENT to advance in part or in full any amounts necessary to cover the cost incurred or to be incurred in this paragraph.

4. LAWYER'S LIEN: The CLIENT hereby gives the LAWYER a lien on the CLIENT'S claim, cause of action and any sums that may be received or recovered for the LAWYER'S fee and all costs expended as covered in this agreement. The CLIENT understands and agrees that he/she will make not settlement of the claim or accept any sum or other consideration as compensation or reimbursement for any claim unless the LAWYER is present and receives his/her contingency fee share in accordance with paragraph 5 below and the cost & other expenses as contained in paragraph 3 above.

5. CONTINGENCY FEE PROVISIONS: LAWYER'S fees are not set by law, but are the result of negotiations between the LAWYER and the CLIENT. The contingency fee is different between lawyers but the majority of contingency fees range between 33 1/3% to 40%. Some fees run as high as 50% on unusual cases where there is a serious doubt about potential recovery. In connection and relationship to the CLIENT'S claim the LAWYER agrees, in lieu of charging an hourly fee, to charge the CLIENT for his/her services an amount of 33 1/3% of any amount received or recovered if the case or claim is settled without a lawsuit filed, or 40% of any amounts received or recovered if the matter is settled after a lawsuit is

filed. The contingency fee shall be based on the amount of the GROSS RECOVERY. The CLIENT agrees that this contingency fee agreement shall be binding on their heirs, executors, and legal representatives.

6. POWER OF ATTORNEY: The CLIENT hereby gives the LAWYER a POWER OF ATTORNEY to file any legal actions or lawsuits that may necessary; to execute all documents connected with the CLIENT'S claim which shall include pleadings, contracts, settlement agreements, releases, dismissals, orders; and all other documents that the CLIENT could properly execute. However, CLIENT reserves the right to approve any document or pleading before such is filed.

7. SCOPE OF SERVICES: The CLIENT understands and agrees that the services contemplated herein do not include an appeal of the CLIENT'S case or claim. If an appeal should be necessary, a new and separate agreement between the LAWYER and the CLIENT shall be necessary to establish the LAWYER'S fees for such services. The CLIENT understands and agrees that the fees herein relate only to the immediate action, and do not include any legal services which have to be rendered to settle or resolve other issues which may arise out of or in some manner be related to this action contemplated in this agreement.

8. FAVORABLE OUTCOME NOT GUARANTEED: The CLIENT acknowledges that the LAWYER has made NO PROMISE OR GUARANTEE as to the successful outcome of their case or claim, nor any prediction relating to the outcome of the CLIENT'S case.

9. COOPERATION BY CLIENT: The CLIENT agrees that he/she will keep the LAWYER advised of his/her whereabouts at all times, appear on reasonable notice at any trial or hearing, or other legal proceedings as requested by the LAWYER, and to comply with all reasonable requests in connection with the preparation and presentation of the CLIENT'S case or claim. The CLIENT also acknowledges that such request to cooperate by their LAWYER may interfere with or take away substantial

time from their personal, business, and professional affairs. BOTH THE LAWYER AND THE CLIENT will use their best efforts in furthering the purposes of this agreement and in obtaining the necessary evidence and the attendance of witnesses relating to the case or claim.

10. SUBSTITUTION OR DISCHARGE OF LAWYER: The CLIENT shall retain the right to terminate the services of the LAWYER at any time for good reason. However, should the CLIENT discharge the LAWYER prior to the time a recovery is received he/she will be responsible for paying the LAWYER the reasonable value of their services based on the hours expended in behalf of the CLIENT, the legal and financial complexity of the case or claim and the experience, reputation and ability the LAWYER, together with all expenses incurred by the LAWYER at the time of such termination.

11. WITHDRAWAL FROM CASE BY THE LAWYER: The LAWYER shall retain the right to resign as legal counsel at any time for any of the following reasons: a. if CLIENT fails or refuses to cooperate fully, directly, or indirectly in any manner with the LAWYER in failing to supply written or oral documentation, evidence or assistance as requested by the LAWYER; b. if the CLIENT misleads the LAWYER, directly or indirectly, regarding any material fact; or c. if after through investigation of the CLIENT'S case or claim by the LAWYER, the LAWYER determines, in his/her opinion that the CLIENT'S claim does not have merit.

12. THIS AGREEMENT REPRESENTS THE UNDERSTANDING: The LAWYER and the CLIENT both agree that this agreement represents the entire contract between the parties and that no other understandings, agreements, conditions, terms, or representations have been made. The LAWYER and the CLIENT agree that no such covenants exist and any other ideas, suggestions, speculations, or conjecture are notwithstanding and have no influence, force and effect to the understanding between the parties expressed herein.

I, THE UNDERSIGNED CLIENT, HAVE READ, UNDERSTOOD AND AGREED TO EACH OF THE FOREGOING PARAGRAPHS EXPRESSING THE TERMS, CONDITIONS AND MY UNDERSTANDING OF THIS AGREEMENT. IN WITNESS TO MY AGREEING AND UNDERSTANDING OF THIS "LAWYER'S RETAINER AND FEE AGREEMENT", I AM SUBSCRIBING MY SIGNATURE BELOW ON THIS THE DAY OF _____,20____.

_____
CLIENT

I, THE UNDERSIGNED LAWYER, DO HEREBY ACCEPT REPRESENTATION OF THE CLIENT ON THE TERMS AND CONDITIONS AS HEREIN EXPRESSED ON THIS THE ____DAY OF _____, 20____

_____
LAWYER

APPENDIX B

WHAT CAN YOU PRACTICALLY AND REASONABLY EXPECT FROM YOUR LAWYER?

1. To have your telephone calls returned within 24 hours unless he/she is out of town, unavailable, or in court. If your lawyer does not call you back within 24 hours, you should be able to expect that his/her office would call you back to advise of the situation.

2. To receive a prompt response to all correspondence you have addressed to your lawyer. If promptness is not delivered, you should be advised by his/office when you may expect a response and be given the reasons for the delay.

3. To be furnished a copy of your written fee agreement at the time of your signing it irrespective of the size of the fee, the nature of the case, or the number of pages contained in the agreement.

4. To be provided a copy of everything in your file regardless of what it is, which may include photographs, statements of witnesses, depositions, research, traffic accident reports, correspondence, case pleadings, expert witness reports, list of current expenses expended on your case, and your lawyer's chronology of accomplishment and progress in your case.

5. To be provided a totally documented scenario complied chronologically of everything your lawyer has performed and accomplished in your case on a regular basis.

6. To be promised absolutely no potential outcome of your case. A lawyer suggesting that you have a good case is not predicting the outcome of the case. Be wary of a lawyer who attempts to equate the value of your case in dollars and cents on your first visit to a lawyer.

7. To be kept informed about everything in the case and a status report about when the case will come to trial, when the case is delayed, and for what reasons.
8. To be provided a written detailed explanation for all expenses incurred for work performed in behalf of the client.
9. To never have your case or claim settled without your expressed written consent. Permission for your lawyer to settle your case should always be given in writing.
10. To be provided with a complete copy of your file with all original documents if you fire your lawyer. A lawyer may not hold up giving you your file back because you owe money for lawyer's fees or expenses.

APPENDIX C

LEGAL FEES: TEN THINGS YOUR LAWYER MAY NOT WANT YOU TO KNOW

Americans spend over $100 billion in legal fees every year. Fees have increased at double the rate of inflation since 1990, and have shown no signs of slowing down despite a sluggish economy. While most of these fees are collected by ethical attorneys providing valuable, efficient services to their clients, many fees are paid after incompetent lawyering, purposeful padding of bills, ethical violations, or improperly coerced collections. This article provides ten tips for clients who believe their lawyer has over-billed them.

At first glance, the prospect of fighting your lawyer over the propriety of his fees may seem like a daunting task. You are likely to be dependant on your lawyer to represent your interests in ongoing matters. If the representation is over, you may feel compelled to pay outstanding bills, even if they are outrageous, since your lawyer is the last person you want as an adversary in litigation. You recognize that your lawyer possesses superior knowledge about the legal system that will determine any billing dispute. Even if the lawyer was an incompetent sloth in representing your interests, you figure he will probably turn into a 21st century "Matlock" if he has to collect his fees. Spending money on another lawyer—assuming you could even find one willing to oppose another lawyer's fee request—does not appeal to you. Finally, you may feel that the legal system will protect its own, and uphold the fee with little regard for the facts of your case.

For the client who receives an unreasonably high bill that is the result of unethical lawyering, waste or incompetence, these concerns can be overcome with a sensible, managed approach. There are steps you can take both during and after the engagement to communicate your concerns to your lawyer.

Appropriate questioning of bills often leads to a mutually-agreed upon reduction, and can even strengthen the attorney-client relationship. Should all else fail, fee dispute litigation provides substantial relief from some relatively common examples of attorney overbilling, while protecting an attorney's right to a reasonable fee. Ten points for clients to consider:

1. The Retention Letter Or Agreement Cannot Be Used To Justify An Unreasonable Fee

Lawyers will often refer to agreements they have with clients, typically drafted by the lawyer at the beginning of the engagement, as evidence that a client agreed to certain payment terms. For example, there may be agreement as to hourly rates, staffing, or contemplated courses of action. These provisions will be enforced, but only to the extent that the agreement is fairly negotiated, and the fee is reasonable under the circumstances. If either the agreement or the fee is later found by a court to be unfair, the court may either impose a smaller fee or disallow the fee in its entirety. Courts recognize that clients seldom have the experience or the inclination to negotiate every detail of their engagement agreement. Lawyers have form agreements that clients typically sign with little or no explanation, much less negotiation.

In an effort to ensure that lawyers do not use superior experience or negotiating skills in drafting agreements with their clients, the Code of Professional Conduct and Responsibility that applies to all lawyers in New York State (other states have similar or identical codes) provides that an attorney "shall not enter into an agreement for, charge or collect an illegal or excessive fee." DR 2-106[A].

2. Any Promises Made By A Lawyer To A Client Will Be Enforced

While promises to a lawyer may be reviewed by a court, promises to a client will almost always be enforced. Despite this, lawyers often tell their clients they are entitled to a "bonus" over the agreed-upon fee because the matter has become more difficult than expected or because of an unexpectedly favorable result. It is common for such a lawyer to "negotiate" the increased fee in the middle of an engagement. Courts and bar associations will review such "negotiations" for evidence that the attorney asserted improper leverage.

You should not feel compelled to pay your lawyer more than what you agreed to pay him. Of course, there is nothing wrong with paying the lawyer a bonus to reward work well-done, but this is the client's call.

3. Diligence In Reviewing A Bill Can Save Money

Clients are best served by addressing a fee problem sooner rather than later. Good and honest lawyers will explain why your bill says what it says. They will admit mistakes if warranted, and suggest ways to minimize costs without jeopardizing results going forward. If your lawyer is unwilling to discuss the bills, you should put your concerns in writing, and consider ending the relationship.

The downside of not raising billing concerns with your lawyer is substantial. You lose the chance to obtain a mutually-agreed upon reduction. The billing practice that offends you will no doubt continue. Finally, if the fee dispute ever gets litigated or arbitrated, your lawyer will claim that you consented to the disputed billing practice.

4. Courts Have Invalidated Many Methods Of Attorney Billing In Recent Years

While a summary of the law surrounding legal fees is well beyond the scope of this article, a steady stream of state and federal court decisions in recent years have invalidated certain billing practices that are still relatively common. Some examples of billing practices often found to be improper:

Overhead, administrative charges, and clerical services. Unless specified in the retainer agreement or other agreement, you should not have hourly charges for non-legal personnel such as photocopy operators, secretaries, messengers, librarians or receptionists. Nor should you be paying for heating, air conditioning or word processing;

- Time spent on billing and collections. For example, if you call your lawyer to discuss your bill, and you see that call reflected on your next bill;
- Bills that have not been itemized to reflect services rendered. If you are being billed by the hour, you have a right to a bill that shows what your lawyer was doing, and when he was doing it;
- Excessive time to complete a task. While this can be subjective, courts have not hesitated to use their legal expertise to declare work on a given matter to be excessive;
- Excessive staffing of a case or transaction. From a law firm's perspective, the more people billing, the better. Courts may evaluate a matter and determine whether the staffing was reasonable or excessive;
- Not enough delegation. Where a senior partner is billing at sky-high rates but spending a lot of time on routine legal work, such as preparing filings or reviewing documents, a Court may find that the bill is allowable, but at a lower rate;
- Evidence of double-billing. This is where a lawyer bills two or more clients for the same effort;
- Unannounced hourly rate increases;
- Time spent on training new lawyers, or lawyers unfamiliar with a certain field of law; and
- Undisclosed mark-ups on "contract" or "temp" lawyers hired by the law firm.

5. A Lawyer Cannot Necessarily Quit Representing You Because Of A Fee Dispute

Lawyers will often threaten to withdraw from a case or transaction when a client misses a payment or two. The client than has two potentially unpleasant options—either pay the lawyer what is possibly an unreasonable fee or spend even more money to hire another lawyer and get the second lawyer up to speed for the representation. A savvy client may consider a third option—state a written objection to the reasonableness of the fee, pay some reasonable portion if warranted, and ask that the lawyer continue with the representation.

Lawyers do not have an automatic right to stop representing a client in the event of a fee dispute. Model Rule of Professional Conduct 1.16, which applies in New York and many other jurisdictions, permits a lawyer to withdraw if "the client fails substantially to fulfill an obligation to the lawyer regarding the lawyer's services and has been given a reasonable warning that the lawyer will withdraw unless the obligation is fulfilled." Since the client is only obliged to pay the portion of the attorney's fee that is reasonable, a lawyer cannot cease representing a client because of a client's refusal to pay an unreasonable or excessive fee.

Of course, if you believe you have been overbilled, you may wish to fire your attorney, or the relationship may be soured on both ends to the extent that it does not make sense to continue. However, keeping your lawyer may be preferable to trying to find another one—the lawyer will have fiduciary responsibilities, malpractice exposure, and a duty of zealous representation as long as he represents you.

6. A Lawyer Is Strictly Limited In What He Can Do To Collect His Fee

Like other businesses and professions, attorneys can take steps to collect accounts receivable. However, the lawyer's unique role as fiduciary and legal advisor subject him to more limitations on their conduct than other professionals.

A New York State ethics opinion prohibits lawyers from hiring a credit bureau to collect their accounts receivable. Moreover, a lawyer cannot use information learned during the course of the attorney-client relationship to apply pressure on a client for payment. Exceptions to this rule apply in attorney fee litigation and malpractice disputes, as the attorney can reveal information as necessary to defend himself or his fee. A lawyer is also prohibited from misleading the client into thinking that the lawyer's claim for fees will prevail in fee dispute litigation.

Lawyers frequently try to coerce payment by asserting an "attorneys' lien" on all or part of a former client's case file pending receipt of payment. Depending on whether the case or transaction is over, this can leave the client in the unenviable position of having to pay the fee to get much-needed papers for an ongoing legal matter. However, in practice a client operating in good faith has little to fear. If the client has a need for the documents in an ongoing matter, and a good faith basis for not paying a portion of the fee, lawyers cannot withhold critical papers. Even after the attorney-client relationship is over, the lawyer has a duty to assist in an orderly transition to replacement counsel to minimize prejudice to his former client.

7. A Lawyer Has Many More Reasons Than A Client To Avoid
    Fee Dispute Litigation

This does not suggest that fee dispute litigation is fun for anybody. Both sides should seek to settle such disputes whenever possible. Clients should certainly avoid fee litigation where they do not believe they have a strong case, or the amounts in dispute are not worth the effort. Lawyers have a right to make a living. Clients also run a substantial risk of losing a fee dispute, and paying the entire fee plus whatever fees they incurred in the fee dispute litigation. For lawyers, however, the stakes are much higher. A lawyer's professional judgment is at issue in every fee dispute case. Failure to collect a large legal fee can endanger the lawyer's standing in his firm and within the larger legal or client community. Fee collection claims often lead to ethical complaints, and counterclaims for malpractice, fraud, breach of fiduciary duty, or breach of contract. Even if a malpractice claim is weak the lawyer must ordinarily disclose the claim to his partners and malpractice insurer. It is often more palatable for the lawyer and the firm to strike a deal which allows them to collect some of their fee rather than go through the uncertainties of a court or arbitration process.

Nor should the client be overly concerned that the "system" will protect the lawyer. Given the legion of cases disallowing legal fees, it is hard to make the case that the system is biased against the client. Judges are former lawyers who often take a pay cut when they leave the business of law. To be sure, some judges will identify with the lawyers. Others will recall their greedy former colleagues and be inclined to favor the client. Most will simply preside over the case without prejudice to either side.\

8. Even If You Have Already Paid Your Lawyer, You May Be Entitled to Get Your Money Back

Fee disputes occasionally arise after the client has either (1) advanced money in anticipation of services to be rendered (often called a "retainer" or "advance") or (2) tendered full payment for legal services already rendered. In either case, the client is ordinarily entitled to receive his money back if the lawyer has charged an unreasonable fee.

Where money has been advanced in anticipation of future services, the lawyer is usually required to keep the money in a client trust account. The trust account money is considered property of the client in most jurisdictions. The lawyer has a right to withdraw the money after the fees are "earned" by the lawyer.

Client trust accounts raise ethical headaches for lawyers. If the lawyer/client relationship is terminated by either party, or the lawyer's services are completed before the advance is exhausted, the lawyer must refund the balance promptly to the client. If a fee dispute arises over money held in trust, lawyers should freeze the disputed funds in the trust account pending resolution of the dispute. These are tough rules to follow for a cash-strapped lawyer, and many ethical complaints arise out of the handling of client trust accounts. Just remember that it is your money unless and until legitimately earned by your lawyer.

As for cases where the client has already paid in full, the client can seek a refund if facts coming to light after the payment lead the client to believe that the fee was unreasonable. The client will probably not be able to obtain a refund if (1) the client had awareness of relevant facts and paid his lawyer, or (2) the applicable statute of limitations has expired.

9. Any Unethical Behavior May Be Grounds For Total or Partial Forfeiture Of Fees

A lawyer is ordinarily not permitted to profit from unethical conduct that harms his client. This provides another ground for potentially challenging legal fees, even where the lawyer's fees are otherwise reasonable. If the ethical transgression is slight or not related to the fees charged to the client, courts are less likely to order a forfeiture of fees. Where the transgression is serious and has a closer nexus to the fees, partial or total forfeiture is likely.

As a client questioning the propriety of your bills, ask yourself the following questions:

- Did my lawyer lie to me at any point in the representation?
- Did my lawyer fail to explain how this matter would be billed?
- Did my lawyer reveal any confidential information to third parties without my consent?
- Was my lawyer conflicted in any way from providing me with appropriate representation?

- Did my lawyer disobey any of my lawful instructions (not including disagreements which were discussed and resolved)?
- Did my lawyer treat advance or retainer payments as his own funds, or otherwise misappropriate my property?
- Was my lawyer incompetent in his performance of legal services?

If you believe a "yes" answer is appropriate for any of these questions, and there is a lot of money involved, you should consult with another lawyer.

10. Arbitration Provides A Cost-Effective Approach To Small Disputes

Many state bar associations now provide fee arbitration that streamlines the entire process so that the parties can obtain a judgment without the tremendous expenditure of time normally associated with commercial litigation. In New York State, the fee dispute arbitration program applies to all fee disputes except for criminal matters, where the contested fee is greater than $1,000 and less than $50,000. The program is voluntary for clients but mandatory for lawyers. Both sides have an opportunity to file a lawsuit after the bar association panel renders a decision. If neither side files a lawsuit within 30 days, the panel's determination becomes final.

These arbitration programs can save legal fees since discovery and motion practice are virtually nonexistent. In traditional litigation, or even other forums for commercial arbitration, legal fees can easily exceed $25,000. Therefore, in cases where a relatively small amount is in dispute, the bar-sponsored arbitration programs provide the best way for a client to contest a fee.

The downside of these programs is that many of them (including New York's) limit their jurisdiction to fee disputes, and refuse to hear cases involving more serious allegations of attorney misconduct. The limited or nonexistent discovery can also be a negative, since courts would ordinarily allow clients to obtain relevant information from the law firm, including records that may be used to verify time entries or expenses, and attorney work product that the law firm has otherwise chosen to withhold. Finally, the proceedings are conducted in private, which at best makes it difficult to judge the fairness of the decisions rendered in those proceedings, and at worst raises the possibility that lawyers are protecting their own. For larger disputes, or disputes where the client has a valid malpractice or breach of fiduciary duty claim, traditional courts are the best option for a client.

Appendix D

Guidelines for Professional Conduct*

Attorneys who engage in litigation should strive for prompt, efficient, ethical, fair and just disposition of litigation. In fulfilling this obligation the lawyer should adhere to the standards of practice as set out below.

1. In fulfilling his or her primary duty to the client, a lawyer must be ever conscious of the broader duty to the judicial system that serves both attorney and client.
2. A lawyer owes to the judiciary, candor, diligence and utmost respect.
3. A lawyer owes, to opposing counsel, a duty of courtesy and cooperation, the observation of which is necessary for the efficient administration of our system of justice and the respect of the public it serves.
4. A lawyer unquestionably owes, to the administration of justice, the fundamental duties of personal dignity and professional integrity.
5. Lawyers should treat each other, the opposing party, the court, and members of the court staff with courtesy and civility and conduct themselves in a professional manner at all times.
6. A client has no right to demand that counsel abuse the opposite party or indulge in offensive conduct. A lawyer shall always treat adverse witnesses and suitors with fairness and due consideration.
7. In adversary proceedings, clients are litigants and though ill feeling may exist between clients, such ill feeling should not influence a lawyer's conduct, attitude or demeanor towards opposing lawyers.

8. A lawyer should not use any form of discovery, or the scheduling of discovery, as a means of harassing opposing counsel or counsel's client.
9. Lawyers will be punctual in communications with others and in honoring scheduled appearances, and will recognize that negligence and tardiness are demeaning to the lawyer and to the judicial system.
10. If a fellow member of the Bar makes a just request for cooperation, or seeks scheduling accommodation, a lawyer will not arbitrarily or unreasonably withhold consent.
11. Effective advocacy does not require antagonistic or obnoxious behavior and members of the Bar will adhere to the higher standard of conduct which judges, lawyers, clients, and the public may rightfully expect.

*Used with permission by the Mississippi State Bar

APPENDIX E

A LAWYER'S CREED*

To my clients, I offer faithfulness, competence, diligence, and good judgment. I will strive to represent you as I would want to be represented and to be worthy of your trust.

To the opposing parties and their counsel, I offer fairness, integrity, and civility. I will seek to fairly resolve differences and, if we fail to reconcile disagreements, I will strive to make our dispute a dignified one.

To the courts, and other tribunals, and to those who assist them, I offer respect, candor, and courtesy. I will strive to do honor to the search for justice.

To my colleagues in the practice of law, I offer concern for your reputation and well being. I will extend to you the same courtesy, respect, candor and dignity that I expect to be extended to me. I will strive to make our association a professional friendship.

To the profession, I will strive to keep our business a profession and our profession a calling in the spirit of public service.

To the public and our systems of justice, I offer service. I will strive to improve the law and our legal system, to make the law and our legal system available to all, and to seek the common good through effective and ethical representation of my clients.

ASPIRATIONAL IDEALS

As a lawyer, I will aspire:

(a) To put fidelity to clients and, through clients, to the common good, before my personal interests.

(b) To model for others, and particularly for my clients, the respect due to those we call upon to resolve our disputes and the regard due to all participants in our dispute resolution processes.
(c) To pursue the goals of equality and fairness in my personal and professional activities.
(d) To preserve and improve the law, the legal system, and other dispute resolution processes as instruments for the common good.
(e) To make the law, the legal system, and other dispute resolution processes available to all.
(f) To practice with a personal commitment to the rules governing our profession and to encourage others to do the same.
(g) To preserve the dignity and the integrity of our profession by my conduct. The dignity and the integrity of our profession is an inheritance that must be maintained by each successive generation of lawyers.
(h) To achieve excellence in my work.
(i) To practice law not only as a business, but as a calling in the spirit of public service.

As to clients, I will aspire:

(a) To expeditious and economical achievement of client objectives.
(b) To fully informed client decision-making. As a professional, I will:

(1) Counsel clients about various forms of dispute resolution;
(2) Counsel clients about the value of cooperation as a means towards the productive resolution of disputes;
(3) Maintain the sympathetic detachment that permits objective and independent advice to clients;
(4) Communicate promptly and clearly with clients; and
(5) Reach clear agreements with clients concerning the nature of the representation.

(c) To fair and equitable fee agreements. As a professional, I will:

   (1) Consider and discuss with clients alternative fee arrange-
       ments as may be appropriate in the circumstances;
   (2) Reach fee agreements with clients as early in the
       relationship as possible; and
   (3) Determine the amount of fees by consideration of many
       factors and not just time spent by the attorney.

(d) To comply with the obligations of confidentiality and the
    avoidance of conflicting loyalties in a manner designed to
    achieve the fidelity to clients.
(e) To achieve and maintain a high level of competence in my
    fields of practice.

As to opposing parties and their counsel, I will aspire:

(a) To cooperate with opposing counsel in a manner consistent
    with the competent representation of my client. As a
    professional, I will:

   (1) Notify opposing counsel in a timely fashion of any
       canceled appearance;
   (2) Grant reasonable requests for extensions or scheduling
       changes; and
   (3) Consult with opposing counsel in the scheduling of
       appearances, meetings, and depositions.

(b) To treat opposing counsel in a manner consistent with his or
    her professional obligations and consistent with the dignity
    of the search for justice. As a professional, I will:

   (1) Not serve motions or pleadings in such a manner or at
       such a time as to preclude opportunity for a competent
       response;
   (2) Be courteous and civil in all communications;

(3) Respond promptly to all requests by opposing counsel;

(4) Avoid rudeness and other acts of disrespect in all meetings including depositions and negotiations;

(5) Prepare documents that accurately reflect the agreement of all parties; and

(6) Clearly identify all changes made in documents submitted by opposing counsel for review.

As to the courts, other tribunals, and to those who assist them, I will aspire:

(a) To represent my clients in a manner consistent with the proper functioning of a fair, efficient, and humane system of justice. As a professional, I will:

(1) Avoid non-essential litigation and non-essential pleading in litigation;

(2) Explore with clients and opposing parties the possibilities of settlement of litigated matters;

(3) Seek non-coerced agreement between the parties on procedural and discovery matters;

(4) Avoid all delays not dictated by a competent presentation of a client's claims;

(5) Prevent misuses of court time by verifying the availability of key participants for scheduled appearances before the court and by being punctual; and

(6) Advise clients about the obligations of civility, courtesy, fairness, cooperation, and other proper behavior expected of those who use our systems of justice.

(b) To model for others the respect due to our courts. As a professional, I will:

(1) Act with complete honesty;

(2) Know court rules and procedures;

(3) Give appropriate deference to court rulings;

(4) Avoid undue familiarity and any appearance or claim of any undue influence with members of the judiciary;

(5) Avoid unfounded, unsubstantiated, or unjustified public criticism of members of the judiciary;

(6) Show respect with my attire and demeanor;

(7) Assist the judiciary in determining the applicable law; and

(8) Seek to understand the judiciary's obligations of informed and impartial decision-making.

As to my colleagues in the practice of law, I will aspire:

(a) To recognize and to develop our interdependence;

(b) To assist my colleagues to become better people in the practice of law and to accept their assistance offered to me.

(c) To defend my colleagues against unjust criticism; and

(d) To offer my colleagues appropriate assistance with your personal and professional needs.

As to our profession, I will aspire:

(a) To improve the practice of law. As a professional, I will:

(1) Support high-quality continuing legal education;

(2) Participate in organized activities of the bar and other legal organizations;

(3) Assist when requested in the education of future lawyers; and

(4) Promote understanding of professionalism and ethical standards among members of the profession.

(b) To protect the public from incompetent or other wrongful lawyering. As a professional, I will:

(1) Support high standards in bar admissions; and

(2) Assist in the enforcement of the legal and ethical standards imposed upon all lawyers.

(c) To support diversity in the profession, especially the practice of law by members of historically underrepresented groups.

(d) To promote the understanding of and an appreciation for our profession by the public. I will:

(1) Use appropriate opportunities, publicly and privately, to comment upon the roles of lawyers in society and government, as well as in our system of justice; and

(2) Conduct myself always with an awareness that my actions and demeanor reflect upon our profession.

(e) To devote my time and skills to activities that promote the common good.

As to the public and our systems of justice, I will aspire:

(a) To counsel clients about the moral and social consequences of their conduct.

(b) To consider the effect of my conduct on the image of our systems of justice including the social effect of advertising methods.

(c) To provide the pro bono representation that is necessary to make our system of justice available to all.

(d) To support organizations that provide pro bono representation to indigent clients.

(e) To improve our laws and legal system by, for example:

(1) Serving as a public official;

(2) Assisting in the education of the public concerning our laws and legal system;

(3) Commenting publicly upon our laws; and

(4) Using other appropriate methods of effecting positive change in our laws and legal system

*Used by permission from the Mississippi Bar Association